Reforming China's Public Finances

Reforming China's Public Finances

editors
Ehtisham Ahmad
Gao Qiang
Vito Tanzi

Papers presented at a symposium held in
Shanghai, China, October 25–28, 1993

International Monetary Fund
Washington • 1995

Cover and interior design by IMF Graphics Section

Library of Congress Cataloging-in-Publication Data

Reforming China's Public Finances / editors, Ehtisham Ahmad, Gao
  Qiang, Vito Tanzi.
     p.   cm.
  "Papers presented at a symposium held in Shanghai. China,
October 25–28, 1993."
  Includes bibliographical references (p.).
  ISBN 1-55775-511-6
  1. Finance, Public—China—Congresses.   2. China—Economic
policy—1976—Congresses.   I. Ahmad, Ehtisham.   II. Gao, Qiang.
III. Tanzi, Vito.
HJ1401.R44   1995
336.51—dc20   95-25328
                                                        CIP

Price: US$24.00

Address orders to:
International Monetary Fund, Publication Services
700 19th Street, N.W., Washington, D.C. 20431, U.S.A.
Telephone: (202) 623-7430
Telefax: (202) 623-7201
Internet: publications@imf.org

Foreword

In recent years, China has taken steps to promote sustainable growth, with greater reliance on market mechanisms and institutions that facilitate orderly macroeconomic controls. The International Monetary Fund has been assisting the authorities in this endeavor. IMF participation has been particularly active in various fiscal areas such as tax policy, tax administration, budget management processes and the budget law, and fiscal relations between different levels of government.

In preparation for the introduction of major tax reforms and a new system of fiscal relations between different levels of government, the Ministry of Finance asked the Fiscal Affairs Department of the IMF to help prepare a seminar at which these issues could be discussed. The World Bank joined this effort, and Bank staff prepared a number of papers based on their own work in related areas. The conference, hosted jointly by the Ministry of Finance and the Shanghai municipal government, made possible an exchange of views between senior officials from the central and provincial governments in China and staff and experts from the IMF and the World Bank.

The reform of Chinese public finances is essential to the success of the efforts undertaken to ensure what the Chinese authorities call a market socialist economy and to the continued prosperity for the Chinese people. The conference discussed various policy options that might be considered by the Chinese authorities and the provinces in determining a sequencing of key fiscal reforms. I trust that this volume will contribute to the reform process in China and to its understanding by observers and scholars in other parts of the world.

MICHEL CAMDESSUS
Managing Director
International Monetary Fund

Acknowledgment

The introduction of a new tax system and budget laws to generate adequate resources for the government and to create a "level playing field" in China will have consequences for fiscal relations between the central and provincial governments. The close interrelationships between these reforms was brought out in the seminar, which also provided a forum for discussion between the central and provincial governments, with presentations by the IMF and World Bank staff on international experiences and their own work in China.

The Vice-Minister of Finance, Mr. Jin Renqing, opened the seminar, stressing the importance that the central government attached to the deliberations. A great deal of preparatory work was done by officials of the Budget Management Department of the Ministry of Finance. We would like to thank in particular Ms. Feng Xiuhua, Deputy Director, and Mr. Wang Weixing, Division Chief. A Chinese version of this volume has already been published by the Ministry of Finance, in collaboration with the IMF's Fiscal Affairs Department (FAD).

We would also like to thank the Mayor of Shanghai and the Finance Bureau of Shanghai Municipality for their excellent arrangements in hosting the seminar and for their hospitality during our stay in Shanghai. The presence of a large number of participants from various provinces and central government agencies contributed to a rich exchange of ideas.

World Bank staff presented a number of key papers, reflecting their own work and interest in related fields. Senior Bank staff, including, among others, Mr. Pieter Bottelier, the Resident Representative in Beijing, Mr. Ramgopal Agarwala, Division Chief, and Mr. Vinod Thomas, Chief Economist (Asia), addressed the seminar and chaired sessions.

Mr. Douglas Scott, the Fund's Resident Representative played a key role in arranging and attending the seminar. A number of FAD staff presented papers and chaired sessions during the seminar. In recent years, FAD has provided technical assistance in the areas of tax policy and administration, budget laws and management, as well as in the area of fiscal relations between different levels of government. Special thanks are due to Juanita Roushdy of the Fund's External Relations

Department, who worked hard to prepare the volume for publication, and to Fawzia Dossani who typed numerous drafts of the manuscript.

EHTISHAM AHMAD
GAO QIANG
VITO TANZI

Contents

Revenue Assignments—Tax Policy and Administration

Grants and Transfers

1

Overview

Ehtisham Ahmad, Gao Qiang, and Vito Tanzi*

The reform of fiscal relations between different levels of government is crucial to the success of China's current structural transformation to a social market economy. The reform will profoundly affect macroeconomic stability, growth prospects, and the effectiveness of providing public services and interregional equity. In order to review international experience in this regard and to clearly identify the policy options for China in the short to medium term, a conference was held in Shanghai in October 1993. The papers in this volume include those presented at the conference and a few that supplement it. They embrace the full range of fiscal relations between different levels of government—the background to the current policy choices; national budget policies and the legal and institutional role of different levels of government; expenditure assignments; tax assignments and administration; and transfers and grants from higher levels of government.

The conference was organized by the Chinese Ministry of Finance and the Fiscal Affairs Department of the International Monetary Fund, with the cosponsorship of the World Bank and the Shanghai municipal authorities. The conference program was drawn up by the Ministry of Finance and the IMF, and officials from both institutions presented a large number of papers. The World Bank staff also presented a number of papers and acted as discussants. The Shanghai Finance Bureau hosted the meeting, providing excellent conference facilities, interpretation, and translation, as well as a paper on local finances. The conference was attended by officials from the central departments, including the State Tax Bureau, the State Planning Commission, and the Commission for Economic Restructuring, as well as from a number of provinces.

---

*Ahmad and Tanzi, International Monetary Fund, Gao Qiang, Ministry of Finance, China.

1

As described in the introductory speeches by the Vice-Minister of Finance, and by Gao Qiang, Director of the Budget Management Department (Chapter 2), the reform of intragovernmental fiscal relations is critical to the stability and sustained growth of the Chinese economy in the years to come. In this context, a number of fiscal reforms will be needed simultaneously. The conference sought to highlight the main avenues and to illustrate these with examples from other countries, intertwining them with specific proposals and discussion of Chinese problems. As will become clear, the evidence from the international context displays a variety of institutions and outcomes that reflect the economic and historical backgrounds of the countries concerned. Yet there are common themes—including the importance of budgetary discipline, a clarity of budget laws and procedures, the importance of appropriate expenditure and revenue assignments, and the crucial role of objectively determined patterns of grants and transfers. Within each of these areas are also many ways of tackling specific issues that arise. Clearly, the solutions to China's problems must display Chinese characteristics and the preferences of Chinese policymakers. It is important, however, to ensure that the chosen paths, and subpaths, are consistent and display an overall coherence.

Background

The Chinese authorities have foreseen that sustainable growth with equity, in an economy that is increasingly integrated in the world trade and financial system, must be accompanied by widespread reform of public sector policies. This includes modernization of taxation policies and administration, together with new approaches for formulating and implementing public expenditure policies. The authorities also recognize that such reforms must take account of China's size and diversity, thus changes to intergovernmental financial relations are essential in ensuring that policies to achieve national objectives blend with policies that take account of specific regional and local needs.

A technical assistance team from the Fund visited China in July 1993 and argued that a continuation of contracting arrangements between the central government and the provinces could be a source of macroeconomic instability in the future. A move to establish greater central government control over revenues through a National Tax Administration would be desirable. This would invariably affect the tax assignments. A greater central government share in total revenues would be sustainable only if accompanied by a system of transfers to local governments, based on scientific criteria.

China's recent experience with fiscal reforms, as well as with some problem areas and policy options for the future, described by Gao Qiang, on behalf of the Ministry of Finance, in Chapter 2. The short-comings of the system of contracting revenues between different levels of government are emphasized and some policy options to reform the system are highlighted. Gao Qiang explains the difficulties with the current contracting arrangements regarding taxation in China and sets out the main axes for reform that have been adopted by the government to increase revenues and provide the basis for a rational tax system. These involve both tax assignments, with the determination of central and local tax bases, and tax sharing—relating to the major sources of revenue. As pointed out in Chapter 14, this arrangement of revenue-sharing is equivalent to the establishment of non-equalizing general grants. A second major reform, presented by Gao Qiang, is the establishment of a central tax administration (State Administration of Taxation), to minimize the possibilities of local government exemptions and preferences with respect to such taxes. The service would be responsible for the central taxes and the major sources of revenues. An important question is whether "shared taxes," which are likely to be the most important in terms of revenues, should be administered by the State Administration of Taxation. A related question is whether the corporate income tax on centrally owned enterprises should be allocated to the central government, and whether the corporate income tax on locally owned enterprises should be administered by and allocated to local governments. In most countries, the administration of the corporate income tax is invariably carried out by a single authority.

The differences between different regions of China are summarized in Chapter 3 by Mr. Zhenjun of the State Nationalities Commission. It focuses on the requirements of inter-regional equity and the policy importance of providing access to a minimum standard of public goods and services throughout China.

When the conference took place, the full extent of the planned fiscal reforms had still to be decided. As a result of the discussion at the conference, and a subsequent workshop organized by the Fiscal Affairs Department, the authorities have made a number of modifications in the proposed fiscal arrangements affecting relations between different levels of government. The most important modifications have been with respect to proposed tax assignments and revenue-sharing arrangements. These changes are reflected in the subsequent guidelines from the National People's Congress, and the decisions of the State Council.

New Taxation Arrangements

As described in Chapter 2, an overriding objective of the reforms is to replace a system of taxation, based essentially on negotiation and contracts, with a uniform application of taxes based on a legal foundation. The introduction of a modern tax system should remove special disincentives and create a "level playing field" so that investment and labor market decisions are not biased. Initially, it was proposed that the main revenue sources, as described above, would be shared taxes, and the proportions to be shared could vary across taxes and across regions; in addition, there would have been purely central and purely local (provincial) taxes. The revised system, introduced as of January 1, 1994, is described later in the volume in Chapter 9 by Xu Shanda and Ma Lin of the State Administration of Taxation (SAT).

The main difference between the announced system and the proposal discussed at the conference is a much sharper delineation in tax assignments; the value-added tax (VAT) is the main revenue source to be shared, with a 75 percent share going to the central government and the rest to the local governments.[1] The central taxes and the shared taxes—that is, the VAT—are to be administered by SAT. This arrangement will increase the initial share of central government revenues, in total revenue collections, from under 40 percent to around 60 percent. To protect local government expenditures, as an interim measure, the central government has agreed to provide transfers that would maintain the provinces's 1993 level of nominal revenue collections. This interim measure is to be replaced by a "scientific" grants mechanism as soon as practicable.

Budget and Legal Framework

The workings of a market-based economy require a mechanism for budgeting and control that differs from that needed in a centrally planned economy. The budget plays a central role in a market economy. It provides the levers for macroeconomic control; whereas in the former centrally planned context it played a passive role in providing

---

[1]As described in Chapter 2, the revenues from the natural resource tax are to be assigned to the province in which the resource occurs, although the revenues from offshore oil will be assigned to the central government. While the natural resource tax is described as being "shared," the sharing is effectively an assignment of different taxes from different types of resources to different levels of government. A transfer tax on share transactions will also be shared, but this is unlikely to generate significant revenues.

the financing for predetermined plan targets. The Chinese case is surveyed in Chapter 4 by Shahid Yusuf and Bert Hofman, based on the extensive work of the World Bank in this area. In Chapter 5, Ehtisham Ahmad, Maurice Kennedy, and Ingrid Klering set out the main issues that arise in establishing and clarifying budget laws. The experience of many countries of the Organization on Economic Cooperation and Development (OECD) is summarized. The authors note that it is important to clarify the relative roles of the legislature and the executive, the scope of government activities, the importance of the Minister of Finance, the relationships between different levels of government, and the mechanisms for achieving macroeconomic control and accountability of officials.

In connection with the overall macroeconomic management of the economy, the importance of the *effective* control over all types of borrowings by subnational levels of government needs to be stressed, including indirect methods such as the buildup of arrears and IOUs, the burgeoning of unaccounted for extrabudgetary funds, and the setting up of "dummy" organizations to borrow and perform government tasks. It is evident that a proper classification of revenues and expenditures (stressed in both papers) is crucial if the budget is to perform the functions needed in a market-based context. It would, in fact, be quite straightforward to reclassify the Chinese budget into a format consistent with the *Government Finance Statistics* conventions of the IMF, which are generally being followed elsewhere.

Expenditure Assignments

The assignment of expenditure responsibilities is typically the first step in determining different forms of intergovernmental fiscal relations. There is extensive debate on the degree of centralization or decentralization that may be relevant in a given context. Much of the literature, however, is based on models of the economy that depend on the mobility of factors, particularly labor and capital, which may not be relevant for China. As Gao Qiang illustrates in Chapter 2, the recent experience of China is based on "contracting" arrangements between different levels of government, which appear to have outlived their usefulness; thus, a study of the Chinese context may involve a somewhat different paradigm from that used in other countries. Important lessons may still be drawn from international experience, however; although in assessing this experience, it would be useful to keep in mind the difference between *policy, administration*, and *financing* responsibilities. These issues are stressed in Chapter 6 by Ehtisham Ahmad, in a review of international experience with respect to expenditure assignments, illustrating the diversity of experience in this regard and some of the principles that might be relevant for China.

The paper by Ahmad also examines social protection reform in China. A major issue is that a corresponding rationalization of payroll contributions for social security should accompany reform of the tax system. Thus, regions such as Shanghai should not be penalized because of the higher concentration of the aged, relative to the working population, than the average. The main issue for discussion is the case for a high level of pooling of risks for pensions and unemployment insurance, not only to reduce "tax competition" across localities, but also to ensure uniformity of provision for the main contingencies that require state support. Different considerations apply in the case of social assistance, which could continue to be provided effectively by local governments, as is presently the case in China. Interregional comparisons should be handled in the context of horizontal equalization. The issue of China's present system of grants and transfers is raised in this context. As described in Chapter 3, the current transfers are based on comparisons of per capita incomes of the mid-1980s. The transfer system would need to better account for price changes if horizontal equity is to be appropriately addressed; this issue is taken up later (see Chapters 14–16).

The subsequent papers are devoted to different aspects of expenditure assignments in China. A major issue relates to the responsibility for large or "lumpy" investments. The paper by Bert Hofman and Richard Newfarmer (Chapter 7) sets out the principles and suggests applications for the Chinese context. Somewhat different considerations apply in the context of social expenditures, and the case of health care differs from education, or the provision of housing. Zuliu Hu in Chapter 8 assesses the scope for government intervention and that of the private sector. He also examines the issue of which level of government in China should be responsible for the social expenditures and stresses that intrasectoral considerations may be important. The difficulties with the application of the benefit principle, to guide expenditure assignments, are also discussed.

Tax Policy and Administration

At the conference it was pointed out that sharing taxes in varying proportions could reintroduce the "bargaining" between tax collecting and recipient governments that the new system sought to eliminate.

The distinctions between tax assignment, relating to control over tax rates and bases, administration, and revenue allocation could allow a nondistortionary system of tax assignment and administration, which would need to be supplemented by revenue-sharing and transfer arrangements. The revised arrangements are described in Chapter 9, by Xu Shanda and Ma Lin, of the State Administration of Taxation, rewritten after the conference to reflect the tax system introduced in China as of January 1, 1994. In principle, the new arrangements would limit the possibility of local government exemptions to central or shared taxes—which had in the past eroded central government control over tax bases and effective rates.

Xu Shanda and Ma Lin outline the thinking behind the proposed taxation reforms, subsequently approved by the State Council. As they explain, the guiding principles were the need to create "a uniform tax code, equitable tax burdens, a simplified tax system; a rational division of powers, straightening out of the apportionment of tax monies between the national government and local governments, and building a taxation system that is consistent with the needs of a socialist market economy." The paper outlines the reforms proposed for enterprise profits tax, including the unification of the laws applying to state enterprises, private enterprises and other similar organizations, and introduction of measures that bring the treatment of interest and depreciation charges more into line with international practice. Measures to standardize the income tax and value-added taxes are explained, as is the rationale for proposed consumption and business taxes, which may be seen as largely complementing the coverage of the VAT. They also discuss prospective new, or amended, taxes on natural resources, urban construction, property, securities, a possible social security levy, and the readjustment, merger, simplification, and possible abolition of a host of smaller taxes, some of which have an exotic flavor (e.g., a banquet tax and animal trading tax) but in the end may be a "nuisance," in the sense that they are unpopular, are hard to administer, and do not raise a great amount of revenue. Finally, the authors argue for more thought to be given to possible local government taxes that might be seen as linked to financing activities at that level of government.

The paper by Shi Yaobin of the Ministry of Finance, Chapter 10, concentrates on the background and reasons for enterprise tax reform. The paper complements the earlier presentation by Xu Shanda and Ma Lin, and includes a valuable account of the complexities and difficulties of the former profit-sharing system.

The discussion of the State Administration of Taxation paper stressed the importance of a centralized tax administration, as well as some potential difficulties in its establishment. Ahmad raised the issue of insulating SAT officials from local influences. It was also argued that the assignment of the enterprise income tax should not be based on the ownership of enterprises—this assignment generates duplicate administration functions and would also pose increasing difficulties for administration as patterns of ownership begin to diversify. However, the arrangements implemented as of January 1, 1994, retain the assignment of the enterprise income tax by ownership type—reflecting the otherwise relatively weak own-tax bases of the local governments. As suggested by Vito Tanzi, the tax reforms and tax assignments should be reviewed periodically, and this issue could be taken up again at a later stage.

In his own paper (Chapter 11), Vito Tanzi has a dual task. First, he surveys international experience in tax assignments, blending theoretical concepts with a policy focus and administrative realities. A pragmatic approach that recognizes the importance of stabilization policy and combines with the need for uniform administration had led a number of countries to assign responsibility for setting rates and administration of some of the major taxes to the central government level. While some taxes, such as sales and personal income tax may be operated at the subnational level, the only tax that was widely applied at the local level was the property tax.

Tanzi expresses his strong support of the thrust of the tax policy reforms proposed by the Chinese authorities, while mentioning some concerns in regard to the design aspects of some specific measures. In particular, he suggests a preference for a single rate for the enterprise income tax, rather than two. There is also a possible concern that the design of the income tax, including the relatively high deduction for living allowances, may restrict the yield of this prospectively important tax. He also cautions that the business tax, and similar taxes, should not be allowed to erode the VAT base, which is so vital to future revenue collections.

With regard to another important subject, local government taxes, Georgio Brosio, of Turin University in Italy, provides in Chapter 12 a comprehensive account of local taxation in an international context. His paper shows that, despite the inherent difficulties of defining and administering local taxes, the share of local revenues in industrial countries has risen in recent years. One factor in this rise was the emergence of local business taxes, especially in Germany and France, which had complemented traditional property taxes. He argues that successful local taxes should strictly adhere to the benefit principle—linking revenue burdens to observed local services provided—and should be levied on as broad a base as possible to minimize distortions to the local economy.

During the conference, Yu Zichong of the Shanghai Municipal Tax Administration reviewed practices in local taxation in China and possible reform directions. His independently derived conclusions echoed Brosio's comments. In particular, he remarked on the fragmented nature of the current tax system, which makes it difficult to administer. He argued that tax bases should be based on the benefit principle, made consistent within jurisdictions, but not necessarily across jurisdictions (since some diversity is desirable), and be broadened via the assignment of taxes, such as the local business tax, the interest income tax, and natural resource taxes to the local level. He saw a need for a division of tax powers between central and local governments—with local governments given greater freedom to move into certain areas, not utilized by the central government, and to set their own tax rates and determine the relevant bases. In this context, he suggested that it would be desirable for personal income tax revenues to be shared between central and local governments. He endorsed the development of separate national and local taxation administrations and urged the development of self-assessment and withholding taxes.

In Chapter 13, Manuelyan Atinc and Bert Hofman deal with the issue of taxation of natural resources. The authors argue that the "economic rent" generated by the development of the resources—defined as the market value of the resource exploited minus all costs necessary for exploitation—should accrue to the government, and that special taxation measures may be needed to achieve that result. The paper canvasses the taxation options available—ranging from a pure resource rent tax and cash flow taxes to royalties, auctioning, and production-sharing arrangements. Atinc and Hofman express a preference for a modified cash flow tax and suggest that China may wish to consider implementing such a tax. They also argue that the immobility of the tax base makes natural resource taxes a potential candidate for local government taxation. At the very least, this tax base might be shared with the central government, in a manner that would allow local governments to cover development of local infrastructure, associated with resource development, and environmental clean up costs after project completion and implementation.

Discussion of the issues raised by these papers was lively. One question was the extent to which the taxation reform would bring China closer to international experience and the relative benefits that it might bring for economic management and accountability by various levels of government. Another controversial issue was the advocacy of cash flow taxation. Tanzi noted that whatever their theoretical merits, such taxes were as yet untried and there was a question therefore whether China would wish to place itself in the vanguard of experimentation with such taxes, especially in view of possible revenue loss in the short to medium term. The Chinese participants also expressed reservations about the applicability of such taxes at this time and, more generally, questioned the view that potentially complex natural resource taxation issues could be adequately handled at the local government level.

Grants and Transfers

The session on Grants and Transfers opened with a selective review of international experience with intergovernment grants and transfers by Anwar Shah (Chapter 14). The paper lists four main objectives of such arrangements: (1) correcting for fiscal gaps—often labeled as vertical imbalances—in the availability of resources to different levels of government; (2) encouraging the use of national minimum standards of service by subnational governments; (3) corrections of potential underprovision of some services at subnational level where the benefits of programs spill over into other jurisdictions; and (4) the presence of differential fiscal capacities between different subnational governments—which may impede a subnational government's ability to provide a reasonably comparable level of service at standard levels of taxation. He also lists a number of desirable design characteristics of grants and transfers.

Shah's review of practices in selected developing countries suggests that the actual practices followed often fail to meet the objectives and design principles he outlines. In order to help policymakers avoid mistakes, he sets down a decision framework that links the type of arrangement to be followed to the policy objective set; revenue sharing to deal with fiscal gaps; conditional nonmatching grants to deal with minimum standards; open-ended matching transfers to deal with benefit spillover; and unconditional block grants using equalization criteria to deal with horizontal imbalances in fiscal capacities.

After the conference, a technical assistance team from IMF's Fiscal Affairs Department focused on institutional and information requirements for the establishment and implementation of a comprehensive system of grants and prepared a report. The report (Chapter 15) Ehtisham Ahmad, Jon Craig, and Dubravko Mihaljek, is included in the volume to complete the policy options that would need to be considered by the authorities. The paper points out that a comprehensive system of grants would include both special purpose and equalization grants. In some countries, there is an independent Grants Commission, as in Australia, whereas in others, such as Canada, the equalization exercise is carried out by the Ministry of Finance. The methods of estimating equalization grants could be restricted to an assessment of revenue capacities of different regions, as in Canada, to one which includes both assessments of revenue capacities as well as differential expenditure needs. The information requirements differ with the method of estimation chosen.

A paper by Jon Craig (Chapter 16) deals solely with the techniques used by governments to address their horizontal equity objectives. It provides an analytical framework for designing grant arrangements, including the quantification of the vertical and horizontal balances within the system of intergovernment finances. The policy efforts to correct one imbalance can often have implications for the resolution of the other. Craig also refers to a number of case studies.

Sequencing of Reform

The conference introduced a full range of issues and options relating to intragovernmental fiscal relations in a country the size of and as complex as China, with references to international experience. It is our hope that the discussions have served to highlight the options for reform and the sequencing of the steps to be taken in the short to medium term.

The devolution of expenditure responsibilities in China is likely to be maintained and could even be strengthened. At the same time, greater central control is likely to be exercised over the revenue base. Typically, once expenditure assignments are determined, the question of revenue assignments can be addressed in a meaningful fashion. Indeed, this principle was reflected in the structure of the conference. There was disagreement, however, about whether *further adjustments* to the current expenditure assignments were needed prior to the determination of the revenue assignments and of transfers. At a closed session, Ahmad took the view that the changes proposed by the authorities on the revenue side were fundamental to the reform process and should not be delayed to await further refinements in expenditure assignments—especially since this is likely to be a lengthy process involving a changing role for state-owned enterprises. Thus, a transfer system would be developed on the basis of current expenditure assignments, and this could be adjusted as expenditure assignments change over time.

A crucial feature in the reform of intragovernmental fiscal relations in China concerns the establishment of a separate "State Administration of Taxation." The institution of the administration based on modern tax administration functions, the likely time frame involved, and whether the officials of such a service can actually be insulated from "local" pressures and influence are among the most important questions for the reform.

Intragovernmental Fiscal Issues in China

2

Problems in Chinese Intragovernmental Fiscal Relations, Tax-Sharing System, and Future Reform

Gao Qiang*

This paper outlines the main problems in Chinese intragovernmental fiscal relations and the main difficulties to be faced in future reform.[1] It also presents a discussion of the tax-sharing arrangements envisaged. These issues cover the division of fiscal revenues between different levels of government, the responsibility for fiscal expenditures, and other fiscal relations.

Current Intragovernmental Fiscal Relations

China's present fiscal system was set up in 1988. It includes six kinds of contracting methods: The first is "contracting of progressive increases in revenue." This method is based on the 1987 local government final accounting of revenues and local government obligations, the rate of increase in revenue and withholdings, and the percentage to be paid to the central government determined on the basis of the increase in revenues during the previous several years. Revenues within the progressive rate of increase are divided between the central government and local governments at a prescribed retention and payment percentage. Revenues in excess of the progressive rate of increase are retained entirely by local governments. When revenues do not meet the

---

*Ministry of Finance, China

[1]Given that China is a unitary state, the term "intragovernmental" is used by the authorities in preference to the term "intergovernmental" fiscal relations. *Ed.*

progressive increase rate, the shortfall in payment to the central government is made up out of local governments' own financial resources. Ten areas practice this method.

The second is "dividing up the total amount." This method is based on approved base figures for fiscal receipts and expenditures for the previous two years. Local government total fiscal revenues as a percentage of total expenditures are used to determine the ratio between local government retention and payment to the central government. Three areas practice this method. The third method is to "divide up the total amount, and any increase." This means that in addition to dividing up the total amount, the amount of revenue increase over the previous year is also shared proportionately. Three areas practice this method.

The fourth is "contracting of a progressive increase in the amount to be paid to the higher authority." This method uses the base figures for revenue payments to the central government in 1987; the amount to be paid increases progressively at a certain rate each year. Two areas practice this method. The fifth method is "payment of a fixed amount to the higher authority." This method is based on previously approved revenue and expenditures base figures, and a fixed amount of the portion of revenues in excess of expenditures is paid to the central government. Three areas practice this method.

The sixth method is the "fixed amount subsidy." This method uses a base figure for previously approved revenues and expenditures, and the central government provides a fixed amount subsidy to cover expenditures in excess of revenues. Sixteen areas practice this method. Because the central government has no uniform regulations to cover fiscal contracting among governments below the provincial level, all jurisdictions suit general methods to specific circumstances, and the practices vary greatly.

Unlike the previous fiscal system's "unified state control over revenues and expenditures," the fiscal contracting system has greatly stimulated local governments' interest in increasing revenues and reducing expenditures. It has also provided favorable fiscal conditions for the development of the local economy. Nevertheless, the fiscal contracting system is still an unstandardized, incomplete method that does not meet the needs for building a socialist market economy. Its inherent shortcomings are becoming increasingly apparent as time goes by.

Weakened Central Government Macroeconomic Regulation and Control

The most important characteristic of the contracting system is that it sets unequivocally the revenues that local governments are to pay to the central government. Except for a stipulated percentage to be paid to the central government, local governments retain all increments to fiscal revenues. Consequently, central government revenues are inelastic. Since the implementation of the fiscal contracting system in 1988, local governments' annual revenue increases paid to the central government have been less than 10 percent. More than 90 percent of increased revenue has been retained by local governments. In addition, because tax revenues are collected mostly by local tax agencies, and because local governments have substantial authority to grant tax reductions or exemptions, a decline in the share of central government revenues is difficult to avoid. Consequently, in 1992 central government "own" revenues (exclusive of liabilities) amounted to only 28.7 percent of national fiscal revenues. This has weakened the central government's macroeconomic regulation and control capability and has been detrimental to financing central government expenditures, such as key national construction projects.

Contracting Losses But Not Profits

The fiscal contracting system provides that local governments may retain all increased local governments' fiscal revenues, except for the amount to be paid to the central government in accordance with regulations. However, in the implementation of the contracting system, for various reasons (such as the floods in parts of east China two years ago), fiscal revenues in some areas do not reach the contracted progressive increase level. In such cases, the central government is obliged to reduce or exempt the amount due from such areas. In addition, the expenditures assigned to local governments, under expenditure contracting, may also require the central government to provide special subsidies or transfers. This increases the central government's fiscal difficulties.

Detrimental to Adjustment of the Industrial Structure and Implementation of Industrial Policy

The fiscal contracting system divides both enterprise income taxes and the turnover tax between the central government and the local government jurisdiction in charge of collection. This closely links industrial and commercial enterprise taxation to local fiscal revenues. Thus, in order to broaden their own sources of revenue, jurisdictions frequently vie with each other to develop projects that show quick results and that produce high revenues and large profits in order to gain the greatest fiscal returns for their own area. They also protect the sale of products from these local projects; for example, state policy restricts development of tobacco and alcoholic beverage industries. However, since the tax rate on these products is high and returns are great, each jurisdiction seeks to expand their output. Not only does this cause duplication of construction and skewing of the industrial structure, but it hinders formation of a unified domestic market and wastes resources.

Large Amount of Discretion in the Contracting System

The fiscal contracting system was worked out through negotiations between the central government and the provinces, autonomous regions, and municipalities under direct central government administration. Because of the "horse-trading" done concerning a fairly large number of matters, policies are not uniform, the system is not standard, and strict legal restraints are lacking. This is not in keeping with requirements for building a socialist market economic system or for expressing the rule of law, openness, systematization, and fairness.

Thanks to many years' study and reference to prevailing international practices, the distribution of fiscal responsibilities between the central government and local governments will be solved through a tax-sharing arrangement. Thus, during the second half of 1992, the central government selected nine localities, namely, Liaoning Province, Zhejiang Province, Shenyang, Dalian, Tianjin, Qingdao, Wuhan, Chongqing, and the Xinjiang Uygur autonomous region, as pilots for reform. The tax-sharing system that is being experimented with contains both certain elements of a general tax-sharing system and also retains certain methods of the fiscal contracting system. Its basic configuration calls for the division of existing fiscal revenues into three categories: permanent central government revenues, permanent local government revenues, and revenues to be shared between the central government and local governments.

Revenues to be shared between the central government and local governments include the product tax, the value-added tax, the business tax, the uniform industrial and commercial tax, and the resources tax. Two ratios are used for the division of the shared revenues, namely a "50-50" division between the central government and local governments in general, and an "80-20" division between the central government and minority nationality areas. In the pilot areas, the portion of local government permanent fiscal revenue plus jointly shared revenue, that is, revenue greater than the base figure for local government expenditures, is contracted for payment to the central government at an annual increment of 5 percent. If the portion of permanent local fiscal revenues plus shared revenues is less than the base figure for local fiscal expenditures, the central government provides a fixed sum subsidy. Appropriate care is accorded to minority nationality areas.

The situation in the pilot areas shows some inadequacies in this plan, mostly that the amount of shared revenues is too large, that the main kinds of taxes to be shared by the central government and local governments have not been clarified, and that central government macroeconomic regulation and control capabilities have not improved markedly.

To promote the building of a socialist market economic system, the State Council has decided to enhance the reform of the revenue-sharing and transfer systems. Beginning in 1994, with the nationwide dismantling of the existing fiscal contracting system, the tax-sharing system is to be implemented across China. This reform requires that tax system reform, state-owned enterprise profit distribution system reform, financial system reform, and investment system reform proceed in tandem. This reform has a bearing on readjustment of the economic interests of all. It requires solving several major difficulties and crucial problems: one, how to divide equitably the main forms of taxation between the central government and local governments; two, how to set up separate central government and local government tax agencies; three, how to define clearly the division of fiscal and other powers among governments; and four, how to be fair in setting local fiscal revenue and expenditure base figures, as well as in central government transfers to local governments.

Policy Orientation of China's Tax-Sharing System

The Fourteenth Party Congress spelled out reform goals for the establishment of a socialist market economy system, and a widespread consensus has also been gradually reached among governments at all levels about the establishment of a fiscal system in which tax sharing is the main feature. At the end of August 1993, the State Council Standing Committee convened and approved in principle a tax-sharing system and fiscal reform plan; it also called for further amplification and improvement of the plan. The following covers basic principles and ideas for the fiscal system reform in the near future.

Basic Principles

A reform of the tax-sharing system affects adjustment of the interests of all and has a bearing on the overall macroeconomic situation. Proceeding from Chinese realities, and with reference to international practice, the following basic principles have been emphasized by the government.

The implementation of tax system reform is to be simultaneously accompanied by the distribution of tax revenues among governments. The establishment of a scientific, equitable, and stable taxation system provides the foundation for pursuing the tax-sharing system. The State Council has already approved, in principle, reform plans for China's tax system for the near future, the basic ingredients of which are across-the-board promotion of value-added tax (VAT), uniformity in the domestically owned enterprise income tax, amplification of the individual income tax, the merging of various small taxes, and the introduction of new kinds of taxes as economic development requires. A simultaneous reform of the tax-sharing system and a complete reform of the taxation system pose great difficulties and risks, but until the taxation system is sound, a scientific reform of the tax-sharing and transfer system will be difficult. After a tax-sharing system is instituted, separate central government and local government agencies for tax collection and administration will be set up to ensure the separate revenues of the central government and local government; each jurisdiction will collect its own taxes. At the same time, tax legislation and administrative authority will also be spelled out.

Rationally adjust the distribution of financial capacity among regions. In the division of tax revenues among governments, consideration must be given to both the need to enhance central government macroeconomic regulation and control capabilities, and local governments' need for financial resources to develop economic and cultural, educational, and scientific research endeavors. This would stimulate the interest of both the central and local governments.

On the basis of the foregoing principle, all taxes are divided into central government taxes, local government taxes, and taxes shared by the central and local governments. Assigned to the central government are all taxes closely related to the maintenance of national rights and interests and helpful to the exercise of macroeconomic regulation and control. Taxes that produce a large amount of revenue, and that can steadily increase tax revenues, are to be shared between the central and local governments, with most of such revenues going to the central government. Local tax assignment is suited to local government collection and administration. This division both helps establish and perfect a system for the central government's macroeconomic regulation and control, and also takes into account the Chinese realities of a vast area, a large population, and the very numerous economic and social functions that local governments perform. It also ensures that local governments can play a full role and regularly discharge functions in providing regional social services.

Establishment of a standard system for central government transfers to local governments, together with a special disbursements system. Economic development varies greatly between one area and another in China (see Chapter 3). Following the division of taxes, a substantial portion of the central government's increased revenues will be returned to local governments through grants and transfers. The principle used in such transfers is that they must help economically developed areas continue a fairly high speed of development and must gradually increase the financial resources of economically undeveloped areas.

Adherence to the principle of unified policies in combination with control by different levels of government. Dividing tax revenues requires not only consideration of the distribution of revenues between the central and local governments, but also consideration of the regulatory role of taxation on economic and social development and social distributions. After tax sharing, the main function of the central government will be diligent maintenance of a unified nationwide market that protects fair competition among enterprises. The formulation of all principal forms of taxation, the kinds of items to be taxed, and tax rates, should be the responsibility of the central government, along with the responsibility for maintaining nationwide uniformity. At the same time, local governments can be given a certain amount of flexibility in the administration of small taxes that provide revenues for local governments.

Highlighting important points and paying close attention to principal contradictions. A reform of fiscal functions among governments affects a broad spectrum and sparks conflicts of various kinds. It cannot be accomplished in a single step, nor can all problems be solved simultaneously. Priorities must be set. The main forms of taxation used for macroeconomic regulation and control must be differentiated, and various technical problems, or problems resulting from conditions not being appropriate, may be gradually solved during implementation.

Content of New System

The concrete content of the new tax-sharing system is as follows.

Assignment of mandates and expenditure responsibilities between the central government and local governments. According to the present distribution of mandates between the central and local governments, the central government is responsible for expenditures relating to national security and foreign affairs, administrative expenses for the central government departments, the necessary expenditures in adjusting the national economic structure, coordinating regional development and executing macroeconomic control, as well as the development expenses for the sectors that come under the direct control of the central government. The specific categories of expenditure are national defense expenses; armed police administrative expenses; expenses for foreign affairs and financial aid to other countries; administrative expenses for central government departments; capital construction investment under the control of the central government; expenses for technical innovation and new product pilot production of enterprises that belong to the central government; geological prospecting expenses; expenses for supporting agriculture; expenses for debt service on domestic and foreign debt incurred by the central government; expenses for police, procuration, and courts at central levels; and administrative expenses for culture, education, and health care.

The local governments are responsible for their administrative expenses and the relevant necessary expenditures of the development of the local economy and sectors, which include local administrative expenditure; expenditure for public security; procuration organization and court; part of the armed security force expenditures; administration expenditure for civil militia; capital investment of local government; technical renovation and new product experiment expenses of local enterprises; expenditures for assisting agriculture; urban maintenance and construction expenditures, some administration expenses for local culture, education, and health care; and price subsidies and other expenses.

Revenue assignment of central and local governments. Central government revenues include customs duty, consumption tax, and VAT collected by customs, consumption tax, income tax of central enterprises, income tax of local banks, foreign ventures in banks and nonbanking financial institutions, revenue submission from railway transportation departments, head offices of all banks and all insurance companies (including business tax, income tax and profits, and tax on urban maintenance and construction), as well as profit from the enterprises of the central government. All tax rebates on exported goods are to be borne by the central government.

Local government revenues include the business tax (not including the business tax from railway transportation department and all head offices of all banks and insurance companies), income tax of local enterprises (except the income tax of the above-mentioned local banks, foreign investment banks and nonbanking financial institutions), profits from local enterprises, personal income tax, urban and town land use tax, investment orientation adjustment tax for fixed assets, urban maintenance and construction tax (except the payment from the railway transportation department, and all head offices of all banks and insurance companies), house property tax, vehicle and vessel use tax, stamp tax, slaughter tax, agricultural (animal husbandry) tax, deed tax, fertile land use tax, inheritance and gift taxes, land value increment tax, and payment for the use of national land, and so on.

The revenue shared by central and local governments will include the VAT, natural resource tax, and transfer tax. As for the sharing of the VAT, 75 percent will be allocated to the central government and 25 percent to local governments. After the reform of the industrial-commercial tax, the VAT will become the most important indirect tax, and will apply to all stages, from industrial production to commercial wholesale and retail trade.

The rationale for including the resource tax in revenue sharing is that the state is the owner of all resources and the central government retains the right to share part of the revenue. However, the actual situation is that most of the mineral resources are located mainly in midwest regions and in poor areas (see Chapter 3). Thus, distribution is to be according to the types of resource: most of the resource tax will go to the local governments. However, the resource tax on offshore oil will be allocated entirely to the central government.

The transfer tax will be shared equally by central and local governments. The reason for sharing the tax in this manner is that, although the stock exchanges are located in large cities, the tax revenue comes from all over the country. Therefore, it is inappropriate to allow the local government, where the exchanges are located, to retain all the revenues. Consequently, the tax is to be shared by central and local governments.

Fix the amount of tax repayment from the central government to the local governments. In order to maintain the present activity levels of local governments, and achieve the objective of the reform gradually, a part of the taxes collected by the central government is to be returned to local governments on the base of 1993 local revenues. Thus, according to the actual revenue of local governments in 1993, given the new tax reform and revenue assignments, the net sum to be turned over by the local governments to the central government would be determined by the consumption tax plus 75 percent of VAT revenues minus established transfers from the central to local governments. Thus, if the net amount to be turned over is equal to the 1993 transfer, this amount will be retained by the local government—thereby ensuring 1993 levels of aggregate local resources. After 1994, the transfer will increase annually given the 1993 base. The increment would be determined by a 1:0.3 coefficient, based on the average rate of increase of national VAT and consumption tax revenues; that is, an increase of 1 percent of the above-mentioned two taxes would lead to a 0.3 percent increase in the central government transfer to the local governments.

Treatment of the central and local government transfers. In order to implement the tax-sharing system reform smoothly, after its introduction in 1994, the distribution pattern of the old system will be reformed gradually. Thus, the central government subsidy (or transfer) will remain in practice, and the turnover system for local governments will be retained as well. Those areas with a "payment of a fixed amount to the higher authority," and "progressive increase in the payment to the higher authority" will still practice these methods. Those areas with "dividing up the total amount" and experimenting with the new tax-sharing system will practice the method of "progressive increase in the payment to the higher authority."

In general, after the introduction of the tax-sharing system reform, the initial central government revenue is expected to increase to 57 percent of the total national revenue. However, the amounts equivalent to the increment will be transferred to the local governments given the base-year formulation described above. Therefore, the central government's own revenues will initially remain unchanged, and the center will not benefit directly from the newly introduced tax system reform. But from a long-run perspective, the central government will have approximately little more than half of the increment of the VAT. This practice embodies the principle that the central government will eventually control most revenues, achieved on an incremental basis.

There are also some weaknesses in this reform scheme. First, the base figure is determined in the hope that local financial capability will be secured. There is no large adjustment between regions; therefore, the existing disparity between regions in financial capacity cannot be eliminated. Second, more studies are needed in order to establish a more scientific and reasonable transfer system in China.

Generally speaking, the basic objective of the intergovernmental reform in China is to adjust the fiscal system, to adapt to the need of building a socialist market economy, and to get closer to the established international practices. This is an important and time-consuming task and will require major efforts on the part of the central and provincial governments.

3

China's Financial Policies for Minority Nationalities and Poor Areas

M. Zhu Zhenjun*

At present, China is devoting itself to setting up and perfecting a socialist market economy system, by using the successful experiences of other countries. A series of significant reforms in planning, investment, finance and tax, monetary and foreign trade have been made. Among these, the reforms of the financial and tax system are the key links. This paper provides background information on a major element in the relations between different levels of government: policies concerning minority and poor areas.

Concept of Minority and Poor Areas

China is a unitary state but, with 56 nationalities, is a multinational country. The Han people form the majority, accounting for 91.96 percent of the population. The other 55 nationalities are known as the "minority nationalities." The minority nationalities of China have been living in the country for generations. As members of the Chinese national family, they, together with the Han people, form the multifaceted culture of China. After the founding of the People's Republic of China, the status of minority nationalities was described in the Constitution, and regional national autonomy was assured. Thus, the rights and status of the minority nationalities are protected under the highest legal authority in China.

At present, there are 158 national autonomous areas in China, comprising 5 autonomous regions, 30 autonomous prefectures, and 123

*State Nationalities Commission, China.

autonomous counties (banners). Among the 55 nationalities, 45 have established autonomous areas, forming 78 percent of the total minority peoples in China. The area of the "minority nationalities" with regional autonomy amounts to 64 percent of the land area, with a population of 160 million, accounting for 13 percent of the population. In addition to guaranteeing the autonomous right of the minority people inhabiting the scattered and sparsely populated areas, there are about 1,700 autonomous villages (townships). In 1984, the "Law of Regional National Autonomy of the People's Republic of China" was promulgated and implemented. In law, it is stipulated that the "minority" autonomous areas will enjoy wide rights of legislation, economy, science and technology, culture, education, public health, and managing local finances. These rights differ from the standard local constitutions and legal provisions. In 1993, China again issued and enforced the "Urban National Working Rules of the People's Republic of China" and the "National Village (Township) Working Rules of the People's Republic of China." These established a national relationship of equality, unity, mutual cooperation, joint development, and common prosperity.

China, with a vast territory and large population, is a developing country. Given factors of history, geography, and so on, the economic development of each economic region is obviously in a state of imbalance. The economically undeveloped areas are mainly scattered in the desert, mountainous, and karst areas of southwest and northwest China. These areas have concentrations of poor people, and because of the factors of history, most of the population of these areas are minorities. Thus, the national minority areas are also the poorest areas in China. Until 1992, 27 million were classified as having unmet basic needs. Of these people, more than 80 percent were in the national autonomous areas. Another 80 million could be classified as poor. In recent years, the Chinese government has made strenuous efforts to address the problems of the poverty-stricken areas of the national autonomous regions.

A state of comparative prosperity is likely for the people of China by the end of this century, given current growth rates. However, some pockets of poverty are likely to remain in areas of central and western China. Moreover, the gap in social and economic development levels, in comparison with the eastern coastal areas, is getting wider. This is because of the relatively fast growth of the economy of the coastal areas, given the reforms and open policy of the past fifteen years. In order to address this problem, the Chinese government proposed a plan to eliminate the poverty of 80 million people in the central and western areas of China over a period of seven years. To accomplish this, the targets of the ninth five-year plan envisage that the Chinese government would provide additional resources to meet measures to reduce poverty in such areas by the end of the century. According to this plan, direct financial support to the poor will be supplemented by measures related to economic restructuring.

Financial Support Policies for Minority and Poor Areas

After the founding of the People's Republic of China, a series of special policies and measures for the minority and poor areas were instituted, by the Constitution and law, in order to realize the goals of equality, unity, mutual cooperation, joint development, and common prosperity of various nationalities.

The national autonomous areas had the right of financial management. In 1963, when China operated under a planned economic system, the central government specially set up a financial management system for the national autonomous areas. It included the following:

• The balance of expenditures by the state would be made up by transfers, after local revenues and expenditures were checked and ratified by the state.

• Subsidies given to the national autonomous areas were to increase by 5 percent of final expenditures on administrative and institutional expenses of the previous year.

• The allocation of a reserve fund was 2 percent higher than in non-autonomous areas.

• Grants to the minority areas were provided in the state budget each year.

• The local governments' surpluses of the previous year, and excess shared revenue in the process of implementing the budget of a given year, were to be retained by the local governments.

• Subject to the basic principles of the national tax law, the autonomous regions could influence tax rates in their areas, when necessary, subject to State Council approval.

In 1980, during reforms of the planning system, the Chinese government implemented the fiscal contract system (as discussed in other chapters—see, e.g., the discussion in Chapter 2). Under the new system, it was stipulated that the national autonomous areas would carry out their own fiscal management, while some special transfers for these areas would remain in the state budget. The resources of five autonomous regions, and Yunnan, Guizhou, and Qinghai provinces (hereinafter called eight poor provinces and regions), increased at an average rate of 10 percent a year. Meanwhile, a special fund from the central budget known as the "development fund supporting the undeveloped areas" was also set up. In 1992, for example, central transfers to the eight poor provinces and regions were 14 billion yuan and accounted for about 40 percent of total revenues, or 31.83 percent of the expenditures of these poor regions. In addition, the Chinese government established a number of special funds in the budget items of the central and local governments. These included the "development capital for supporting the economic undeveloped areas," "grants-in-aid for minority areas," "flexible fund for minority nationalities," "subsidy for the construction of border areas," "subsidy for capital expenditure of the border areas," "Wu-bao (basic needs) fund for the poverty-stricken counties of the minority areas," "special funds for the education of minority nationalities," "agricultural construction funds supporting Sanxi" (namely, Zihaigu in Ningxia, Hexi, and Dingxi regions in Gansu), and "construction funds for the 'Sanzhou' autonomous prefectures in Sichuan" (namely, Liangshan, Aba, and Ganxi), and so on.

At the same time, policy measures were taken to reduce and exempt taxes in the poor areas, and to encourage more credits and loans of financial institutions to be invested in the minority and poor areas. Subsidized interest was provided for "special loans for the economic development of the poor areas," "special loans for the township enterprises in the central and west of China," and so on, set up by the central financial institutions.

At present, with a transition from a fiscal contract system to a separate tax system, transfers will be needed to support policies in minority and poor areas. First, the interests of minority and poor areas should be kept in mind with the new tax system. The objective of tax reforms in China is to set up a new financial management system, which is suited to the demands of the socialist market economy, and to further strengthen macroadjustment and control by the central government. But, in design, it is not meant to adversely affect local interests. Attention, however, is needed to ensure that resources of the poorer areas are not reduced but are increased normally. The overall growth in revenues will permit an increasing increment for the poorer areas. Thus expenditure responsibilities should be clarified, for local governments, to ensure that there is no need for borrowing to meet local outlays, thus reinforcing macroeconomic management.

The stipulations in the proposed revenue-sharing system are that the base year for the local revenue level, to be assured by the central government, is taken as 1993. Thus, local taxes will be supplemented by the central government, out of its own taxes and shared revenue (e.g., 75 percent of VAT collections), so that 1993 nominal revenues for local governments are maintained. The local governments will have a complete and independent tax system and the legislative power on assigned taxes, after the implementation of the new tax system. The specification of the local taxes, to have a wide tax base, will also have a direct bearing on local economic development. Thus, local governments will emphasize local tax resources, tap the potentialities, and enforce effective collection. It is expected that local revenues, overall, will increase as a result of the reform.

Second, central government resources would continue to provide strong support for the undeveloped areas. As in Japan, and other countries, the central government plays an important role in redistribution across regions, to provide greater support to the poorer and less developed provinces. Since China is a large and diverse country, the central government also has a redistributive role but has lacked the resources to reasonably regulate the distribution of revenues between the regions. With additional revenues accruing to the central government, the systemic reform of fiscal relations should not only support the development of the developed areas but also the economic development of the undeveloped areas, through revenue sharing, transfer payments, and special appropriations (special purpose grants) by the central government.

Third, sharing the natural resources tax will greatly increase the financial revenue of the minority and poor areas and promote development of the regional economy. China has a vast territory and abundant resources, but natural resources are mainly concentrated in remote and mountainous areas, especially in the minority regions. Such regions, which form 64.3 percent of the total territory of China, account for 94 percent of the grassland; up to 41.6 percent of forest resources; and 52.5 percent of the water reserves of the whole country. Moreover, the regions have more than 90 percent of the deposits of rare metals, magnesium, and chromium; and over 35 percent of coal, copper, lead, zinc, and antimony; as well as abundant reserves of oil and natural gas. With effective use of this resource base, local governments should have ample revenues for rational development of the region.

Fourth, the existing special funds and transfers will be maintained in the short to medium term, to protect local activity levels, and will be standardized gradually through the tax-sharing and transfer system. The new revenue-sharing arrangements, however, are likely to confer benefits to the more advanced regions, and a new system of grants and transfers is still to be specified. The base period method of transfers is to be continued as an interim measure, but lacks a sound basis.

Policy Reforms in the Minority Areas

In the transition period between the new and old economic systems, the direction of the policies should support and provide preferential treatment to the minority areas.

A Factor-Based Method for Support to Minority Areas

The base number method adopted, taking the year 1993 as the base year, is an interim measure. Eventually, this method should be replaced by the factor method. The factor method would be based on the determinants of local finance, such as population, land area, cultivated land per capita, GNP per capita, proportion of minorities, geographical condition, natural resources, and circumstances of social development (as used by Australia in the determination of grants). Relativities would be determined by the government, taking into account relative disabilities on both the expenditure and revenue sides.

A comprehensive assessment of the various factors is needed to evaluate central and local government responsibilities. Both quantitative and qualitative analyses are needed to delimit the classification of central or local activities.

Guarantee of Minimum Levels of Public Services

In order to sustain the basic needs of social development of poor areas, and narrow the gap in social and economic development with other areas, different types of financial aid have been given to the local governments in different periods. In the past decades, there has been some experimentation to improve the economy in the minority and poor areas. Central government support has been used to improve the investment climate of these areas and to help them promote development of social services. The per capita incomes and expenditures in the minority and poor areas, however, are lower than the average for China. In many remote areas, minimum basic public services are still not met.

In many countries, the main objectives of transfer policies are to solve the problem of local fiscal disequilibria and to ensure a minimum standard of basic public services. The disequilibria of the local governments include vertical and horizontal imbalances, and a system of grants is needed to address such imbalances (see also Chapter 15).

Tax Administration, Assignments, and Revenue Sharing

The objective of the reform of the system of tax assignments and administration is to encourage local governments to increase revenues by expanding the tax base, reducing arbitrariness, and raising the transparency of the tax system. This system should provide for adequate social services and provide incentives to restrain expenditures.

In China's tax reform (see Chapter 9), it has been decided to extend the scope of local taxes, to include resources, together with a simplification, amalgamation, and elimination of some tax categories. This reform can address both the issue of higher prices for raw materials of energy and the rational use of resources. More resources would then be forthcoming to the poor regions, thus narrowing the gap between east and west China. Despite this tax assignment, additional transfers may be needed, as noted above. These would include both "equalization" grants, as well as special purpose funds, but more work is needed to specify these transfers more precisely.

The Budget, Macroeconomic Control, and Legal Framework

4

Budget Policy in China

Bert Hofman and Shahid Yusuf*

Budget policy in conjunction with the planning mechanism was the most powerful instrument available to governments in socialist economies. Its importance was magnified by the passive role played by money and the degree to which credit management was an extension of the budget and the plan. Saving was to a large extent redistributed throughout the budget, according to plan priorities. With progressive decentralization and the spread of market institutions, the role of budgetary policy has changed. Moreover, the emergence of the socialist market economy has fundamentally altered the role of the budget in macroeconomic management. There is a need to redefine budgetary policy goals and to overhaul the making, as well as the implementation, of this policy.

This paper addresses the changing role of budgetary policy in China. It describes the main budgetary trends over the reform period and analyzes the various government functions performed with budgetary means. It then examines factors influencing the future direction of budgetary policy and the consequent need for change in scope and function of the budget. The paper concludes with policy recommendations.

Trends in Expenditures and Revenues over the Reform Period

Narrowing the scale of central government activities has brought about a decline in budgetary expenditures from 31 percent of GNP in 1978 to 20.4 percent in 1991 (Table 1). The deepest cuts have been in

* The World Bank.

Table 1. Revenues and Expenditures as Percent of GNP

	1978	1979	1980	1981	1982	1983	1984	1985	1986	1987	1988	1989	1990	1991
Budgetary expenditures[1]	30.96	31.86	27.13	23.36	22.21	22.25	22.21	21.53	24.04	21.67	19.35	19.26	19.84	20.39
Central	14.21	16.19	14.56	12.62	11.08	11.06	10.61	9.76	9.92	9.13	7.58	7.00	7.89	8.05
Local	16.75	15.68	12.57	10.74	11.13	11.19	11.6	11.77	14.11	12.53	11.77	12.26	11.95	12.34
Budgetary revenues[2]	31.25	27.60	24.28	22.83	21.64	21.50	21.57	21.78	23.31	20.96	18.79	18.67	19.04	19.25
Central fixed revenue		3.95	3.88	4.71	4.98	6.40	7.53	8.26	9.45	8.02	7.48	7.00	7.86	7.36
Central revenue after tax sharing				13.99	11.90	11.48	11.94	11.27	11.82	10.91	9.40	8.94	9.77	
Local revenue		23.65	20.39	18.12	16.67	15.10	14.04	13.52	13.86	12.95	11.32	11.67	11.18	11.89
Local revenue after tax sharing				8.83	9.75	10.02	9.64	10.52	11.49	10.05	9.40	9.73	9.27	
Adjusted budgetary expenditures[3]	36.8	39.5	35.2	32.4	31.1	31.7	30.5	30.5	30.6	28.1	25.7	26.3	26.0	25.6
Central	16.7	19.8	18.4	16.6	15.0	15.6	14.5	14.2	12.8	11.8	10.3	9.8	8.8	
Local	20.0	19.6	16.8	15.8	16.2	16.0	16.0	16.4	17.8	16.2	15.4	16.5	17.2	
Adjusted budgetary revenues[4]	37.1	34.3	32.0	31.7	30.0	30.3	29.2	29.9	28.7	26.4	23.5	24.2	23.9	22.1
Central				17.7	15.3	15.4	15.2	14.8	13.6	12.6	10.5	10.2	9.4	
Local				13.9	14.8	14.9	14.0	15.1	15.1	13.8	13.1	14.0	14.5	

Source: China Statistical Yearbook, 1990 (English) Tables T6.13 and T6.14, and update from China Statistical Yearbook, 1991; Ministry of Finance data; authors' calculations.
[1]Expenditures refer to administration of expenditures.
[2]Include debt issue.
[3]Exclude debt issue.
[4]For adjustments, see text.

capital expenditures, from 12.6 percent of GNP in 1978 to 3.9 percent in 1991, as reforms transferred the bulk of investment responsibilities to state-owned enterprises. Further sharp cuts took place over those same years in budgetary defense spending, from 4.7 percent of GNP to 1.8 percent. Against the general trend, nondefense current expenditures rose slightly, from 13.7 percent of GNP to 14.7 percent; social expenditures, administration, and price subsidies all grew moderately in terms of GNP, while debt service grew very rapidly, albeit from an extremely small base. Decentralization of government functions enlarged the budgetary presence of local government, and the devolution of decision power increased the importance of local government in the budgetary process. The central government's share of budgetary expenditure is now below 40 percent, down from a peak of 54 percent in 1981.[1]

Some of the most rapidly rising expenditure categories have increasingly fallen on local authorities, which in turn have developed extrabudgetary sources of income to finance their current and capital expenditures. The decline of the public sector's economic functions is reflected in the reduced share of investments (capital construction and technological transformation). This has been particularly sharp at the local government level: in 1978, the central-to-local split was about 56:44; in 1991, it was 74:26. Culture, education, science, and health enlarged their share of the budget, and price subsidies increased from nil to 10 percent of the budget. Budgetary revenues have declined in parallel largely because of price and enterprise reforms. By 1991, the ratio of revenues to GNP was little more than half the level in 1978 (Table 1).

Recasting the Budget

Chinese fiscal statistics do not follow international practice, and for meaningful comparison certain adjustments have to be made. The main ones of concern are (1) Subsidies to state-owned enterprises are treated as negative revenues rather than expenditures; (2) Debt issue is treated as revenue rather than as a financing item; (3) Debt repayment is treated as expenditures; (4) Extrabudgetary funds are a part of general government revenue because only about 20 percent are revenues of local finance bureaus and administrative or nonprofit units. Adjusted for these accounting differences, expenditures *including fiscal extrabudgetary expenditures* show a declining trend in terms of GNP, but government has a much higher share: this fell from 36.8 percent in

---

[1]For a more thorough discussion, see World Bank, "Budgetary Policy and Intergovernmental Fiscal Relations," Report No. 11094-CHA (Washington: World Bank, 1993).

1978 to 25.6 percent in 1991. The decline in revenue is on the order of 10–22.3 percent of GNP in 1991. The adjusted figures for expenditures shed a different light on the scale of the government's activities: a 26 percent share of GNP is comparable with other Asian developing countries, which averaged 27.0 percent in 1988 (Table 1).

Quasi-Fiscal Activities of the Central Bank

The incomplete delineation of the budgetary and monetary sector enabled the government to make ample use of quasi-fiscal activities of the central bank, and of para-fiscal activities of the specialized banks. Throughout the 1980s, seigniorage obtained was very high. Seigniorage from currency alone reached as much as 4.8 percent of GNP in 1988 and 1992. The seigniorage from reserve money—currency plus reserves of the banking system at the central bank—amounted to over 7 percent of GNP in 1990 (Table 2).

Scope and Policy of the Budget

The scale of the budget and the policy environment are affected by several forces: revenue mobilization and budgetary balance, development function, and industrial restructuring.

Revenue Mobilization and Budgetary Balance

Until the early 1980s, revenue was raised primarily through the state-owned enterprises by way of tax payments and profit remittances. To facilitate the extraction of surplus, state-owned enterprise income was augmented by fixing relative prices so as to transfer resources from other sectors to industry. Control over industrial wages and enterprise spending served as additional implicit taxes, which helped to further raise the (taxable) profits of state-owned enterprises. This system of enlarging the pool of resources in one sector and using price, wage, and expenditure controls to maximize the state's command over them was responsible for the high rates of saving in the socialist economies, most notably in China.

Reforms required a radical alteration in the scale of the budget and its role as a policy instrument. Fiscal decentralization, increased enterprise autonomy, and the emergence of a large nonstate sector have lessened both the mobilization and the allocation of resources through the budget, without significantly diminishing the resources at the command of various state entities. Over the reform period, China's

Table 2. Seigniorage in China

	1984	1985	1986	1987	1988	1989	1990	1991	1992
	(In billions of yuan)								
Currency	79.2	98.8	121.8	145.4	213.3	234.2	264.1	317.4	432.9
Change in currency		19.6	23.0	23.0	67.9	20.9	29.9	53.3	115.5
Reserve money		228.6	282.7	322.3	405.5	501.7	657.2	825.2	971.1
Change in reserve money			54.1	39.6	83.2	96.2	155.5	168.0	145.9
GNP	696.2	855.8	969.6	1,130.1	1,406.8	1,599.3	1,769.5	1,985.5	2,387.6
Inflation (in percent)	4.5	9.0	4.8	5.1	11.8	8.9	6.3	4.2	7.3
	(In percent of GNP)								
Seigniorage from currency		2.3	2.4	2.1	4.8	1.3	1.7	2.7	4.8
Inflation tax over currency		0.8	0.5	0.5	1.2	1.2	0.8	0.6	1.0
Real currency expansion		1.5	1.9	1.6	3.6	0.1	0.9	2.1	3.8
Seigniorage from reserve money			5.6	3.5	5.9	6.0	8.8	8.5	6.1
Inflation tax over reserve money			1.1	1.3	2.7	2.3	1.8	1.4	2.5
Real reserve money expansion			4.5	2.2	3.2	3.7	7.0	7.1	3.6

Source: Bert Hofman, "Seigniorage in China" (mimeograph, Washington: World Bank, March 1993).
Note: Seigniorage is estimated as the expansion of money as a percentage of GNP; end-of-year figures are used for money. The inflation tax is estimated as the money stock of the previous year times inflation in the current year. The real money expansion is calculated as a residual of seigniorage and inflation tax. Inflation is the percentage change in GNP deflator. All estimates should be considered as preliminary; the use of annual figures overestimates the amount of seigniorage.

budgetary revenues have declined significantly, from 31.3 percent of GNP in 1978 to 16.8 percent in 1991.[2] The main factor behind the decline in revenues has been the reduced budgetary contributions from state-owned enterprises—direct tax payments and profit remittances—which fell from 20.6 percent of GNP to less than 5 percent during the period, while enterprise losses—registered as negative revenue—grew strongly. Enterprise income reached 55 percent of total revenues through the mid-1970s before tax reform reduced this component to virtually zero in the mid-1980s.[3]

This shift of resources out of the budget was essential for sharpening incentives to reform and developing support for reforms at the provincial level, but it has curtailed the power of budgetary policy and reduced the volume of resources that the government can directly commit for building infrastructure. The budget now plays a minor part in resource mobilization and savings. Government savings are a small fraction of the total, as they are in other East Asian economies. However, China's current tax system does not adequately serve even the government's much narrower expectations regarding budgetary policy. The revenue base is shrinking for a variety of reasons having to do with tax coverage, exemptions, and collection problems. Further, tax revenue has a modest income elasticity. Access to funds from other sources has enabled the various levels of government to avoid a revenue crunch. But this makes budgetary planning very difficult and fiscal functioning is rendered inefficient.

Development Function

When the budget served as the conduit for the bulk of investment funding, budgetary policy defined the tempo and direction of development activity. In China, industrial development, which attracted a disproportionate share of resources for capital spending, was closely keyed to budgetary decisions, and the government's sectoral or regional priorities could be implemented with minimal lags through budgetary initiatives. Allocational decisions, however, were concentrated in the hands of planners, and market forces were excluded from playing a vital part in investment allocation. On balance, the reduced scale of the budget, and within it a redistribution toward public services and away from capital spending, has been a healthy trend and makes China's budget-driven development activities more nearly com-

---

[2]Chinese definition, excluding debt issued.

[3]C. Wong, "Fiscal Reforms and Local Industrialization: The Problematic Sequencing of Reform in Post-Mao China," *Modern China*, Vol. 8 (April 1992), pp. 197–226.

parable with those of other East Asian countries. A further reduction at this stage would be disadvantageous because, as emphasized by several cross-country studies, capital spending, particularly on infrastructure, financed through the budget, can be vital for removing bottlenecks, encouraging investment in productive activities, and attracting foreign capital, all of which raise growth rates.

Industrial Restructuring

Budget policy had been used as an instrument for industrial development in the past, and it is inevitable that to some degree, postreform industrial restructuring must be financed through the budget. This is especially the case in the early stages of reform when the banking system is still immature and direct state intervention is necessary to motivate restructuring and absorb some of the shocks. A shrinkage in budgetary resources, however, has drastically curtailed the government's ability to support restructuring directly, but budgetary funds continue to play a catalytic role. In China, as in other former socialist countries, they are supplemented by resources the government directs through extrabudgetary channels and the financial system. With industrial restructuring, the state is beginning to use mergers, group formation, and closure to far greater effect, as the buoyancy of the economy makes it easier to absorb redundant labor in other activities. As is inevitable given revenue trends, much of the transient costs of restructuring are being borne by the financial system, as are some of the long-term costs of industrial change. Together they absorb a large part of the seigniorage acquired by banks. Under the current decentralization procedures, industrial financing, which draws on seigniorage, cannot be differentiated adequately from other types of lending activities, directed or otherwise. The government is actively trying, however, to contain the cost of restructuring, and the trend of such expenditures is likely to be downward. But a clearer delineation of the banks' quasi-fiscal expenditure and their incorporation into the budget would enhance the efficiency of budgetary policy and relieve banks of a considerable burden.

Regional Policy

Fiscal decentralization and a smaller resource envelope have reduced the scale of regional policy, whether for fiscal equalization or industrialization. This is to be expected given the spirit of reforms and the greater labor mobility now permitted. Development in China is more likely to proceed along lines of comparative advantage and is increasingly a provincially financed affair. Poverty alleviation and infrastructure building in the interior provinces, however, still require fiscal support from the center so that some of the benefits from past balanced growth can be sustained. While the central government has continued to assist the poorest provinces, it has been unable to arrange for an interprovincial resource transfer on a sufficient scale to meet their needs. Further poverty reduction and avoidance of a progressive widening in interprovincial disparities require larger transfers. To do this, the center must generate more budgetary resources and arrive at new central and provincial sharing arrangements (see Chapter 3).

Macromanagement

Prior to the start of reforms, macroeconomic balance and price stability were achieved through planning, administrative controls over spending, and price regulation. Budgetary policy did not make a significant independent contribution. Since the early 1980s, with the gradual dismantling of planning, budgetary policy has increased its actual and potential role in the sphere of macromanagement. Because of relatively prudent fiscal management, which has entailed scaling back government expenditures as revenues have fallen, plus the availability of resources from seigniorage averaging 5–6 percent of GNP, budgetary deficits were held to an average of 2 percent of GNP and financed in large part by noninflationary means. Thus, budgetary policy has not been a significant source of inflationary pressure. By the same token, it contributed little toward stabilizing the economy in 1985 or 1988–90. Direct controls over investment, credit, wages, and prices of consumer items and industrial intermediates were principally responsible for deflating the economy. The nature of tax-contracting arrangements and the rigidity of most expenditures in the short term has also meant that these have not served as automatic stabilizers. A number of developments described below, however, suggest that budgetary policy may need to be used more aggressively for macromanagement and that this function might come to dominate resource mobilization and developmental roles.

Factors Influencing the Future Role of Budgetary Policy

In spite of declining tax revenues, the various levels of government have been able to pay for capital construction, subsidies, and state-owned enterprise deficits by mobilizing extrabudgetary funds that utilize the resources yielded by seigniorage and drawing on abundant household savings. Demand shocks have been controlled by administrative means and through the application of price controls. Over the medium term, it is likely that extrabudgetary revenues will remain stable while resources from seigniorage decline. In addition, making full use of the market as an allocation mechanism requires reducing the use of administrative controls. The stripping away of administrative controls will affect the government's ability to put a lid on demand pressures using its traditional instruments. Both of these trends signal the need for strengthening macromanagement through the budget.

Access to Extrabudgetary Funds

Local authorities were successful in raising extrabudgetary funds from the enterprise sector, because of the control they exercise over the burgeoning collective sector. With the spread of market institutions, a changing structure of ownership has increased the countervailing power of those owning or managing China's nonstate enterprises. There is more resistance to the raising of rates and surcharges by local governments. With greater market integration and competition between localities for business, the share of extrabudgetary resources is unlikely to rise and may gradually decline.

Changing Money Demand

As indicated earlier, the Chinese government has augmented its fiscal resources through the seigniorage obtained by the People's Bank of China and the specialized banks. Seigniorage derives from the increase in money balances and inflation, which erodes their value. During the early stages of reform, forced saving may have influenced the demand for money. But, by and large, demand for liquid assets, which has pushed monetary velocity from 1.65 in 1985 to 0.94 in 1992, is the outcome of precautionary and transactions needs linked to income growth.

Monetization of agriculture, marketization of state-owned enterprises, and strong growth in the less integrated nonstate sector increased the number of market transactions per unit of GNP, and thus fueled demand for money. Moreover, until very recently, monetary assets, such as cash and bank deposits, were the only assets available for a population eager to save in the light of increased income growth. Generally, positive real interest rates made this form of financial repression relatively benign and prevented flight into real assets. Increasing liberalization raised the consumption-based interest rate in China even higher than the measured real interest rate, because postponement of consumption not only yielded good returns, but delay allowed consumers the option to choose from a wider variety of goods, many of a higher quality.

Cross-country experience suggests that velocity might not decline much further. Financial liberalization, which is in itself highly desirable for efficient allocation of savings, has led to a rapid increase in the supply of alternative assets, besides bank deposits. Stocks, enterprise bonds, land, and foreign currency are beginning to provide alternatives for deposits in the banking system, and monetary expansion now triggers speculation in urban real estate and demand for foreign exchange, which pushes down swap market rates for the renminbi. Since early in 1993, these developments were fueled by disintermediation from the banking system, not least due to negative real interest rates on bank accounts. Such asset diversification is in principle desirable from the standpoint of resource allocation, as it provides a variety of financing instruments with a range of risk characteristics, but it can be destabilizing for the banking system in the short run. The message for monetary and fiscal policy is that to minimize inflationary pressure, much less reliance on seigniorage is mandatory, as asset diversification is likely to increase the level and variability of money velocity. Hence, China's government must reduce its demands on the banking system to meet fiscal needs. Fiscal reform is thus a necessary complement to stricter monetary control.

Enterprise Independence

Although government control over state-owned enterprises is being curtailed, it remains fairly extensive. In times of macroeconomic instability, these regulatory powers have reinforced the effectiveness of administrative measures. Thus, state-owned enterprises have been rationed in large part by administrative means; whereas monetary measures have been used to check the growth of nonstate enterprises. With the adoption of "The Regulations for Transforming the Operating Mechanism of the State-Owned Enterprises," direct government control of enterprises will erode further and provincial finance bureaus will be able to exert less influence than they currently can over the state-owned enterprises under their jurisdiction. At the same time, substantial efficiency gains will be realized, as investment and production decisions are delinked from political considerations. Further, a hardening of the budget constraint of enterprises will speed up adjustment and should in principle reduce the need for budgetary subsidies to cover losses of state-owned enterprise. The upshot of all this will be that government will be less and less able to use enterprise spending as a macroeconomic stabilization tool in the future. More of the burden of macroeconomic management will fall on the budget, but budgetary policy will also not be hamstrung by obligations to the state sector.

Changing Social Protection

With the acceleration of price reforms, and growing household income, budgetary subsidies will rapidly diminish. But, over time their place will be taken by new forms of social protection, as most of the social security and pension delivery is shifted off the enterprises' books. Although, in principle, the finance for such functions is there—the enterprises have paid for it thus far—the central government, in conjunction with provincial authorities, will have to impose new levies to raise additional resources for social security payments.

Increasing Regional Disparities

Since 1992, cross-provincial growth rates have diverged even more than in the past, with poorer provinces registering lower growth and hence relatively weaker fiscal performance. Both for efficiency and for equity reasons, regional redistribution is a priority. The present fiscal system is ill-equipped for this increasingly important task, and new ways to redistribute fiscal resources among regions should be developed in the context of overall reform (see Chapter 3).

Policy Recommendations

China's fiscal system served the country well under a regime of central planning. In the context of overall fiscal reforms, however, China's budgetary process and intergovernmental relations need fundamental change to support fiscal policy that promotes macroeconomic stability, efficiency, and equity. Fiscal reforms are more likely to succeed if all parties perceive some gains. This argues for comprehensive reforms. Budgetary reforms and changing intergovernmental relations should therefore go hand in hand with broadening the tax base, creating a local tax base, rationalizing the tax collection system, and giving the central government greater macroeconomic control by way of indirect instruments. The experience with fiscal reforms over the recent past suggests that the experimental, regionally limited, piecemeal reform method, successful in many areas, may not work with fiscal reforms. A gradual nationwide implementation of an established reform plan might yield better results.

The Budget and Scope of Government

Budget reforms must change the scope, content, and objectives of the budget and budgetary policy. In the long run, the budget should clearly reflect the government's role. Nongovernment activities should be removed from the government budget and fiscal accounts, including enterprise extrabudgetary funds. Budgetary investment expenditures should concentrate on government functions. As far as possible, fiscal extrabudgetary funds should become an integral part of the budget. Government activities now performed by enterprises, such as social security, should be included. Quasi-fiscal activities of the banking system should be made transparent in the budget. As soon as this is feasible, policy lending by the banks should be curtailed and to the extent possible handled through the budget. Unifying government activities in the budget is a precondition for the budgetary process to become a meaningful mechanism for allocating scarce resources across government objectives. A unified budget will also greatly increase the effectiveness of macroeconomic policy.

The government's share of the economy should be an outcome of the change in budgetary scope instead of being a goal in itself: there is no objectively optimal share of government in an economy. More important is the ability to finance the desired share of government in a noninflationary way: tax reforms and tax administration reforms should in the long run achieve that goal and eliminate recourse to the banking system.

Broadening the Tax Base

For the government to find sustainable finance for its activities, the tax base needs broadening. China's plans to unify the enterprise income tax and abolish repayment of debt before taxes, to accelerate the introduction of an economywide VAT, and to introduce various other taxes is a step in the right direction. However, for these plans to succeed, satisfactory arrangements in intergovernmental finance need to be found. China's authorities should clearly assign functions over levels of government, with efficient service delivery and fiscal equity as guiding principles. Control over government functions crucial for macroeconomic stability should be recentralized, including control over aggregate government borrowing, and overall tax burden.

Own-Tax Base

China's authorities should assign each level of government a substantial own-tax base, to finance those functions for which it has full responsibility. Assigning local governments a local tax base would raise the level of accountability and provide incentives for better and cheaper public services. Own-tax bases can also serve to absorb variations in expenditure needs without periodic renegotiation of intergovernmental fiscal relations. Finally, extension of the local tax base would iron out many of the current problems with the system of intergovernmental fiscal relations. For local government, property taxes would be an excellent own-tax source, which is thus far hardly exploited in China.

Tax Sharing and Equalization

A full separation of tax bases in China is probably not feasible, nor desirable in the light of efficiency of collection, given the establishment of the State Administration of Taxation. The fiscal gap between expenditure needs and revenues from the own-tax base can be filled by tax sharing, general grants, specific grants, or a combination thereof. The divergence in economic performance and fiscal capacity among regions calls for a fiscal system with equalizing properties. Horizontal equalization of fiscal capacity between localities can be achieved though tax-sharing arrangements or through equalization grants.

The Budget as a Policy Tool

The budget's importance as a macroeconomic policy tool needs to be explicitly recognized. One way of doing this would be to issue a background document on the economic outlook along with the budget, which defines the macroeconomic assumptions underlying the budget and explicates their implications.

Multiyear budgeting, and a stronger coordination of the budget and the Development Plan, would improve assessment of the macroeconomic impact of government policy. Development of automatic stabilizers, both on the expenditure side and on the revenue side, would enhance the responsiveness of fiscal policy to fluctuations in output and employment.

Budget procedures and techniques should allow for shifts in expenditure categories, in line with the changing needs of China's society. This requires abandoning the incremental "base number" technique of budgeting and adopting budgeting techniques that are program oriented.

China's budget classification and presentation need adjustment to accommodate multiple users and uses. Adoption of the international standard of budget categorization and presentation is strongly recommended. The presentation of the budget should incorporate an economic analysis of government plans. In addition, the functional and administrative classification should be such as to assign spending authority to specific ministries, units, and levels of government. A wider publication of a more detailed budget would signal the government's policy intentions, and the fiscal stance of the budget, to sectors that are no longer under direct government control. This would improve coordination and speed up desired adjustment to new policies in the rest of the economy.

5

Budget Laws, Control, Review, and Management in China

Ehtisham Ahmad, Maurice Kennedy, and Ingrid Klering*

The development of a framework of budget laws in China is important in clarifying and managing the financial resources of the government and is crucial in establishing levers of macroeconomic control. A framework of laws that contain or have an impact on the development of the budget, its approval by the National People's Congress (NPC) and the corresponding arrangements at local levels of government, the management of its execution and adjustment, and the processes for the accountability of those responsible for the administration of government programs will affect almost everyone who has a role in government. Of themselves, laws cannot ensure effective financial management. It requires both political will and an awareness of policy-makers and managers at each link in the chain from the highest level of government to those delivering the services. But laws are the levers of change.

China had no organic budget law until 1994.[1] Although interim regulations were issued in October 1991, they are inadequate in dealing with the relationship between the NPC and the government, and between the central and local governments (defined here to include all subnational levels).

---

*Ahmad and Klering, International Monetary Fund, and Kennedy, Ministry of Finance, Australia.
[1]This paper was written before the budget law was considered by the National People's Congress in 1994. However, principles in this paper could be used to guide future amendments. *Ed.*

Major Principles of Public Expenditure Management

The budget should be seen as an instrument of macroeconomic management and a mechanism to ensure the efficiency of government resource allocation. Macroeconomic management can be greatly influenced by budget laws: in the way powers are distributed among the executive and legislative branches, and between different levels of government; limitations on activities funded through extrabudgetary funds; and whether constraints on borrowing or deficit are included in the legislation.

Different approaches to budget management have been taken by different countries, with varying degrees of emphasis on the powers of the ministry of finance within the executive, and between the executive branch and parliament. The legal aspect is a requirement that there should be an adequate machinery to ensure allocation of resources and payment of monies for specified purposes and their accounting. A key consideration in each stage is that specific responsibilities be allocated to designated officers to execute tasks according to defined procedures. In addition, the law should specify that budget execution shall be subject to audit by an independent auditor reporting directly to parliament. A primary task of the audit is to ensure that the designated officers perform the tasks according to the defined procedures. Such a function is designed to give parliament an assurance that the executive is using appropriated funds properly.

Legal Framework of Budgeting

Budget legislation can be viewed at several levels: constitutional, organic budget law, annual appropriation and special appropriation budget laws, and financial regulations and executive instructions issued by the Minister of Finance. Countries differ greatly in the extent to which their laws in this area are formally codified. Common law countries, such as the United Kingdom and countries of the British Commonwealth, rely heavily on established administrative practice and the procedures of parliament as a basis for budgeting rules. By contrast, civil law countries, such as Germany, Italy, and France, have extensively codified their budgetary law.[2]

---

[2]In France, the relevant legislation is given in a few documents: (1) the Constitution, (2) the Organic Budget Law, and (3) the Public Accounting Act, 1989. By contrast, in the United Kingdom, in addition to common law and administrative precedents, relevant legislation includes: (1) the Public Revenue and Consolidated Fund Charges Act, (2) the National Audit Act, (3) the Local Government Planning and Land Act. By far the most important document is the "Government Accounting Guidelines," which is, however, not an act. For the United States, the relevant legislation includes: (1) the Constitution, (2) the Act of Congress and the Treasury Act, 1789, (3) the Budget and

The *constitutional provisions* for budgeting present the highest level in the legal hierarchy and, compared with ordinary legislation, have the greatest binding force due to the special requirements regarding procedures for amendment. A constitution would deal usually only with the broadest matter of principle, such as the requirement that all public funds should be paid into designated accounts and that these accounts can only be spent under the authority of a law, and provisions relating to the relative powers of the executive and legislative branches with respect to public finance legislation. The definition of the financial relations between national and subnational levels of government is explicitly stated in the constitutions of some countries, such as Germany, Australia, and India.

The *organic budget law*, which may take the form of a single law, or several general laws, is drafted, like any other law, to be in force for an indefinite period of time. It provides binding principles for budget management and auditing. It provides, in greater detail, the framework of control that governs the processes of the annual appropriation of funds, as well as accounting for use of the funds by the legislature. As an integral element of the process, the responsibilities of each organization are also specified.

Annual appropriation laws, which are enacted under the provisions of the constitution or organic budget law, primarily serve the purpose of obtaining authorizations from the legislature for public funds to carry out government programs. Other laws may also have budgetary implications over an indefinite period, such as, inter alia, for social security payments, government borrowing, and debt. To cover such open-ended expenditures, there are often special or standing appropriations (see below on budget "lock-ins").

To ensure uniform application of the budget legislation and the government financial operations between different ministries and spending agencies, the minister of finance generally issues more detailed budget regulations and instructions on behalf of the government.

Structure of a New Budget Law for China

In addition to an organic budget law, there should be a provision for supporting rules and regulations to facilitate day-to-day administration. These could be at two levels: (1) regulations issued by the Ministry of Finance under the authority of the State Council that

Accounting Procedures Act, 1921 and 1950, (4) the Congressional Budget and Impoundment Act (the Budget Act), (5) the Balanced Budget and Emergency Deficit Control Act, (6) the Budget Enforcement Act, 1990, and (7) the Chief Financial Officers Act.

could deal with matters subject to a degree of variability, and (2) instructions issued by the Ministry of Finance concerning matters of procedure to be binding on agencies and enterprises. It is important to note here that the budget law should provide that the regulations be consistent with it, and the instructions with the regulations. In this way, all three tiers of laws and rules would, between them, form a comprehensive and cohesive framework for budgetary and financial control and management.

General Principles and Objectives

A budget law should deal clearly with objectives and matters of principle. It would be beneficial if the objectives were also to include a reference to "the achievement of efficient, effective, economical and moral (ethical) performance in the management of the state's financial resources." By including these particular matters as part of the budget law's objectives, the sections in the law relating to legal responsibilities and obligations can, and should, then include a complementary requirement that the heads of agencies must manage the resources made available to their organizations through the budget in ways that ensure that the law's objectives are met. This would expressly strengthen the process of calling them to account for their performance as financial resource managers and, in turn, the performance of their employees who are accountable to them. This would be a key concept in raising the awareness for better financial management by all in the chain of control over budget resource use. Key technical definitions should be stated explicitly in the budget law. It should in its introductory section identify the main actors responsible for implementing the budget law and then state specific responsibilities in following sections. Any breach of these responsibilities should incur a penalty. The very central role of the minister of finance should be highlighted. Moreover, to ensure that both government and the legislature focus on a clear analytical definition of the budget deficit, the definition of the deficit should be included in the budget law.

Table 1 shows that, from a sample of the countries of the Organization for Economic Cooperation and Development, the budget law identifies the main actors, and especially the Ministry of Finance, responsible for the administration of the law. A technical definition of the budget deficit, however, is not always included in the budget law. For example, France, Portugal, and the United Kingdom do not include any explicit provisions on the deficit.

A central feature of a budget law, as a control mechanism, is its specification of the way in which the use of public money is to be authorized.

Table 1. Examples of Technical Definitions in Organic Budget Laws

Country	Technical Definition of Budget Deficit Comparable with Fund Accounting[1]	Administrative Agencies Administrating the Budget Law	Extrabudgetary Funds
Australia	Budget deficit defined in accordance with Fund accounting. No explicit provisions on definitions on revenue and expenditure (AA).	The Executive Council; Department of the Prime Minister and the Cabinet Officer; Minister of Finance and his Secretary of State; Treasury Department; and the Auditor General (CFMH par. 2.25).	There are funds that do not go through the annual appropriation process (needs a special instruction). All funds are presented in the annual estimates (C par. 81, 83, FMAB 38).
France	Organic budget law contains no explicit provision on technical definitions.	The Council of Minister; Minister of Finance and the Secretary of the Budget; Planning Commission; The National Institute of Statistics; and, the Office of Regional Development (LDF).	There are no funds that do not go through the annual appropriation process (needs a special instruction). All funds are presented in the annual estimates (LDB sec. 4).
Germany	Budget deficit defined in accordance with Fund accounting. The law includes provisions defining revenue and expenditure (LBP par. 38, FBC par. 25, 81).	The Federal Council; Financial Planning Council; Budget Committees; Federal Minister of Finance; The Federal Revenue (LBP, FBC).	There are funds that do not go through the annual appropriation process. All funds are presented in the annual estimates (C par. 12, FBC par. 37–39).
New Zealand	The law contains no explicit provision on technical definitions on budget deficit. Revenue and expenditure is defined (PFA par. 2).	The Executive Council; Minister of Finance; and the Treasury (PFA).	There are funds that do not go through the annual appropriation process. All funds are presented in the annual estimates (PFA par. 8, 9–12).
Portugal	Organic budget law contains no explicit provision on technical definitions.	The Plenary of the Republic; Minister of Finance and ministers of departments; and the Audit Court (AL par. 21, 22).	There are funds that do not go through the annual appropriation process. All funds are presented in the annual estimates (AL par. 3).

Table 1 *(concluded)*

Country	Technical Definition of Budget Deficit Comparable with Fund Accounting[1]	Administrative Agencies Administrating the Budget Law	Extrabudgetary Funds
Sweden	Budget deficit defined in accordance with Fund accounting. No explicit provisions on definitions on revenue and expenditure (GAG).	The Minister of Finance; Secretary of the Budget and the Budget Department; National Debt Authority (Treasury); and the National Audit Office (C chapter 9).	There are no funds that do not go through the annual appropriation process. All funds are presented in the annual estimates (C chapter 9).
United Kingdom	The law contains no explicit provision on technical definitions.	The Treasury and Chief Secretary to the Treasurer; Treasury Officer of Accounts; Management and Personnel Office; Paymaster General's Office; Principal Finance Officer; and the National Audit Office (GAG section D, E).	There are no funds that do not go through the annual appropriation process. Not all funds are presented in the annual estimates (GAG section A, B).
United States	Budget deficit defined in accordance with Fund accounting. The law includes provisions defining revenue and expenditure (BSC page 32–34, CBP section 3).	The Congressional Budget Office; Treasury and its Secretary; Office of Management and Budget; heads of departments and agencies; and the Comptroller General (BSC page 2–4).	There are no funds that do not go through the annual appropriation process. All funds are presented in the annual estimates (BSC page 3–4).

Note: See appendix for sources, p. 73.

[1] In principal an analytical definition of the budget deficit that excludes borrowing and use of bank balances from receipts and repayment of principal from expenditure and is equal to net financing.

The budget law should stipulate that no money is to be spent unless there is an appropriation (an authorization to spend moneys received in the public account, specifying both the amount and the purpose of the spending). Such provision will be the basis for ensuring control over all money and limiting the possibility of establishing funds not subject to budget laws or any misuse of funds. Thus, a budget revision is needed to authorize expenditures in excess of the initial appropriation.

The budget law should in this area also include provisions that appropriations under any law, other than the annual appropriation law, shall be included in the budget estimates presented to Parliament and accounted for in the same manner. Any earmarking should be clearly specified. The law should also specify the basis on which transactions are recorded—for example, on a cash or accruals basis.

The government's legal rights to collect revenues (taxes, fines, various levies, and so on) should be authorized by various laws intended to apply equally to all persons and enterprises. The budget law should contain a provision to ensure that such obligations to the government shall not be waived or forgiven by officials without the express, or delegated, authority of the minister of finance, and in accordance with conditions that the minister may impose.

The budget law should legally define the difference between those bodies that carry out the functions of government (also known as agencies), and those that function in their own right (defined as entities)—even if they are government controlled or owned. The above distinction relates to the scope of the budget, which would deal with the receipts and appropriations only for the functions of government. The establishment of this distinction is particularly important for China because of the blurred delimitations between enterprises and "state functions" particularly at the subnational level and the banking system. In most market-oriented countries, entities, such as state-owned enterprises, pay dividends to the government, as well as taxes, which are both included in the budget. The budget also includes appropriations for the working capital and subsidies paid to the state-owned enterprises by the government. The day-to-day receipts and payments of the enterprises as they undertake their business operations are not included in the state budget.

In developing or refining a system of budget law, the ability to classify each government body properly and consistently according to its status as well as the correct classification of budget receipts and payments and their consequent control and management is an issue of the greatest importance.[3] Under the conventions of *Government Finance Statistics*, cash operating surpluses of state-owned enterprises are shown as nontax revenues, whereas losses are treated as subsidies.

Power Over Budget Management

The way in which power over the budget is shared between the executive and legislative branches and within the executive branch is a reflection of political forces. Thus, a fundamental requirement of a budget

---

[3]See International Monetary Fund, *A Manual on Government Finance Statistics* (Washington: IMF, 1986), Chapter III, pp. 93–108.

law is to define the rights, powers, obligations, and responsibilities of those to whom the law applies. In budget law, there are normally five distinct functions, within *each* tier of government forming the bounds of "fiscal legality," which are performed by the following different players: the political body (NPC or subnational congress), the executive or administrative arm (committees or individual ministries), the Ministry of Finance or treasury, heads of agencies, and, the Auditor-General.

Paramount Political Body

The role of the NPC or subnational congresses (as specified in the Constitution) is to formally enact the principal matters (and matters of principle) that it wishes to permit or compel the executive government or administrative arm to undertake. In most countries, proposals for budget legislation emanate from the executive arm for the consideration of the paramount political body. As indicated in Table 2, the power of the legislature to amend the budget prepared by the executive varies substantially among countries. In Germany, Sweden, and the United States, the legislature has unlimited powers to amend the budget, whereas the powers of the legislature are relatively limited in this regard in the United Kingdom, and most of the countries of the British Commonwealth, and France. The powers of the legislature over the budget are most extensive in the United States, and this situation has given rise to a series of attempts to establish legislative limits on the budget deficit (e.g., the Balanced Budget and Emergency Deficit Control Act, 1985 and the "Gramm-Rudman-Hollings Act") and the establishment of the Congressional Budget Office to assist Congress to review the President's budget proposals and initiate its own proposals.

Executive or Administrative Arm

The role of the executive or administrative arm is to propose budget legislation and to carry out and implement the laws enacted by the supreme legislature. The formal authority is exercised by individual ministers (or heads of executive committees) but is normally passed to individual officials, to undertake the financial functions that the paramount body has sanctioned. Desirably, such authority should be expressed in formal instruments of delegation or authorization to the officials concerned.

Ministry of Finance or Treasury

The role of the Ministry of Finance or treasury should include the right and obligation to issue binding rules to officials in all other

Table 2. Examples of Power Over Budget Management

Country	Power of Legislative Branch	Power of Minister of Finance or Treasury	Subnational Financing
Australia	The legislature has no power to come up with new proposals. It may amend in executive proposals as long as the Parliament does not increase the burden on the people (CFMH par. 1.3, 1.4).	To be responsible for economic, fiscal, and monetary policy; draft and propose the budget; evaluate and review government programs, expenditure, and proposals. Be in charge of financial administration and control accounts, including the Public Account (AAO); to give warrants; and, to require all necessary information (CFMH).	The law does not cover such provision. However, the Australian Loan Council determines the total public borrowing, which is then shared between different tiers of government.
France	The legislature has no power to come up with new proposals. Although Parliament may raise expenditures if other expenditures are reduced (LDF par. 67, 68, 82, 83).	As above but more emphasis on the overall control of public expenditure (C, LDF par. 84–89).	There is a binding balanced budget requirement for subnational levels (LDF par. 36, 37).
Germany	The legislature has unlimited power to come up with new proposals or propose amendments to the executive proposals (FBC par. 28–33).	As above (LBP, FBC).	There is a binding balanced budget requirement (C par. 109–110).
New Zealand	The legislature has no power to come up with new proposals. Although proposals may be amended as long as the Parliament does not increase the burden on the people (C).	As above but also to provide for such other matters as are necessary for giving full effect to the proposals and for due administration thereof (PFA par. 79–81).	The law does not cover such provision.
Portugal	The legislature has no power to come up with new proposals, but proposals can be amended without limit (AL).	As above and emphasis on the ongoing system of budget management (PAL par. 1).	The law does not cover such provision. However, there is in practice a balanced budget requirement, and all tiers of government may contract loans only within limits set by the Assembly (AL).

Table 2 *(concluded)*

Country	Power of Legislative Branch	Power of Minister of Finance or Treasury	Subnational Financing
Sweden	The legislature has power to add new proposals and amend executive proposals without restrictions (C chapter 9).	As above (C chapter 9, GD 1992).	There is a balanced budget requirement. Subnational levels borrow on their own behalf (in any bank) (GD 1992).
United Kingdom	The legislature has no power to come up with new proposals. Taxes and expenditure may be reduced by the legislature but not increased.[1]	As above (GAG)	The law does not cover such provision. However, there is a general balanced budget requirement: total deficit may not exceed investment expenditure or more than 10 percent over their total allocation. Borrowing (by any bank) must be authorized from higher level.
United States	The legislature has power to come up with new proposals and amend executive proposals without restrictions (CBP Title I, II).	As above, mainly performed by the Treasury and the Office of Management and Budget (CBP par. 502).	The law does not cover such provisions. However there is a state balanced budget requirement (GRHA).

Note: See appendix for sources, p. 73.
[1]From "Summary and Guide to the Estimates"; Chapter 5, Parliamentary Procedures.

agencies,concerning the policies and procedures for financial management, controls, and reporting. This role should be based on powers expressly conferred on it by the paramount body or under delegated authority. Organizational patterns vary, and in a few countries the treasury is separate from the Ministry of Finance. In China, it may be appropriate for the Minister of Finance to exercise the treasury functions, as opposed to the banking functions that need to be specified (see below).

Heads of Agencies

The role of the heads of agencies reflects their responsibility for the overall management of their agency—including, inherently, the conduct of its financial affairs. In this role, they will be required to issue detailed operating instructions to their own personnel on financial procedures and practices that provide a local context to support rules issued from the ministry of finance or treasury. Their powers (whether ceded or inherent) to issue financial instructions and undertake financial management activities within their agency should be expressly limited so as to give no scope for conduct inconsistent with ministry of finance or treasury rules.

The Auditor

In most countries the auditor-general's task is to supervise the performance of the budget. Since the audit is, in effect, of the government's performance (see also below), the auditor-general should play a crucial part in making government accountable to the National People's Congress in China. The budget law should require that the accounts are audited properly. A separate law may be desirable to define the powers and responsibilities of the auditor-general. He should be compelled to report on the financial activities of each agency periodically (e.g., annually). To that end, the auditor should have a mandate and access powers, conferred by law, to examine and report on whatever aspect of an agency's operations he considers desirable, in order to facilitate evaluation and ensure efficiency.

Consideration should be given to make the auditor-general more independent, than at present, by making him formally responsible solely to the NPC rather than to the State Council (of which he is a member). Under such an arrangement, the auditor-general would furnish reports directly to the NPC, or a committee of the NPC. The government would remain responsible for rectifying any shortcomings in management or administration that have been identified by the auditor. Indeed, how well and how quickly the government responds to such reports or recommendations of the auditor is a significant strand in the accountability framework of the government to the NPC.

Subnational Levels

The division of responsibilities between the central and local level of governments, and the level of autonomy that local governments exercise, varies between countries. In China, under Article 99 of the Constitution, local people's congresses at and above the county level have the power to examine and approve the plans and budgets of their respective administrative areas. Under the current arrangements, the state budget, which consolidates the budgets of central and local governments, is considered by the NPC. This greatly complicates budgetary practices, since not all local congresses meet before the NPC considers the state budget.

An alternative, that might be feasible in China, is for the NPC to consider only central government revenues and expenditures, along with grants and transfers to local level governments; local people's congresses would then be responsible for the expenditures at their level, subject to their own resources plus centrally determined grants and transfers. This would greatly simplify the budget making and control processes, and permit decentralized expenditure decisions provided that borrowing by local governments is effectively controlled.

It has been recognized that the stipulation concerning zero net borrowing by subnational levels of government has been somewhat unrealistic, and that loopholes have permitted considerable indirect borrowing by local governments. Tightening the loopholes, involving a clearer distinction between the agencies of government and entities, such as enterprises owned by local governments, would be important. However, legitimate borrowing requirements of local governments should be recognized. Thus the budget law should permit borrowing by subnational levels of government, but restrict this to resources made available by the next higher level of government, or instruments approved by the central government. All forms of borrowing must be reported. Annual limits on overall borrowing would need to be specified by the central government in consultation with the relevant local governments, facilitating central control over aggregate borrowing and credit.

In many countries, the subnational levels of government are required by the budget law to submit their budget estimates to the Ministry of Finance—not for incorporation into a consolidated budget, but for the purpose of determining revenue shares and distribution of grants—and also to report outcomes periodically to the Ministry of Finance.

The Treasury

The budget law should define the role of the treasury. As indicated in Table 2, the role and power of the ministry of finance or treasury, in most OECD countries is well defined in the budget law. However, emphases vary—France, for instance, places greater weight on the overall control of public expenditure, while New Zealand emphasizes all matters necessary for providing full effect to the budget and for its administration.

The treasury should be responsible for all the assets and liabilities of the agencies of the government, including inter alia amounts of receipts that have not yet been banked, amounts held in bank accounts operated by agencies, and cash advances (amounts not yet spent). These amounts deemed to be in the treasury cannot be spent without an appropriation to ensure financial discipline. The treasury, within the ministry of finance, becomes the center of the government's system of budget implementation and collection of revenues, execution and control of expenditures, as well as maintenance of internal and external debt. While the exact institutional form differs markedly between countries,[4] the treasury's functions typically include the closely interconnected areas:

• budget execution (in terms of tax revenues, expenditure needs, and the financing of any deficit);

• the control of budget execution, and information flows for this purpose;

• the management of cash, assets and liabilities; and

• the accounting for all government operations according to standard rules; maintenance of central accounts.

A treasury could incorporate purely cash management and accounting functions. Maintaining the accounting of government transactions in the treasury, rather than the banking system, could speed up and improve the quality of information available to the Ministry of Finance for policy purposes. In some countries, a treasury plays a more "active" role in enforcing expenditure control through regular monitoring or cash limits on commitments and expenditures made possible by the recording of all stages of the payment process in the system. All extrabudgetary accounts should be brought into the treasury system, and local governments could also utilize the system to carry out and control the execution of their budgets. This would facilitate speedy information flows to the ministry of finance, even with decentralized decision making on expenditures and some revenue bases.

The budget law should specify that all the monies legally owned by the government must be paid as soon as practicable into a treasury bank account. This requirement would facilitate the introduction of active cash management and control functions by the Ministry of Finance or treasury.

The budget law should declare the minister of finance to be nominal custodian of the treasury and require him to safeguard, manage, and account for the treasury. All bank accounts opened and operated by agencies for dealing with monies of the treasury should be on the minister's behalf. Thus the budget law should give the Minister of Finance the exclusive power to arrange for the banking of treasury monies.

---

[4]The British Treasury carries out most of the functions of the Ministry of Finance. In France, the Treasury is one of the most important Directorates of the Ministry of Finance, again providing a mechanism of tight control. Control functions are more dispersed in the United States, where the Treasury shares responsibilities with many other influential players in the executive branch and Congress.

The maintenance of all government accounts by the treasury, and the consolidation of these transactions in the treasury account with the People's Bank of China (PBC) would minimize the level of unused cash balances, and put any such balances to the most effective use as determined by the treasury. While the main bank account of the treasury would still remain with the PBC, the relationship between the government (through the Minister of Finance) and the PBC would be changed to one between a client and a banker. The PBC would pay market interest rates on deposits, but charge the government for the services provided.

The budget law should also provide the Minister of Finance (treasury) with the power to require reports on any public account set up outside the budget framework and to control expenditure and use of credit within deficit limit, specified in the appropriation law.

Preparation and Approval of the Budget

The budget law should specify the principles and outline the processes whereby the expenditure plans of the budget are prepared, presented to parliament for review and approval, and appropriated by parliament. In this area, the law should specifically cover the proposed macroeconomic strategy for the budget period and periods in the future. Estimates should be prepared for each annual appropriation law, providing details of the amounts to be drafted to each head of expenditure, the purpose of each head and performance to be achieved during the budget year.

A feature common to most of the OECD countries is that the budget is prepared within a multi-annual planning framework (see Table 3). Thus the budget is considered in the context of a detailed analysis and statement of the government's medium-term economic policy. In some cases, the multiannual planning requirements are included in the law. In others, such as Australia and the United Kingdom, multiannual planning is a central feature of the budget process, even though there is no explicit legal requirement for this.

While some countries, such as France and the United States have specified limits to the budget deficit, such a target may not be appropriate to include in a budget law for China, given the difficulty of defining a sustainable deficit,[5] which may vary over time. However, each annual budget law should specify a target deficit for the year, and set

---

[5]The question of the appropriate definition and concept of the budget deficit is an issue of considerable importance (see, e.g., M. Blejer and A. Cheasty, "The Measurement of Fiscal Deficits: Analytical and Methodological Issues," *Journal of Economic Literature*, Vol. 29 (December 1991), pp. 1644–78).

Table 3. Examples of Preparation and Approval of the Budget

Country	Provisions on Budget Period and Multiannual Planning	General Budget Constraints	Contingency Funds
Australia	Budget year is July 1–June 30. There is no provision on multiannual planning, and no plan is approved by Parliament although the budget bill includes three-year estimates.	No constraints defined by law, but by political strategy described in the budget speech (e.g., the federal government shall have a budget surplus in 1996).	The Appropriation and Supply Acts include provisions for contingency funds to cover expenditure in advance for unforeseen or urgent need. The Parliament gets monthly reports (CFMH par. 1.16).
France	Budget year is the calendar year. Multiannual planning (three-year) is requested but not approved by Parliament (LDF par. 23–25, 61–62).	No constraints defined by law. Although there have been two major principles as a base for the political strategy; the central deficit must not exceed 3 percent of GDP and the tax burden shall be lowered by 1 percent a year.	The Finance Act includes provisions for the use of contingency funds to cover expenditure in advance for unforeseen and urgent need (LDF par. 49–51, 71).
Germany	Budget year is the calendar year. Multiannual planning (five-year) is requested but not approved by Parliament (LBP par. 51, 52).	Medium-term financial plans have restricted the growth of federal government expenditure to 3 percent a year in current prices.	Excess and extrabudgetary expenditure may be given by the Ministry of Finance only in the event of unforeseen and unavoidable need. Bundestag and Bundesrat shall be informed every three months (FBC par. 37).
New Zealand	Budget year is July 1–June 30. No provision on multiannual planning (PFA par. 46).	The law does not cover such provision.	The government has the power to meet the need of unappropriated expenditure and emergency expenditure and costs (PFA par. 37).
Portugal	Budget year is the calendar year. Multiannual planning is performed occasionally and is not approved by Parliament (AL par. 2).	The law does not cover such provision.	The law does not cover such provision.

Table 3 *(concluded)*

Country	Provisions on Budget Period and Multiannual Planning	General Budget Constraints	Contingency Funds
Sweden	Budget year is July 1– June 30. Multiannual planning (five-year) is requested but not approved by Parliament. The "plan" is more of a scenario, including all government obligations and commitments (PD 1974).	No constraints defined by law but by political statement; medium-term plans to cut expenditure by 10 percent over a period of three years, ending 1995.	The Ministry of Finance has power to make money available for expenditure during the year in the event of unforeseen and unavoidable need. Parliament gets reports every six months (C chap. 9).
United Kingdom	Budget year is April 1– March 31. The law does not cover provisions on multiannual planning, however, a three-year plan is prepared and presented to Parliament but does not require Parliament's approval.	No constraints defined by law, but by medium-term political financial strategy to keep the deficit within the plan.	The treasury has power to make unappropriated expenditure in case of unforseen and urgent needs (GAG section A).
United States	Budget year is October 1–September 30. The budget covers the four years following the budget year; however, these estimates are not approved (BSC page 1, CBP par. 501).	Budget deficit reduction target is set out in the GRH Act that sets an annual reduction target until the budget is balanced. An automatic process takes over that cuts expenditure across the entire budget, although this law has been modified several times (GRHA).	The law does not cover such provision.

the maximum level of domestic credit to be allowed during this period. These targets should be consistent with the desired macroeconomic strategy, for the current year and the medium term.[6]

The need to ensure flexibility in budgeting can present a problem unless there is discipline in the way the estimates are prepared. The procedures for preparing sound budget estimates are not matters for

---

[6]Multiannual financial planning is required in several countries such as Germany (five years), France (three years), and Australia (three years), but is generally not subject to parliamentary approval.

inclusion in the budget law. However, the timing is. Since the NPC does not meet to approve the budget until after the commencement of China's financial year, it is asked to retrospectively approve appropriations that have already been acted upon from the beginning of the financial year. It is not good law to validate past actions—rather, the law should approve future actions. Consequently, the budget law should contain a provision that creates a "standing appropriation" that appropriates, say, four-twelfths of the previous year's budget for ongoing expenditures to lawfully continue until the current year's budget is approved. The current year's budget submitted to the NPC should indicate how much is already authorized under the standing appropriation and how much extra the NPC is being asked to approve to make up the total of the current year's budget.

Execution and Adjustment of the Budget

The powers of the executive and the Ministry of Finance to control budget execution are crucial to enabling the government to adjust quickly to changing economic circumstances. To ensure such powers, the budget law should specify that no expenditure shall be undertaken by any spending ministry without a warrant (i.e., an authority issued by the minister to commit funds for certain purposes in a specified time) from the Ministry of Finance. Other means to enable control in this area are to require that the Minister of Finance shall ensure that funds are authorized by law before issuing a warrant; that transfers between budget heads shall require supplementary appropriation laws; but that the minister of finance may approve transfer of funds between chapters within the same head and may issue regulations in this area; and, that the Minister of Finance shall report back to the NPC if major changes have been implemented.

Adjustment of a budget during the course of a year is a problem that occurs in most countries. The budget law may permit the budget of each year to contain an appropriation line item that permits up to an identifiable amount (possibly set in terms of a small percentage, for example, 2 percent, of the previous year's estimate of budget appropriations) to be spent on urgent and unforeseen expenditures, on the authority of the Minister of Finance. Such expenditures would be reported to the NPC and should be subject to audit by the independent auditor-general.

As indicated by Table 4, the European systems, as a rule, give implicit authority to the executive, through the Ministry of Finance, to limit outlays below the level authorized by parliament if economic circumstances so dictate. In the United States, however, the budget is pre-

Table 4. Examples of Execution and Adjustment of the Budget

Country	Warrant Necessary Before Disbursement	Power for Ministry of Finance to Withhold Expenditure	Rules for Virement	Rules for Carry-Over to Next Year	Expenditure Controlled by
Australia	A drawing right must be issued by the Ministry of Finance before disbursement (FMAB par. 46).	The Executive is authorized to give warrants up to the appropriated amount but is not obliged to (FMAB par. 46).	Virement is possible between subheads and within running costs, however, this is not regulated by the law.	Capital expenditure may be carried over, however, this is not regulated by the law.	The Ministry of Finance, treasury, and officials appointed by the Ministry of Finance (FMAB par. 26).
France	Issued by the Ministry of Finance, any decree or bill of any ministry must bear the countersignature of the Minister of Finance (LDF par. 71, 108).	The law does not cover such provision.	Virement is possible within a limit of 10 percent of the appropriated amount (LDF par. 90).	The law does not include such provision.	Minister of Finance; Finance Comptroller, of the Ministry of Finance represented at each of the various ministries. The treasury and official of Ministry of Finance sit in all committees to ensure due attention to financial matters and enjoy the power of veto (LDF, DB).
Germany	Approval by the Ministry of Finance is required before disbursement (FBC par. 36–37).	Power is delegated to the Minister of Finance to be used if the development of revenue and expenditure so requires (LBP par. 25, FBC par. 41).	Virement is possible within the same chapter, between salaries and wages and from expenditures on civil servants to salaries.[1] Must be approved by the Minister of Finance (LBP par. 15, FBC par. 20, 46).	Investment expenditure and expenditure from earmarked revenue may be carried over[2] (LBP par. 15, FBC par. 19).	Minister of finance; head of departments and agencies (FBC, LBP).

New Zealand	The law does not explicitly require a warrant before disbursement. However, the law gives the Ministry of Finance or treasury a possibility to require any information, which is used as a base for a warrant system (PFA par. 81).	Appropriated amount constitutes the maximum amount to be used (PFA).	Money may be transferred if (1) the amount does not increase an appropriation by more than 5 percent, (2) no other transfer has been made during the year to the same appropriation, and (3) the total amount is unaltered (PFA par. 5).	The law does not cover such provision.	The Ministry of Finance; the treasury; Chief Executives; and heads of departments (PFA).
Portugal	Authority to authorize expenditure is assigned to the officials of agencies and departments to the extent of the powers of current management that they hold (AL par. 23, 24).	Appropriations constitute the maximum amount to be used in making expenditure (AL par. 18).	The law does not include such provision.	The law does not include such provision.	The Ministry of Finance; heads of departments and agencies (DL par. 53).
Sweden	Issued by the Minister of Finance, all bills must bear the countersignature of the Minister of Finance or officials appointed by the minister (GD 1974).	Appropriations other than for mandatory expenditure, constitute the maximum amount to be used. The government is not obliged to use the maximum amount (GD 1986).	Virement permitted within and between votes. Needs approval by the Ministry of Finance. Parliament is informed twice a year (GD 1992).	About 10 percent of all appropriations are accepted to be carried over. In principle, all appropriations to governmental authorities can be carried forward until the end of the third year (GD 1981).	Ministry of Finance; head of spending ministries; the National Debt Authority; and, the National Audit Office (C, PDs, GDs).

Table 4 (concluded)

Country	Warrant Necessary Before Disbursement	Power for Ministry of Finance to Withhold Expenditure	Rules for Virement	Rules for Carry-Over to Next Year	Expenditure Controlled by
United Kingdom	Issued by the Minister of Finance (GAG section D).	Appropriations other than for mandatory expenditure constitute the maximum amount to be used. The government is not obliged to use the maximum amount (GAG section D).	Virement between sub-heads is possible but needs approval by the treasury. The treasury has no power to authorize virement between votes or to meet additional expenditure with virement (GAG section B).	Appropriated funds are in principle made available for one financial year only. If the money is not required to meet expenditure chargeble to that year, it cannot be carried forward into the next. Exemptions can be made for capital expenditure that can be carried forward to the next financial year.[3] (GAG section A, B).	The treasury; accounting officers within departments and agencies; the Comptroller and Auditor General (GAG section C, D, E).
United States	Issued by the treasury (BSC page 6).	The president cannot impound or delay the use of appropriated funds without approval from the Congress (BSC page 4–6).	The law covers no such provision.	The law covers no such provision.	Office of Management and Budget, the treasury, and heads of departments (BSC, CBP).

[1] Expenditure budgeted without detailed purpose may not be transferred to another chapter nor carried forward.
[2] Transfer is accepted within department; between departments needs consent of minister of finance. Only investment expenditure and expenditure from earmarked revenue may be carried over.
[3] With approval by Parliament only for transfers between votes. About 5 percent of capital expenditure and defense expenditure are carried over.

pared on an obligation basis and requires an explicit impoundment to be approved by Congress before the expenditure authority can be withdrawn. In the United States, it is thus difficult to adjust expenditures during the year.

The Ministry of Finance also exercises varying levels of authority over the rights of ministries to move funds from one type of expenditure to another (virement) and to shift spending from one budget period to another. In general, OECD countries have streamlined controls in this area with a view to giving maximum flexibility to managers to allocate resources to achieve the required results. As also shown in Table 4, Australia, Sweden, and the United Kingdom, for instance, give departments substantial freedom to reallocate resources for departmental running costs. In New Zealand, departments and agencies have freedom to reallocate resources within the amounts appropriated to produce a certain class of outputs; other movement needs approval of the Governor-General or the Parliament. Some provision to shift resources between budget years is given in most of the countries shown.

"Budget Lock-In"

The legal effect of the NPC's approval of the budget is to authorize the government to proceed to finance its spending proposals. The basis on which the government proceeds will depend on whether it is being compelled or merely permitted to implement particular programs.

The explanation of this distinction lies in the fact that it is common practice for the framework of appropriations to reflect the policies contained in other nonbudgetary laws (e.g., laws that specify the conditions under which a person qualifies for an entitlement to some benefit; or a statutory commitment of a particular level of expenditure to a project). If there is no discretion for the government but to pay such a benefit or finance the project at that level, it can be said that the appropriation for the payment is a "compulsory" appropriation. On the other hand, an appropriation covering, say, hiring more staff or purchasing some asset can be said to be "permissive" or discretionary—as the government can make choices about whether to proceed, how fast, to what standard, and so on—and it is up to the government to decide not to spend any or all of the amount appropriated.

Governments that are burdened with budgets containing a high proportion of compulsory appropriations experience what can be described as "budget lock-in"—the loss of fiscal policy flexibility. It may assist the NPC's deliberations of the budget and heighten its awareness of that problem if the supporting documentation submitted with the annual budget were to include a table of total proposed receipts and payments showing the compulsory payments separately from the discretionary expenditures (Table 5).

Accounting

The budget law would require that accounts are prepared and audited. The form of accounting should be prescribed by regulations under the authority of the Minister of Finance. These would ensure that each and every operation is recorded in an accurate manner, to provide a continuously updated picture of government operations, with clear advantages for management. Hence, proper definition and implementation of the government accounting framework and methods are essential for budget management. Some of the main principles of government accounting methods include universality (all transactions should be subject to an accounting operation) and double entry accounting, to ensure better control. The accounting plan must be structured to ensure the availability of an appropriate account (or subaccount) for each and every operation. The lack of accounts for recording operations, such as the setting of limits on commitments or payments, would hinder the monitoring and control of the operations. A proper definition of accounting schemes is important to ensure that each stage, in any given operation, is recorded in the appropriate account of the accounting plan. Inadequate definitions of accounting schemes may result in lack of information needed for monitoring and control of government operations.

Table 5. Sample Table of Total Receipts and Payments

Receipts		Payments	
Taxes imposed under law	X	Compulsory payments to existing statutes	X
Other receipts from the operation of law (e.g.,fines)	X	Obligated payments to existing contracts	X
Receipts from the sale of goods and services	X	Additional payments proposed to be undertaken this year	X
Other	X		
Receipts from borrowings*	X		
Total	X		X

*Balancing item.

Audit

In most countries, the budget law includes provisions that ministries should prepare appropriate reports and submit financial documents to an external auditor. As can be seen in Table 6, the budget law typically includes provisions on the reporting of the auditor-general to parliament (e.g., as in Australia, France, the United Kingdom, and the United States). The auditor-general, appointed with the approval of

Table 6. Examples of External Auditing of Accounts

Country	Provisions on External Auditing
Australia	External auditing is performed by the Auditor-General, Director of the National Audit office
	The Auditor-General shall prepare audited financial statements on accounts and records of all departments and agencies' business and report to Parliament annually (CMFH).
France	External auditing is performed by the L'Inspection général des finances and La Cour des comptes.
	They audit government transactions and report frequently to Parliament (LDF par. 19–124).
Germany	The Federal Audit Office is responsible for all external auditing. The Auditor General reports to the Parliament and informs the Minister of Finance and Heads of Ministers once every year.
	Provisions on external auditing specify what shall be audited, functions of audit officers, subjects of audit, and time and form of audit (FBC par. 91–94).
New Zealand	The Audit Office is responsible for external auditing and shall each year prepare a report on the public accounts with comments to the parliament (PFA par. 30, 38, 43).
Portugal	The law does not cover such provision.
Sweden	The National Audit Office and the parliamentary auditors are responsible for all external auditing (C). The law does not cover provisions on how audits shall be performed.
United Kingdom	The National Audit Office ensures that the sums guaranteed by Parliament have been used for the purpose intended. NAO also examines the effectiveness of expenditures. It is completely independent and responsible to Parliament. NAO prepares auditing reports and values for money reports for the Parliament (GAG section c, F-M).
United States	Offices of Inspectors General perform auditing in all major departments and agencies. Heads of department are responsible for performing annual evaluation and reporting the results to Congress. The General Accounting Office is responsible for assisting Congress in its oversight of the executive branch in carrying out enacted programs. The Comptroller General works independently under the Congress (BA).

parliament as head of the audit office, is responsible for audit of all public moneys and assets, and all books of account of other funds or records relating thereto. The audit office establishes accepted accounting practice for preparation of government financial statements in consultation with the treasury department or ministry of finance.

The Chinese Constitution of 1982 established a system of audit.[7] As noted above, the auditor derives his authority and is responsible to the administration, acting under the direction of the premier of the State Council (Art. 91). Auditing bodies are established by local governments at local levels and are responsible to the auditing bodies at the next higher level. The nature of the audit in China is reflected in the 1991 "Regulations on Budget Management," under Art. 54, which states:

> Auditing departments at all levels shall take charge of auditing and supervising the execution of budgets of corresponding departments and People's Governments one level below

and Article 69, which states that

> [a]uditing departments at all levels have the right to audit the final accounts of all corresponding departments and those of People's Governments of a lower level.

The emphasis of the Chinese audit laws and regulations is on auditing the implementation and final accounts at lower levels of government. Local governments are responsible to local people's congresses. However, because of the administrative structure of the Audit Administration, problems with the implementation of local budgets (or their final accounts) must be reported by the auditor-general to the prime minister first before referring problems, through the local people's congress to take corrective actions.[8] There is thus relatively limited scope for the auditors at local levels to suggest corrections. Consideration should thus be given to making the local auditors report directly on the operations of local governments to local congresses, to circumvent the current lengthy procedures for suggesting and implementing corrective actions. This change should introduce greater accountability at the local levels.

An additional issue regarding audits in China stems from the limited ability of the auditor-general to supervise the central budget.[9] Since

---

[7]Under Sections 91 and 109.

[8]Under Art. 68 of the Regulations on State Budget Management.

[9]The central government budget is nominally supervised by the Public Finance Committee of the NPC, but this body has very limited personnel to ensure effective supervision.

the auditor-general is of the same level as other ministers and is a member of the State Council (Cabinet), which proposes and approves the budget, there is limited leverage over particular ministries. The auditor-general needs a request from the Prime Minister to audit such ministries and special funds.

Appendix

Main Legal Provisions Relating to the Budget in OECD Countries

Country	Legal Framework
Australia	The Constitution (C) The Audit Act, 1907, including amendments 1989 (AA) The Commonwealth Financial Management Handbook, 1992 (CFMH) Financial Management and Accountability Bill, 1993 (FMAB)
France	The Constitution (C) Les Lois de Finances (LDF) Les Droit Budgétaire (LDB) Le Comptabilité publique, 1989
Germany	The Constitution (C) The Law on Budgetary Principles for Federation and Länder, 1969 (LBP) The Federal Budget Code (FBC) The Law to Promote Economic Stability and Growth, 1969 (LES) The Law on Federal Audit Office, 1985 (LFA)
New Zealand	The Public Finance Act, 1989 (PFA)
Portugal	The Constitution (C) The Assembly of the Republic Law on Framework of the Budget, 1991 (AL) Ministry of Finance Decree Law, 1992 (DL)
Sweden	The Constitution (C) The Government Budget Decree, 174, 1989, 1981, etc. (GBD) Parliament Decrees (PD) National Audit Office General Accounting Guidelines (GAG)
United Kingdom	The Public Revenue and Consolidated Fund Charges Act (CFA) The National Audit Act (NAA) The Government Accounting Guidelines, 1986 (GAG) National Audit Office Framework for Value for Money Audits
United States	The Constitution (C) The Congressional Budget and Impoundment Control Act, "The Budget Act" 1974 and amendments (BA) The Balanced Budget and Emergency Deficit Control Act, 1985 "Gramm-Rudman-Hollings Act" (GRHA) The Budget System and Concepts of the United States Government, 1993 (BSC) The Congressional Budget Process, 1986 (CBP)

Expenditure Assignments

6

A Comparative Perspective on Expenditure Assignments

Ehtisham Ahmad*

Principles

Expenditure assignments influence the effective provision of certain services, as well as macroeconomic policy, but have important distributional implications. They are often based on a benefit principle, that the responsibility for the expenditure should be accorded to the jurisdiction within which the benefits are contained. The "responsibility," however encompasses (1) policy formulation, (2) financing arrangements, and (3) policy administration or implementation. A number of combinations are possible, given the existing institutional framework. Thus, mandates from higher levels, or given policy parameters, could be effectively combined with local financing and administration. Alternatively, central policies and certain types of financing may be negated by local administrations. This paper focuses on international patterns of expenditure assignment, as well as the possibilities for assigning responsibilities for social protection expenditures between different levels of government in China.

With respect to the nexus between administration and policy, there are three types of government programs. The first covers so-called national public goods that require centralized administration and, by necessity, policy. For example, decentralizing responsibility for macroeconomic stability, redistribution, and national defense would be inefficient. Second are so-called local public goods for which decentralization of administration and policy is feasible and generally con-

*International Monetary Fund. This paper is based on Ahmad, Hewitt, and Ruggiero (1994).

sidered to be desirable for allocative efficiency and administrative efficiency, for example, municipal services. Finally, there are mixed public goods for which there are advantages to decentralized administration but for which some degree of centralized coordination of policy is needed.

With primary education and preventive health care, there are certain efficiency advantages to local supply, such as possibly better quality through local supervision and some allowance for communities to express their preferences and priorities. Tertiary education and research and development, as well as hospitals, have economies of scale and benefits that would accrue to more than one jurisdiction—in such cases, higher levels of administration or finance may be needed. For distributional reasons, a nation might want a global minimum standard to ensure that regional disparities do not reflect income differences rather than different preferences. When conflicting goals arise, such as in this case, the analysis can become quite complicated and subject to normative biases. Therefore, one would expect different arrangements in different countries to arise, depending upon the global priorities of society and the government. The case of infrastructure investment is discussed by Hofman and Newfarmer (Chapter 7).

One of the primary conclusions that emerges is that administrative efficiency and allocation efficiency call for a large degree of decentralization of administration. In practice, industrial countries have more decentralized administration than developing countries on average. Perhaps of more interest, in the more highly centralized industrial nations, France, Italy, and Spain, significant tendencies toward decentralization of services is in evidence. This is combined with a centralization of revenue functions for efficiency of administration and to ensure a capacity for redistribution from richer to poorer regions. The distributional implications of expenditure decentralization, however, are often undesirable; tension often exists between expenditure assignments and financing arrangements. Grants serve as the coordinating mechanism that allows decentralized expenditures along with centralized tax collection. They can enable a large degree of decentralization, while allowing a country to pursue redistribution targets. Grants may cause a problem in that they decrease transparency and lead to fiscal illusion, and a trade-off emerges between the separation of administration from financing.

Once an administrative system is in place, there has to be an overpowering efficiency or budgetary reason to change it. Certain reforms to policymaking and financing arrangements may be needed, however, for macroeconomic control. In practice, there is considerable leeway in determining expenditure assignments, which are governed by a country's historical and institutional background. Thus, expenditure assignments in China should display "Chinese characteristics," given that the international experience is very varied.

The Government's Role

Before assigning duties between various levels of government, the scope for the public and private sectors must be defined. In principle, production and consumption of private goods should be left primarily to market forces. The government should then confine itself to cases where there are externalities and market failure. However, even when substantial externalities and informational constraints exist, as with large infrastructure projects, it is not evident that production of private goods should be carried out by the state. Private provision could be accompanied by other forms of intervention or regulation, such as the establishment of environmental standards and regulations. The case for state provision is strongest for public goods, and defense and public administration are examples of public goods par excellence.

The Central Government

There is little doubt that macroeconomic stabilization has to be the responsibility of the central government, although the allocational and distributional objectives are more debatable. Indeed, a variety of patterns are found around the world. Stabilization is difficult to achieve, however, without control of overall expenditure levels. Thus, assignment and control mechanisms of different types of expenditures are of considerable importance from the macroeconomic perspective.

The central government has significant efficiency advantages over local governments in ensuring income redistribution and the establishment of minimum standards across regions. This is because the ability of localities to provide support for low-income groups is severely limited by mobility of the poor, the rich, and businesses. Redistribution by a given locality in isolation can attract poorer individuals from neighboring localities.[1] In general, the greater the extent of mobility, the more difficult and costly it is to redistribute income within a locality. In countries where mobility is limited, such as China, need may be con-

---

[1]At the same time, if taxes are imposed on local factors of production to finance the redistribution, this can lead to a flight of capital and richer individuals, leading to a shrinkage in the resource base. Fixed factors, such as land, vary considerably across regions, and some localities may have very little scope for attaining minimum standards. Although intraregional redistribution remains a possibility, there are administrative advantages in the local identification of target groups and in mobilizing support for such groups.

centrated in regions that have limited ability to provide even minimum services. The establishment of minimal access to education, health, and other human services across regions may be seen as a socially desirable goal of central government. Such a redistributive policy implies at least a financing responsibility for the central government.

Subnational Levels of Government

Beyond the benefit principle, as described above, are few a priori guidelines on the allocation of responsibilities between the center and the provinces, and between the provinces and lower levels of government. Thus, considerable variety may be expected, in infrastructure, social services, and social protection policies. While there are advantages for decentralized administration, for example, in social protection—the needy are easier to define at the local level (i.e., township in China)—the policy and financing functions may not necessarily be the responsibility of the same level of government.

International Patterns of Expenditure Assignment

The systems of intergovernmental finance in many federations have evolved gradually, much like their market and political institutions, reflecting historical circumstances and cultural traits. Among the six major industrial federations (Australia, Austria, Canada, Germany, Switzerland, and the United States), the share of local expenditures in total government expenditures varies from 7 percent in Australia to 26 percent in Switzerland; the states' or provinces' share of total expenditures varies from 16 percent in Austria, to 48 percent in Canada.[2]

The share of local receipts of transfers from higher-level governments varies from 16 percent of total local revenue in Switzerland to 48 percent in Canada; the share of intergovernmental grants in total receipts of states or provinces varies from 16 percent in Germany to 50 percent in Australia. Each country has unique features. In Australia, state governments depend heavily on federal transfers; Switzerland is characterized by strong local governments with relatively little dependence on transfers; the United States has a pass-through transfer system from the federal government to state government to local government. In Canada, however, provincial revenue collection is relatively high (see Bird (1986)).

---

[2]Figures in this section come from International Monetary Fund, *Government Finance Statistics Yearbook*, unless otherwise noted.

In India, the constitution specifies expenditure assignments, but developmental and infrastructural concerns are addressed through the extra-constitutional Planning Commission, with the Finance Commissions addressing issues of revenue sharing and financing needs of the states. Expenditure control, given India's federal structure, is a major policy issue (see Chelliah, Rao, and Sen (1992)). In China also, overall expenditure control and responsibilities are critical elements of economic stabilization. Existing institutions and methods provide a starting point to determine desirable directions of reform.

A difficulty in assigning expenditure responsibilities lies in the fuzzy distinction between levels of administration in some countries. Moreover, as pointed out by Levin (1991), regulation is difficult to measure, and whereas finance and administration can be identified, neither fully represents the full range of activities carried out by the government. The difference between finance and administration lies in intergovernmental grants, financed by the grantor government and administered by the recipient administration in providing goods, transfers, and services. The financing (administration) of expenditures at a particular level is determined inclusive (exclusive) of grants given and net (inclusive) of grants received. Centralization ratios based on the administration of expenditures are likely to underestimate the role of the central government, particularly with respect to redistributional transfers that are generally made by the central authorities. The appropriate classification of extrabudgetary funds, particularly for social security, would also affect the reported degree of centralization.

The result of differences in control, finance, and administration of expenditures at various levels of government is often a vertical imbalance between the expenditures to be incurred by a subnational government and the resources available to it. Some of the resources, such as shared taxes and revenues, conditional grants, and borrowing options, provide a degree of control to higher levels of government. In some cases, the central government mandates certain expenditures, making for control over local expenditures even when these are administered and fully financed by the lower level of administration. At the opposite extreme are expenditures mandated and financed by the central government, such as minimum educational or health standards. Here, the effective control over the level of expenditures rests with the administering lower-level authority (health care in Italy), even though officials of the central administration are represented at the lower level (social expenditures in Pakistan). The reason for the loss of central control in the latter case lies primarily because of the effective underwriting by the central government of deficits or expenditure overruns at lower levels of government. Thus, in most cases, the form of transfers from higher levels of government and the associated incentives for limiting expenditure growth are important in controlling overall expenditures.

A wide variety of expenditure patterns (and associated grants) can be observed across the world. As Table 1 from Levin (1991) indicates, unclassified grants form a predominant share of transfers in countries such as the United Kingdom, France, and Australia. On the other hand, only 11 percent of grants in the United States and around 20 percent in the Scandinavian countries and Canada could be classified as free of regulations. Among developing countries, very few provide the distinction between different types of grants, although a substantial proportion of total expenditures is financed through grants in countries such as India (27.8 percent) or Indonesia (17.6 percent)—excluding transfers for local expenditures in both cases.

When possible to identify, grants allocated for particular functions provide an indication of the extent to which the higher levels of government wish to promote a particular activity. A substantive proportion of the expenditures on education is financed by grants in countries as diverse as Zimbabwe, the United States, and Canada, but very little in the United Kingdom and Germany. In the latter group of countries, however, unconditional grants are of considerably greater importance than in the former—thus indicating that even in a highly "centralized" system as in the United Kingdom, local authorities have some freedom to maneuver in allocating resources for education, despite the establishment of nationwide norms and curriculums.

Fiscal illusion has been observed in several countries for which a reasonably long time series is available (Winer (1983) for Canada, and Gramlich (1979), for a review of U.S. studies). Evidence is consistent with the hypothesis that the separation of decision making caused by substituting own resources with grants increases local expenditure beyond expectation, although the degree of illusion tends to subside over time.[3] A recent study of decentralization and government size in Latin America (which controls for a positive correlation between rising income and the size of government) finds that decentralization financed by central government transfers rather than by own revenues

---

[3]Brosio, Nyman, and Santagata (1980) tried to capture the effects of the separation of the ability to raise own revenue from expenditure assignments due to the 1970s fiscal reform, and they found that per capita expenditure was indeed positively affected. This increase was immediate, although it tends to decline with time owing to the financial problems soon encountered by the subnational governments, and caused by the central government limiting the amount of transfers granted to them. See also Brosio (1985). Rizzo (1985) also finds a positive impact of decentralization on government size in Italy, when coupled with a decline in fiscal responsibility of local administrators.

Table 1. Portions of General Government Expenditure Financed by Intergovernmental Grants

(Average of latest three years available)

	Ending Year	Total Expenditures[1]	Education	Health	Social Security and Welfare	Percent of Intergovernmental Grants Unclassified
			(As percent of general government expenditures)			
Argentina[2]	1987				88.0	
Australia	1987	24.5	30.6	8.2	1.4	60.0
Austria	1987					
Belgium	1987	6.3				0.0
Bolivia	1986	0.4				
Brazil	1987	14.4				
Canada	1987	16.7	50.2	22.9	9.4	21.8
Chile	1987	2.0			0.0	
Colombia	1984	19.1				
Denmark	1986	27.1	9.1	6.2	47.6	23.5
Finland	1987	16.5				
France	1985	6.8	2.7	1.0	1.1	78.0
Germany	1983	10.3	10.9	3.5	3.5	52.6
Hungary	1988	10.4				
India[2]	1986	27.8				
Indonesia[2]	1988	17.6				
Ireland	1987	16.5				
Israel	1986	3.7	18.1	0.7	2.4	51.2
Kenya	1984	4.3				21.1
Luxembourg	1987	11.5	4.9	23.8		
Malawi	1984	6.1				
Mexico	1984	3.3				
Netherlands	1988	23.5				
New Zealand	1981	2.1				
Norway	1986	15.2				16.2
Pakistan	1979	9.7				
Paraguay	1984	0.0				
Poland	1988	10.6				
Romania	1985	10.3				
South Africa	1986	14.9				
Spain	1986	9.8				
Sweden	1987	10.3				21.2
Switzerland	1984	14.9	21.9	7.3	9.4	19.4
Thailand	1982	3.9				9.8
Tunisia	1982	12.1				
United Kingdom	1987	13.3	3.9	0.0	6.5	66.4
United States	1987	14.9	42.8	18.7	13.2	10.9
Yugoslavia	1987	7.2				
Zimbabwe	1986	8.5	37.6	9.3	0.0	2.3

Source: Levin (1991) based on IMF, *Government Finance Statistics Yearbook,* Vol. 13 (Washington: IMF, 1989).

[1] Includes supranational authorities share of general government expenditures in Belgium (2.2 percent), Denmark (2.2 percent), France (1.4 percent), Germany (1.8 percent), Luxembourg (2.7 percent), and United Kingdom (1.9 percent).

[2] Data for general government do not include local government.

is likely to increase government expenditures (Reid and Winkler (1992)). A number of studies point out that the counterpart of fiscal illusion at the federal level is that grants will tend to lead to lower expenditures by higher level governments (see Hewitt (1986) and (1991)). Therefore, the impact of fiscal illusion on general government expenditures is uncertain.

In Italy, revenue centralization since 1973, coupled with the local administration of major expenditure items, such as health and social assistance (see Table 2), has led to a loss of accountability at the local level, leading to an uncontrolled growth of total public expenditure. The absence of own-revenue sources led to a reliance on ad hoc and gap-filling grants. This process has noticeably reduced the transparency of the transfer system and of the central government budget,[4] and local administrators are devoid of budgetary responsibility. While a considerable part of grants are driven by need, most allocations are based on past expenditure norms. With centralized norms for wages and some prices, it is impossible to determine whether local deficits are due to centralized decisions or to local mismanagement. Local residents are not aware of the local costs of services, since most are borne through general taxation. Thus, preferences between alternative local uses of resources are not revealed, and the allocative advantages of decentralization cannot be obtained.

Furthermore, the technical capabilities of local administrators are often inadequate to meet the budget preparation needs of the multiannual budgets, instituted to improve fiscal coordination and to facilitate central control of subnational expenditures. Thus, measures to adjust grants at the margin, and to require more stringent budgeting procedures, have not per se had much of an impact on controlling overall expenditures in Italy. This points to the need to assess expenditure policy and financing sources together with the allocation of expenditure assignments.

There is considerable diversity of experience relating to the share of expenditures on items such as education, health, and social security administered at each level of government, as seen in Table 3 (from Levin (1991)). Thus, among industrial countries, education is primarily

---

[4]For example, the 1990 budget appropriated grants for Lit 4.2 billion (3.2 percent of total grants disbursed that year) to pay for the deficits of local transport companies. That same year, the central government agreed on salary increases with employees of transport firms. This increased the wage bill of local transport firms and the central government had to disburse grants to share the financial burden. Lit 0.2 billion and Lit 0.9 billion were disbursed in 1990 and 1991, respectively. To pay for the remaining Lit 0.4 billion the local authorities were authorized to get 15-year loans. The repayment of these loans would be the responsibility of the central government.

Table 2. Italy: Arrangements for Financing, Legislating for, and Administrating Major Expenditure Items

	Financing	Legislation	Administration
Center			
Health	X	X	
Education	X	X	X
Social welfare[1]	X	X	X
Regions			
Health	X	For own earmarked revenues	
Education			
Social welfare			
Provinces			
Health			
Education	Support personnel, buildings and furniture, for specific schools in secondary education		For functions specified under financing
Social welfare			
Municipalities			
Health			X
Education	Support personnel, buildings, and furniture in elementary education		For functions specified under financing
Social welfare	Cash and in-kind benefits to people on the municipal poor list		For functions specified under financing

[1]Pensions and family allowances.

provided at the central government level, whereas in the United Kingdom and the United States, it is provided by local governments, and by state governments in Australia and Germany. Among developing countries, education and health are primarily provided by the central government in Indonesia, but by the state governments in India (data on local governments are not available in either country). In other countries, such as Brazil, information is not available for the breakdown of functional expenditures at subnational levels of government, despite the importance of such a classification for overall policymaking.

Social Security and the Social Safety Net in China

Social protection mechanisms in many different types of society embody elements of insurance, together with redistribution. This is true in the industrial societies, where formal social insurance instruments

Table 3. Magnitude of General Government Expenditures and Portion Administered by Each Level of Government[1]

(Average of latest three years available)

	Ending Year	As percent of GDP				Total Expenditures			Education			Health			Social Security and Welfare		
		Total	Educa-tion	Health	Social Security and Welfare	Cent. govt.	State govt.	Local govt.	Cent. govt.	State govt.	Local govt.	Cent. govt.	State govt.	Local govt.	Cent. govt.	State govt.	Local govt.
						(As percent of general government)											
Australia	1987	39.1	5.5	5.5	9.6	52.9	40.4	6.8	8.5	91.3	0.2	43.5	55.6	0.9	92.8	6.2	1.0
Austria	1987	51.8				70.4	13.7	16.9									
Belgium[2]	1987	56.7				85.9		11.9									
Canada	1987	46.0	5.8	6.0	12.3	41.3	40.3	18.4	4.8	34.5	60.7	2.6	89.5	7.9	65.8	31.3	2.9
Denmark[2]	1986	57.6	7.1	5.2	23.1	44.9		52.9	46.8		53.2	7.1		92.9	26.1		73.9
Finland	1987	43.0				54.7		45.3									
France[2]	1985	49.3	4.6	8.3	20.9	82.2		16.5	75.3		24.7	97.0		3.0	91.8		8.2
Germany[2]	1983	50.2	4.2	8.0	21.2	58.7	21.5	17.9	1.0	73.8	25.2	74.4	11.2	14.4	79.0	10.9	10.1
Ireland	1987	55.8				72.5		27.5									
Luxembourg[2]	1987	39.1	4.4	0.7	21.3	81.3		15.9	74.1		25.9	92.0		8.0	97.4		2.6
Netherlands	1988	59.2				70.1		29.9									
New Zealand	1981	43.2				86.9		13.1									
Norway	1986	47.2				66.4		33.6									
Spain	1986	38.2				78.8	9.9	11.3									
Sweden	1987	61.6				59.8		40.2									
Switzerland	1984	37.4	5.3	5.9	13.9	47.5	28.3	24.2	6.2	57.5	36.3	45.5	32.1	22.4	88.5	5.6	5.9
United Kingdom[2]	1987	44.8	5.1	5.1	14.3	70.9		27.2	12.7		87.3	100.0		0.0	84.0		16.0
United States	1987	37.1	5.1	4.3	9.0	60.3	17.3	22.4	4.2	24.5	71.3	50.5	33.8	15.7	78.0	14.6	7.4
Hungary	1988	64.5	5.7	4.2	18.1	77.8		22.2	20.0		80.0	39.2		60.8	95.7		4.3
Poland	1988	48.1				71.1		28.9									

	Year																
Romania	1985	32.3	2.1	2.1	8.9	77.0		23.0	28.0		72.0	10.3		89.7	99.3		0.7
Yugoslavia	1987	25.3	3.2	4.2	7.8	23.2	31.4	45.4	0.0		100.0	0.0		100.0	7.3	75.9	16.8
India[3]	1986	22.6	3.4	0.9	2.3	47.5	52.5		9.0	0.0		30.2	0.0		0.0	100.0	
Indonesia[3]	1988	22.8	3.1	0.5	0.4	88.7	11.3		65.3	90.1		72.8	69.8		0.0	100.0	
Israel	1986	62.9	5.3	2.0	10.0	90.8		9.2	67.2	34.7	32.8	97.0	27.2	3.0	94.9		5.1
Pakistan	1979	26.1	4.1	1.1	1.2	68.2	28.3	3.5	94.8		5.2	93.5		6.5	97.4		
Thailand	1982	21.2	4.0	1.1	9.1	92.3		7.7	33.3			24.4			89.4		2.6
Argentina[3]	1987	33.2				60.3	39.7	3.4		66.7			75.6				10.6
Bolivia	1986	11.1				85.9	10.6										
Brazil	1987	34.1				65.8	24.5	9.6									
Chile	1987	32.3	4.9	1.9	8.8	93.8		6.2	81.7		18.3	98.1		1.9	100.0		
Colombia	1984	18.0	5.5	1.3	3.2	67.4	23.9	8.7	55.5	39.2	5.3	49.0	40.2	10.8	90.0		2.2
Mexico	1984	30.2				90.1	7.6	2.3									
Paraguay	1984	11.3				95.1		4.9									
Kenya	1984	29.3	5.2	2.1	1.4	94.3		5.7	94.0		6.0	91.9		8.1	75.9		24.1
Malawi	1984	29.1	3.7	2.2	0.6	93.7		6.3	98.7		1.3	82.9		17.1	100.0		0.0
South Africa	1986	33.3				74.8	12.5	12.7									
Tunisia	1982	34.0	5.1	2.5	4.7	94.6		5.4	100.0			100.0			100.0		0.0
Zimbabwe	1986	45.0	8.3	2.6	3.0	75.8		24.2	60.2		39.8	86.6		13.4	100.0		0.0

Source: Levin (1991) based on IMF, *Government Finance Statistics Yearbook*, Vol. 13 (Washington: IMF, 1989).
[1] Excluding intergovernmental grants.
[2] Includes supranational authorities' share of general government expenditures in Belgium (2.2 percent), Denmark (2.2 percent), France (1.4 percent), Germany (1.8 percent), Luxembourg (2.7 percent), and United Kingdom (1.9 percent).
[3] Data for general government do not include local government.

cater for old age, and other forms of loss of income, including unemployment, together with family allowances that limit the risk of poverty due to childbearing, and measures to provide for social assistance. Informal arrangements that mimic the above arrangements are also occasionally to be found in traditional societies in developing countries, but these suffer from a number of difficulties that mirror the level at which the service is provided (see Ahmad and others (1991)).

A major element in the provision of cover for life-cycle and employment contingencies is the pooling of risk. Thus, enterprise-level provision for the aged or the disabled, as was the case in the former centrally planned economies (e.g., China or the former Soviet Union), imposed major costs on older enterprises that were inconsistent with the efficient functioning of a market economy. In India, the absence of an effective mechanism to cater for the unemployed forces the continuation of subsidies to keep inefficient public sector enterprises afloat. And while community-based provision for the disabled and aged tends to be very effective in identifying the appropriate recipients, given the lower costs of local information, such methods are particularly vulnerable to covariate risks, where the whole community is affected, say, by drought or other shocks. Thus, by their nature, social insurance mechanisms should not be based on local pooling of risks, and the net should be spread as far as administratively possible.

In very large countries, such as China or the former Soviet Union, where there are vastly different demographic and income levels, the national pooling of risks may lead to a transfer of resources from poor to richer regions.[5] In such cases, it has been argued that provincial or republican level funds may be an alternative (some provinces in China and India have larger populations than most countries of the world). However, the requirement that there should be national standards for pensions and unemployment benefits, together with the need to minimize tax competition across regions, suggests that serious consideration should be given to centralized policy in this connection, with an appropriate pooling of risks. The principal issue relates to interpersonal comparisons, with protection of the aged and unemployed, regardless of where they reside. Interregional transfers should be handled

---

[5]See Ahmad (1993) for a discussion of the former Soviet Union, where the establishment of social insurance in 1990 opened up the possibility of transfer flows from the demographically young, but poorer, Central Asian regions to the European countries with aging, but higher-income, populations. A similar situation exists in China, with regions such as Shanghai, with a high proportion of aged, but higher per capita incomes, in relation to provinces with lower incomes, but a younger demographic profile.

within the horizontal equalization nexus, with an appropriate design of grants.

It is clear, however, that the informational advantages of local provision predominate when there is a need for fine targeting, as with most forms of social assistance. The link with local levels of resources (at the margin) is also clear, with the roots of assistance based on charitable provisions by the church, and the more formalized local provisions based on individual wealth in many Middle Eastern and African countries (see Ahmad (1991)). With financing from higher levels of government at the margin, there is lower incentive to pay, together with a reduced incentive to target the neediest.

The devolution of certain social expenditure responsibilities, for example, for consumer and enterprise subsidies in China, has contributed to an intractable problem associated with expenditure and revenue bargaining at lower levels of government. This has degenerated into a loss of control over such expenditures, together with an increase in the associated overall deficit. An attempt to introduce a degree of control, by moving to matching earmarked grants, has had a regressive impact. This is because the system of price subsidies is more heavily concentrated in more urbanized areas and enterprise subsidies in the older industrial centers. Moreover, the matching ratios for central grants can be as high as two, and poor provinces are unable to comply with the high cofinancing requirements and have to forgo the grants.

Pensions

The present practice provides for a pooling of pensions, generally at the local level. The experience with pooling at higher than county or township level varies by province. The result is a considerable variation in contribution rates across localities, adding to the potential for "tax competition" that is already a major problem in China. Thus enterprises in Shanghai bear a considerably greater contribution burden because of the relatively unfavorable demographic patterns of the province (the highest proportion of the aged relative to the working population, among all Chinese provinces). Furthermore, lax investment guidelines and auditing procedures appear to have permitted the "diversion" of pension funds to other uses in some cases. Such an arrangement would result in uneven benefits and coverage in due course.

An alternative is a two-tier system. The first tier would be a basic state pension that could provide for a basic level of benefits, determined within a predetermined band (to account for regional variations in the cost of living) for all workers, financed by a relatively low standard rate of contribution. The contribution rates would be set on a

pay-as-you-go basis, with a moderate level of reserves necessary to ensure payments on a timely basis. A flat rate for contributions and benefits would facilitate administration. This could facilitate an early
extension of coverage to the rural areas, and the sections of the population that are not at present covered.

Pooling could be at the national level for a basic pension arrangement, to minimize the differences in overall tax burdens across provinces, and to ensure that a "level playing field" for new investment is
created. However, an interim measure could be pooling at the provincial or regional levels. As an additional part of this scheme, a "second"
tier of voluntary "defined contributions" could be funded localy. Here,
pension fund safeguards would have to be instituted. Additional work
would be needed to specify the sorts of investment instruments the
private pension funds might be allowed to use. For both tiers, administration may, however, continue as at present.

Unemployment Benefits

China has a system of unemployment benefits, but pooling is organized at the local, and sometimes the city, level. It is very important to
pool risks from the perspective of unemployment insurance, since enterprise restructuring may have significant regional implications. With
a uniform contribution rate, as at present in China, some localities
would have inadequate funds to permit a needed restructuring of enterprises, whereas other localities may have cash reserves together with
a problem of maintaining the value of such reserves. Thus, a national
pool would be needed to ensure a uniform basis for unemployment
benefits.

The level and duration of benefits that might be financed under the
unemployment insurance system would need to be carefully circum-
scribed, in order to avoid the financing problems that have occurred
elsewhere (e.g., in Poland). Consequently, there needs to be a reliance,
at a secondary level, on benefits provided by provinces and local governments, such as through the *wu bao* system and targeted public
works that are used as a social safety net. There is already considerable
experience in the use of public works as a social protection device in
rural China (see below).

Social Assistance

The urban ration networks proved to be an effective safety net during the period that food price reform was being phased in. Now that
food price reform is virtually complete, there needs to be less in the

way of central government *mandates* or policy requirements (involving financial support) in this connection. The infrastructure associated with administration of the urban rations could, however, be used by local authorities to provide more targeted support on a categorical basis, such as to orphans, widows, or the disabled, provided that the local authority feels there is justification for such support. Such interventions would normally be financed through local own revenues.

An important element in the safety net in China relates to targeted public works, through the *"yigong-daizhen"* (or the offer of job opportunities, instead of sheer relief, see Zhu and Zhongyi (1993)). These are applicable in the designated poor regions, with community-identified projects and participants. While such public works have been considered useful in the designated poor areas, it is possible to think of a somewhat modified form of public works forming a more general safety net. The latter social safety net would be seen as a supplement to unemployment insurance, which has to be quite restrictive in terms of the level and duration of benefits provided.

The alternative, social safety net type of public works, essentially offers social assistance through the targeting mechanisms of a low wage and the work test. Under such a scheme, the creation of positive investment would be a bonus but is not essential. One could think of such social safety net public works as being related to operations and maintenance-type activities (roads, irrigation canals, or environmental cleanup) that are primarily labor intensive. Such mechanisms have been an important substitute for unemployment insurance (e.g., in Chile during the 1970s and early 1980s, where unemployment insurance did not exist, and major restructuring occurred, see Ahmad (1991)). In China, such an instrument would be an adjunct to the formal social security instruments and would primarily be financed by local own resources.

A final element in China, the *wu bao*, or five guarantees, provided to the destitute without family or kin support through local targeting and information must necessarily continue as a local function. It appears to be well targeted in the sense that there are few nondeserving recipients of *wu bao* relief, although there are questions as to whether the stigma and identification criteria involved exclude some of the deserving.

Options for China

The main social security instruments would provide an important element in reducing "need" in China, and it is suggested that these be provided in a uniform manner that does not encourage tax competition across regions. National pooling is an option for both a first-tier pension and unemployment insurance. However, additional measures may be needed locally to cater for those who fall through the "national safety net." In China, such measures would include local public works of various sorts, as well as the more traditional social assistance mechanisms that are locally administered, with local determination of benefits, and local financing.

Concluding Remarks

The actual assignment of expenditure responsibilities across different levels of government involves three aspects—administration, policy, and financing. There is considerable variation in international experience, and it is seldom possible to get a definitive assignment of responsibilities in this field. In many industrial countries, including those with sophisticated intergovernmental arrangements, such as Australia, the expenditure responsibilities continue to evolve. The eventual framework, including the revenue assignments and transfer systems, thus should be flexible enough to accommodate changes in expenditure responsibilities over time.

In China, it is unlikely that expenditure responsibilities will be clearly determined before the process of enterprise reform is completed—since many state-owned enterprises still perform several public functions, including schooling, health care, and housing. As discussed in the section on social security and the social safety net in China, the unemployment insurance system is not yet developed to an extent that would allow the employment guarantees provided by the state-owned enterprises to be relaxed to any appreciable extent. Nonetheless, it should be possible to design a system of transfers between different levels of government that defines an appropriate set of "provincial and subprovincial" activities, regardless of which level of government actually carries out the functions.

Control of overall expenditure levels is an important element in a successful macroeconomic strategy. This control is not contingent on the actual administration of various expenditure categories by the central government, rather than on the adoption of appropriate policies that are consistent with the macroeconomic goals, as well as financing mechanisms that provide appropriate incentives for control. Indeed, countries with centralized administration of certain expenditure items are as prone to loss of macroeconomic control as those where the administration is decentralized. However, it is also the case that decentralized administration, with poorly defined policy goals and lax financing mechanisms, almost invariably leads to a loss of macroeconomic control.

References

Ahmad, Ehtisham, "Social Security and the Poor," World Bank *Research Observer*, Vol. 6 (January 1991), pp. 105–27.

——, "Poverty, Demographic Characteristics, and Public Policy in CIS Countries," *Public Finance*, Vol. 48 (1993), pp. 366–79.

——, and others, eds., *Social Security in Developing Countries* (Oxford: Clarendon Press, 1991).

Ahmad, Ehtisham, and Athar Hussain, "Social Security in China: A Historical Perspective," *Social Security in Developing Countries*, ed. by Ehtisham Ahmad and others (Oxford: Clarendon Press, 1991).

Ahmad, Ehtisham, D. Hewitt, and E. Ruggiero, "Assigning Expenditure Responsibilities Across Different Levels of Government" (mimeograph, Washington: International Monetary Fund, 1994).

Bird, Richard, *Federal Finance in Comparative Perspective* (Toronto: Canadian Tax Foundation, 1986).

Brosio, Giorgio, "Fiscal Autonomy of Non-Central Government and the Problem of Public-Spending Growth," *Public Expenditure and Government Growth*, ed. by Francesio Forte and Alan T. Peacock (Oxford, New York: Blackwell, 1985) pp. 53–67.

——, D.N. Nyman, and W. Santagata, "Revenue Sharing and Local Public Spending: The Italian Experience," *Public Choice*, Vol. 35, No. 1 (1980), pp. 3–15.

Chelliah, R.J., M.G. Rao, and T.K. Sen, "Issues Before the Tenth Finance Commission," *Economic and Political Weekly*, Vol. 27 (November 21, 1992), pp. 2539–50.

Gramlich, E., "Intergovernmental Grants: A Review of the Empirical Literature," in *The Political Economy of Fiscal Federalism*, ed. by W. Oates (Lexington, Massachusetts: Lexington Books, 1979).

Hewitt, Daniel, "Fiscal Illusion from Grants and the Level of State and Federal Expenditures," *National Tax Journal*, Vol. 39 (December 1986), pp. 471–83.

——, "Transfers to Local Governments," in *Public Expenditure Handbook: A Guide to Public Policy Issues in Developing Countries*, ed. by Ke-young Chu and Richard Hemming (Washington: International Monetary Fund, 1991), pp. 82–87.

——, and Dubravko Mihaljek, "Fiscal Federalism," in *Fiscal Policies in Economies in Transition*, ed by Vito Tanzi (Washington: International Monetary Fund, 1992), pp. 330–49.

Levin, Jonathan, "Measuring the Role of Sub-National Governments," in *Public Finance with Several Levels of Government*, ed. by Rémy Prud'homme (The Hague: Foundation Journal Public Finance, 1991).

Pisany-Ferry, J., "Maintaining a Coherent Macro-Economic Policy in a Highly Decentralized Federal State: The Experience of the EEC," paper prepared for the OECD Conference on Fiscal Federalism in Economies in Transition, Paris, April 1991.

Reid, Gary, and D.R. Winkler, "Decentralization and Government Size in Latin America" (mimeograph, Washington: World Bank, 1992).

Rizzo, Ilde, "Regional Disparities and Decentralization as Determinants of Public Sector Expenditure Growth in Italy, 1960–1981," in *Public Expenditure and Government Growth*, ed. by Francesco Forte and Alan Peacock (Oxford; New York: Blackwell, 1985).

Tiebout, Charles M., "A Pure Theory of Local Government Expenditure," *Journal of Political Economy*, Vol. 64 (1956), pp. 416–24.

Winer, Stanley L., "Some Evidence on the Effect of the Separation of Spending and Taxing Decisions," *Journal of Political Economy*, Vol. 91 (February 1983), pp. 126–40.

Zhu Ling, and Jiang Zhongyi, "The "Yigong-Daizhen" in China: A New Experience with Relief in Poor Regions Through Labor-Intensive Public Works," *IFPRI Workshop* (Washington, 1993).

7

Infrastructure Provision in a Socialist Market Economy

Bert Hofman and Richard Newfarmer*

There is ample international evidence of the complementarity of infrastructure investment and productive investment. Provision of infrastructure (e.g., roads, railways, power) is therefore a precondition for sustainable growth. Also, lack of infrastructure prevents an integration of the domestic market, causing considerable efficiency losses and uneven regional development. In China, infrastructure development has been lagging behind the phenomenal growth rates of the reform period and is increasingly becoming a bottleneck for further economic development. To illustrate, the volume of freight traffic by rail grew 6.1 percent on average over the period 1980–90, whereas the length of railway lines grew only by an annual 0.6 percent; and freight traffic by road increased at an annual rate of 14.6 percent, whereas road length increased by an annual 1.5 percent over the same period. Besides quantity, the quality of infrastructure seems deficient, not least because of the underfunding of maintenance, but also because of inaccuracies in design.

Perhaps most pressing is the problem of financing China's future investment in infrastructure. Demand is large, not only because the country is opting for a high-growth scenario, but also because there is a deficit situation already. To meet power demand until the year 2000, for example, an annual investment of $15–20 billion is needed, but in 1992, about $12 billion was actually devoted to investment in this sector. At the same time, the forms of financing available to the command economy of the past are dying out: credit allocation through the banking system is bound to shrink during commercialization of the specialized banks and the increasing independence of the central bank.

*The World Bank.

Budgetary financing has already been greatly reduced under pressure of the low tax buoyancy of the tax system. New finance forms will therefore have to replace these waning sources. This paper argues that adequate financing of infrastructure can only be achieved through a proper organization of infrastructure provision.

China's move to a socialist market economy offers new ways to improve the provision of infrastructure. To maximize the benefits of the market as an allocation mechanism, China needs to fundamentally reconsider the tasks of government in infrastructure provision. A crucial step is to separate government from enterprises, which is brought nearer by the "Regulations for Transformation of the State-Owned Enterprises." The government's remaining role in infrastructure, however, is not yet clearly defined; the assignment of functions over government and enterprises is incomplete; and some government functions have not yet found an institutional home. Furthermore, in the context of intergovernmental fiscal reforms, the assignment of government responsibilities in infrastructure over levels of government needs to be addressed. Finally, the financial sector reforms offer an opportunity to address the infrastructure financing problem.

This paper tries to contribute to the rationalization of China's system of infrastructure provision. The first section sets out a normative framework for the government's role in infrastructure provision and discusses how government should organize itself to perform its functions. The second section presents principles of the division of government functions over levels of government. The third derives the implications of the government's role for the financing of infrastructure. The last section spells out China's options.

Because the government's role in enterprises engaged in individual market goods production will diminish—after a period of restructuring that may require some budgetary involvement—this paper will not treat such investment expenditures, even though at present the government is still involved. Nor will it treat capital expenditures necessary for other government tasks, such as education or health care. Space limits prevent the desirable differential treatment of the various sectors that are lumped together as "infrastructure."

What Should Government Do in Infrastructure?

Provision Versus Production

Government has a role in the provision of infrastructure (roads, telecommunication, railways, airports, power, ports, and waterways) because, if left without government intervention, the market is ill-equipped to provide it efficiently. Inefficient provision can be due to a number of characteristics of infrastructure: (1) infrastructure usually requires large, lumpy investments, with many coordination problems in implementation and management; (2) some of these goods (electricity, ports) may show characteristics of natural monopolies, where the minimum optimal scale is close to the market size; (3) pricing of services by the market could be prohibitively costly from an economic perspective (uncongested roads); and (4) the market price could be considered too high from an equity perspective.

In a socialist market economy, government intervention does not imply government production. "Infrastructure" is a bundle of functions, many of which can be more efficiently performed by enterprises, either independent state-owned enterprises, township and village enterprises and collectives, or foreign companies. The art of government policy in infrastructure is to design interventions such that maximum use is made of the allocation through the market mechanism.

Regulation

Government regulation can create conditions for a competitive market. For example, power generation could be treated as a market good, as long as enough competition in supply exists. Effective competition requires the establishment of a national or superregional grid to which competing power suppliers can deliver. Regulations on the conditions of supply, and standardization of regional infrastructure, such as regional rail tracks would greatly enhance competition among nongovernmental suppliers of services. Government would enhance competition also by providing a level playing field for all enterprise—regardless of ownership—by means of a corporate law. Even if competition cannot be ensured, a regulated nongovernmental enterprise often outperforms a monopolistic government agency. Stability and predictability of government regulation is essential for enterprises to engage in long-gestating investments usually involved in infrastructure.

Pricing

Government regulations may equally prevent emergence of a market: price regulation still plays an important role in infrastructure and prevents services, such as power supply and transport, from being fully marketed. Moreover, inefficient pricing has led to inefficient use of existing capacity, and the installation of an inappropriate production structure, geared toward the use of uneconomically priced infrastructure. Infrastructure is more likely to be economically used when charges for infrastructure services reflect economic costs, and adequate pricing can generate investable surpluses for sectors that now depend on China's public finances, such as electricity. Thus, in the move toward the socialist market economy, continued price reform in infrastructure services is essential. Adequate pricing would, therefore, help solve both economic and budgetary problems.

Planning

Even if nongovernmental entities could competitively supply infrastructure and infrastructure services, it is hard for them to generate the information necessary to plan for future needs. Moreover, for numerous infrastructure projects, government policy decisions concerning location, environmental impact, disappropriation of land, overall development policy, and so on need to be taken into account in future needs. This information and planning is basically a public good and needs to be provided by government, as nongovernmental entities will have no interest in generating all the information themselves. In China, the planning of infrastructure investment is situated in the State Planning Commission, the local planning bureaus, and the line ministries. The line ministries, however, have been deeply involved in day-to-day management of enterprises involved in infrastructure production, a task that should gradually disappear. A refocusing of the line ministries toward planning seems, therefore, desirable. The involvement of the Ministry of Finance in planning for infrastructure has traditionally been minimal, even though the budget finances part of the infrastructure investments through the People's Construction Bank of China, and, more important, has often been saddled with recurrent costs. Coordination between the Five-Year Development Plan and the (multiyear) budget would contribute to the attainability of the Plan.

Appraisal

For government, the economic returns should be decisive in providing infrastructure not the private returns of enterprises. Government, therefore, needs project appraisal capacity in order to decide on the need for new infrastructure. In China, the capacity to appraise infrastructure projects is to a considerable extent concentrated in the People's Construction Bank of China, but the stress is on financial appraisal. Economic appraisal seems centered at the State Planning Commission, which can provide subsidized funding and materials for those projects that are economically but not financially viable. The

State Investment Corporations, a 1988 innovation in the planning system, have not been able to play the substantial role in appraisal that was envisioned for them. Their potential role as "investment houses" for certain sectors has not been realized, partially because they only had a single finance channel at their disposal. The Ministry of Finance seems not involved in economic analysis of infrastructure projects, even though these projects compete for budgetary resources with alternative government spending. Financial appraisal is done by the financing agents, such as the People's Construction Bank of China, and is approved by the State Planning Commission as part of the investment approval system. For those projects in which no government finance is required in any form, such approval seems superfluous.

Project Implementation and Service Management

Enterprises are often in a better position to implement infrastructure investment and manage infrastructure services than a government agency. In many countries, construction and management of power generation is done by enterprises. Road construction and maintenance are well-defined functions and can be handled by enterprises, without direct government management. In these functions, the scope for improvement seems the largest, given the often poor implementation record for infrastructure under the planning system and the poor record of maintenance that led to an insufficient level of infrastructure services. Thus, the management of infrastructure services could in many cases be considered for market provision. Managerial autonomy, and full commercial risk for the enterprise, has been shown to be more efficient than more limited forms of enterprise involvement, such as management contracts. Even if the market is found unfit to provide certain infrastructure services (ports, roads), efficiency can be served by delegating responsibility to semiautonomous nonprofit agencies (port authorities, railways), or by devolving responsibilities to lower levels of government. In China, the experience with autonomous port authorities is a promising example.

Supervision

Supervision of the infrastructure investment project is equally an essential task for a government that desires high-quality infrastructure assets, in line with the contracted features. In many countries, supervision is done by the same government agency in charge of project appraisal, as much of the same information is needed for both functions. If the management of infrastructure services is devolved to enterprises, regular reviews on the services delivered by the enterprises is desirable to ensure the regulated or contracted quality and quantity of services is met. Finally, supervision of the general competitive structure of the market for infrastructure is necessary to ensure the most efficient outcome for the users of the infrastructure services.

In China, supervision of government-funded infrastructure investment projects is the task of the People's Construction Bank of China. It oversees the implementation of the project and the disbursements of funds. This supervision has not always been effective, and cost overruns and delays have been persistent in infrastructure investment projects. In the market for infrastructure services, such as the power supply, the government would supervise competitive practices and agreed standards of service. Supervision of the infrastructure services seems to be effected by direct management involvement of the line ministries involved. Again, a retrenchment of these ministries to the task of supervising general regulations and quality standards is necessary to increase the independence of enterprises providing infrastructure services. Supervision of competition is usually done by a separate agency (a cartel bureau, antitrust bureau). China seems to lack such a supervisory agency and has until now opted for direct price control through the Price Bureau.

Subsidization

If the price for which a competitive firm can supply infrastructure is seen as too high—for reasons of equity, efficiency, or development— subsidies can be given, instead of shifting production to government. To minimize the budgetary costs, while leaving producer incentives undistorted, auctioning or competitive bidding may offer a good alternative: the supplier that requires the least subsidy for a given infrastructure service at a given—politically acceptable—price would win the bid. In fact, for the construction of infrastructure projects, this is becoming more and more a common practice in China, but the bidding can be extended to the management and service delivery. The distinction between a government agency and a nongovernmental enterprise becomes vague, if the amount of subsidy on which the enterprise depends becomes high; once the subsidy element dominates, the enterprise could be considered as government.

Potential Competition

Even with a government agency implementing projects, or managing services, competition can play a useful role. The threat of being put out of business by a more efficient enterprise would enhance a government agency's efficiency. Therefore, regular reconsideration of the supplier can greatly enhance efficiency. Such reconsideration could be prescribed in national legislation, but central government could also enhance pressures on local suppliers by making information available on the costs of infrastructure in various localities. A local government that seeks the optimal policy for its constituents would then choose the most efficient supplier.

China's budgeting techniques are not geared toward regular reconsideration of public expenditures: budget formulation is highly incremental, owing to the base-number method, and auditing concentrates on the correspondence of budget and expenditures, and not on the effectiveness or on the output generated with the expenditures. Regular expenditure reviews and more program-oriented budgeting seem, therefore, desirable to increase the quality of infrastructure service delivery. Such reviews should be restricted, however, to the government's own expenditures and should not replace the direct control over enterprises.

Central and Local Tasks: Who Does What?

Local Autonomy in China

In China, fiscal decentralization has given substantial autonomy to subnational government on the expenditure side, although the responsibility for infrastructure is nowhere codified. The constitution merely mentions "regional development" and "economic affairs" as overlapping responsibilities of local government and state council. On the revenue side, however, the local government has, de jure, no autonomy over tax rates or bases. As a consequence, and under pressure of the low revenue buoyancy of the budgetary taxes, a wealth of extrabudgetary fees, charges, and levies have evolved to finance standard government functions, among which is the provision of infrastructure. Moreover, although de jure local governments have no access to borrowing, this is easily circumvented by shifting the borrowing obligation to state-owned enterprises, while reaping the revenues directly by extrabudgetary levies on the borrowing firm, or indirectly by obliging the borrowing firm to perform government functions. China's organization of government still rests on the principle of "dual leadership," making local planning agencies, finance bureaus, railway bureaus, and so on, accountable both to the central government and to the local people's congress. Increased local involvement in infrastructure investment is reflected in the share of locally supported capital construction projects, which rose from 46.5 percent in 1985 to 55.8 percent in 1992, a development contrary to budgetary trends, in which the central government now has over 75 percent of total government capital construction.

Rationale for Decentralization

Conceptually, responsibility for the provision of infrastructure should be put at the level that benefits from it. This implies that the national government should be concerned with national infrastructure projects (national railways, waterways, roads) and overall coordination; whereas the provincial government should be concerned with the same projects but on a local scale, and municipal and lower levels of government should be responsible for municipal, township, and village infrastructure.

Benefit areas of infrastructure are rarely clearly defined, however, national roads can be used for local traffic; ports have benefits beyond the municipality of location; and power stations may supply customers anywhere in the country once they are on a national grid. Responsibility for infrastructure with superregional benefits could be assigned to a higher level of government, whose constituency will benefit the whole area, but this need not be done. In many countries, a wealth of interregional cooperation bodies have responsibility for superregional infrastructure. In China, horizontal cooperation between localities is still rare; most of the coordination takes place at a higher level of government.

The rationale for devolution of responsibility is that local governments will provide the most efficient infrastructure, as they are better aware of local needs and are under closer scrutiny of their constituents than is the central government. Accountability can only be operational, if the local government has a substantial amount of autonomy over its own finance, both on the expenditure side and the revenue side: the fiscal adage for decentralization is that whoever decides on expenditures should pay for expenditures. Financial autonomy is not enough, however: the institutions that should perform the government tasks in infrastructure should be able to operate relatively independently from the central government, as far as local infrastructure is concerned.

User Charges

Assigning responsibility over the infrastructure provision to lower governments is not sufficient in China's context, where substantial local autonomy exists. The incentive for provision should be supplied with the responsibility. A strong incentive for local government to provide infrastructure stems from user charges. If infrastructure supply is no longer a loss-making operation, local governments would be willing to perform the necessary functions to enable nongovernmental production of infrastructure. Economically excludable goods, such as power, ports, airports, and certain roads or bridges, would be able to generate substantial revenue streams. Even if the efficient charge would not total costs of provision, lump-sum charges, for example, for gas or electricity connection, could make public provision a cost-recovering activity.

User charges, if charged by government agencies substantially dependent on general budgetary means, should be in the budget; these funds—except for a share necessary to stimulate collection—are in principle budgetary resources, whose allocation should be decided upon in the annual budget process. In China, many charges and levies by government agencies are kept at the agency as "extrabudgetary funds." This practice distorts efficient allocation of government resources and jeopardizes government budget control. Bringing such charges within the budget could be a start for the creation of a legalized local tax base.

Local Tax Base

Benefit taxes, taxes that are closely related to the use of infrastructure, are a second incentive for local governments to provide infrastructure. Examples are vehicle or license plate taxes, fuel taxes, and driver's license charges, which proxy taxing road use directly; boat taxes and boating licenses for waterways; and passenger taxes for airports. Central government restrictions on local charges should be gradually abolished, if user charges are to be an incentive for local provision of infrastructure.

A third incentive for local governments to provide infrastructure is to assign them a tax base that is highly correlated with the provision of infrastructure. In many countries, property taxes are assigned to the municipal government. Property values, and thus property taxes, vary with the supply of complementary goods, including infrastructure. In China, property markets are still underdeveloped, and most property is directly or indirectly owned by the government and rented out far below economic costs. This does not imply, however, that no user taxes can be levied, either on private agents or on enterprises. Increasing mobility of capital and labor would increase the mechanism by which the tax base is increased, and subnational governments would become more responsive to demands for infrastructure. The central government can promote such benevolent tax competition by increasing the mobility of production factors. An active policy to integrate local capital markets and establish labor markets should, therefore, be the central government's priority, and it should concentrate on the legal structure for local tax bases, including regulations on tax bases, and allowed rates and bases.

Role of Central Government

In a large country like China, most of the infrastructure can be considered as local, and central government involvement need not be large, but could be highly costly. The paramount task for the central government is the integration of the country by national road networks, rail networks, electricity grids, and so on. The tasks of planning, appraising, supervising, and—where applicable—financing such projects should lie with central agents.

National standards and guidelines should guarantee the integration of local infrastructure with national networks. Laws and regulations should set benchmarks for local government taxes and user charges, and budget supervision should ensure sound practices in budgeting for infrastructure, notably, concerning the recurrent cost implications of a government-managed infrastructure service. Central agents can serve as expert advisors for local governments in planning, appraising, and supervising particularly complicated projects. The central government can also stimulate cooperation among regions by serving as facilitator and coordinator of interregional projects.

Finally, the central government should be responsible for the legal framework that allows competition in infrastructure projects and services. Company laws and tax laws that treat each ownership type equally are necessary to level the playing field. Antitrust laws and antitrust supervision are central tasks as well, because they preserve an internal market.

How to Finance Infrastructure Investments

Provided an infrastructure project is economically viable, it will generate a future stream of benefits. Depending on economic feasibility of exclusion, political choices, and choice of organization, this benefit stream is reflected in market prices, user charges, benefit taxation, or budgetary subsidies that reflect the political valuation of infrastructure services. Before the benefits can be substantiated,

Table 1. Financing Investment: Sources of Funds
(In percent)

	1982	1992
Total fixed asset investment		
State appropriation	22.7	7.4
Domestic loans	14.3	21.0
Foreign investment	4.9	6.2
Self-raised funds	47.8	53.8
Other	10.3	11.6
Fixed investment by state-owned units		
State appropriation	35.4	12.4
Domestic loans	14.3	27.4
Foreign investment	6.4	10.4
Self-raised funds	34.8	40.2
Other	9.2	10.3

infrastructure usually requires lumpy investments that need financing. As stated before, the amount of savings is not the bottleneck for infrastructure investment; it is the intermediation. The government's role of direct resource mobilization is shrinking in China. In line with the overall retrenchment of the government, the budgetary role of investment finance has decreased strongly over the reform period, from almost 23 percent in 1982 to 7.4 percent in 1992 (Table 1).[1] Much of the financing has been taken over by domestic loans from banks. Banks obtain most of their funding in the short and medium term and are less suited for the long-term investments required for infrastructure. Moreover, infrastructure finance is still dominated by "policy loans" through the specialized banks, which are incompatible with the desired commercialization of the banks. This makes development of new means of infrastructure finance a pressing problem.

Bonds and Equity

In many market economies, intermediation for infrastructure finance is done by the capital market. Infrastructure that can generate economically a future income stream that covers the investment costs on the project can in principle be managed as a profit-seeking enterprise, either state owned or otherwise. In a perfect capital market, such an enterprise would have independent access to the capital market, and the

---

[1]Although recent data are unavailable, the 1986 figures show a much higher budget participation in infrastructure projects. Economywide, state appropriation constituted 14.5 percent of the investment funding, while transport projects were on average financed for 33 percent from the budget.

Table 2. Securities Market Development
(In percent)

	Issues in 1992
Treasury bonds	31.9
National investment bonds	9.9
Enterprise bonds	29.5
Financial bonds	19.5
Stocks	8.5
Total	100.0

government need not be involved in financing such an enterprise. Even a partial float of equity in state-owned enterprises that implement infrastructure projects or deliver services can be a powerful tool for the owner to monitor its performance, and for competitors to learn which enterprise is efficient in delivery. In China, however, financial market liberalization is still in its infancy, and bonds and equity still play a minor role, funding about 11 percent of total investment. Especially for enterprises, access is limited, with only 7.8 percent of total investment financed by enterprise securities (Table 2).

The primary task for the government in conjunction with opening infrastructure for profit-seeking enterprises is therefore to actively pursue a deepening of the capital market by issuing regulations and instituting the oversight necessary for such a market. At present, a substantial amount of securities issue and trade takes place within an institutional vacuum, which not only affects the quality of the investments financed, but also puts strains on the government's macroeconomic control. In many countries, access to capital markets is regulated, or scheduled according to a timetable, in order to not overburden the capital market, and prudency regulation requires minimum standards of reporting and accounting. Care, however, should be taken that such macroregulation does not interfere with microeconomic efficiency of capital allocation. Clarity of property rights is a necessary condition for increased state-owned-enterprise access to (international) capital markets, and incorporation of those enterprises engaged in infrastructure is indispensable. Since state-owned enterprises are to be considered as independent enterprises, the government should bear no responsibility for their debt issued on the capital market.

Government Guarantees

If carefully handled, government guarantees can be instrumental in enhancing capital market access for enterprises investing in infrastructure. Enterprises with little or no reputation on the (international) capital market may need government guarantees to gain access to those markets. Such guarantees are a government obligation, and it is sound practice in other countries to explicitly take account of them in the budgetary process, by including them as a memorandum item. Moreover, since these guarantees will be called in the event of default of the borrower, provision should be made in the budget to capitalize a fund that will be depleted in the case of default. Failure to do so can seriously destabilize government finance in the future. Providing guarantees requires a solid project analysis—both economically and financially—by government, if no irresponsible risks are to be assumed. Only explicit guarantees, however, should be recognized by government.

Development Banks

A variety of countries have used a special institution to finance infrastructure and other high priority projects, and recently the idea of a "policy bank" has been introduced to China, but the plans are still very much in a state of flux. International experience shows that development banks are rarely successful, but those that are, are neither banks nor do they actively conduct policy. Rather, the institute is designed to implement government policy that requires long-term capital, say, a development bank. Policy choices, such as priority sectors, the total amount of credit the development bank may grant and subsidy on interest or principal repayments cannot be decided by such a bank but are agreed upon in the political process. The agency cannot be used for budgetary tasks such as subsidizing loss-making state-owned enterprises. The development bank can instead concentrate on project selection and the supervision of project implementation and service delivery. Vehicles for investment in infrastructure ıby the agency can be either enterprise-issued bonds or equity, direct loans, or local government bonds or loans. The allocation of funds should be transparent, with economic and financial rates of return as the guiding principles. The development bank could work under commercial criteria, if financially nonviable but economically desirable projects remain in the realm of budgetary finance.

The funding of a development bank should reflect the autonomy perceived for it. If it is to act as a fiscal agent, funding directly from the budget is the most appropriate procedure. The Ministry of Finance would then issue bonds and onlend them to the agency, providing funding for desired interest rate subsidies from the current budget. Alternatively, the development bank can be set at arm's length from government, in which case funding with equity and bonds would be appropriate, possibly with government guarantees as set out above.

The development bank should still receive current funding from the budget for the interest rate subsidies the government sees fit. Finally, the agency could be operated as an enterprise, incorporated, and with its own capital and borrowing, and independent from the budget. Such a corporation would be viable for sectors that will become profitable in the course of reforms, such as the power sector. However, one would hardly consider such a corporation a development bank.

Essential for macroeconomic stability is that the development bank have neither access to domestic commercial bank credit nor credit from the Construction People's Bank of China. Furthermore, credit creation in the monetary sense should be forbidden, and only fully funded investments should be made. Deposit taking by the development bank would be undesirable. Essential for microeconomic efficiency is that the development bank have the capacity and authority to appraise and supervise infrastructure projects, and enforce repayments of its loans. Thus, of the roles of government as spelled out earlier, a development agent can perform three: appraisal, project implementation, and finance. This description comes close to the present role of the People's Construction Bank of China; the biggest difference is that the People's Construction Bank of China takes deposits and has only limited economic appraisal capacity.

Many of the institutions similar to the development bank sought by China have "gone bad" through lax supervision of projects and the absence of provisioning for bad loans. Clear rules on outside portfolio audit, on the publication of accounts and reports, and on loss provisioning will be critical for the long-term viability of such an institution. The governance of the institution would be enhanced by solid rules for the board of directors, financial reporting, and—if applicable—shareholding. Such rules would ideally isolate the agency from direct interference with individual finance decisions, much as a central bank usually functions better when independent of day-to-day politics. A high level of technical expertise of the employees is crucial for success.

Local Government Access to the Capital Market

The major macroeconomic influence of the government stems from the expansionary effect of deficits, as individuals do not fully offset government deficits with private savings. Within a decentralized fiscal system, an additional problem concerning deficit financing arises, when the subnational governments may overissue debt hoping to be bailed out by the central government, if future debt repayments could not be met. However, forbidding subnational deficits altogether leaves possible efficiency gains unexploited, since government infrastructure investments that create long-term benefits and future tax revenue can best be financed by debt issue. Moreover, regulations forbidding local borrowing can sometimes be circumvented, as in China where borrowing for government tasks is sometimes shifted to state-owned enterprises. To maintain macroeconomic stability while allowing at least some local government borrowing, several schemes have proven effective. In most countries of the Organization for Economic Cooperation and Development (OECD), borrowing is restricted to capital investment. Additional regulations usually require interest and amortization to be paid from current income to a certain percentage of current revenue, and so on, and sometimes restrict borrowing to specific purposes (such as energy projects). The aggregate borrowing of subnational governments is often preset by the central government and regularly administered by a special bank for subnational governments.

Local Government and Development Banks

Subnational governments usually have access to development bank lending in countries where such institutions exist, precisely because the local government is heavily involved in those projects that such a bank intends to fund. Development banks could play a useful role in channeling savings to infrastructure investments by enterprises, or by localities. As stated earlier, however, the development banks should be *agencies* rather than banks. For better access to such a bank, a deconcentrated organization seems advisable in a country as large as China. However, compartmentalization and quota disbursement per province should be avoided to maintain overall efficient allocation of capital as much as possible. Local development agencies already exist in China and take responsibility for industrial zone development in a number of localities, such as in Shanghai. Care should be taken that such agencies do not jeopardize central government macroeconomic control.

Capital Grants

Capital grants from central to local government are a means to fund capital projects of local governments. The advantage is that the central government keeps complete control over the general government's access to the capital market; the disadvantage is that grants restrict local governments' accountability of the funds, and they require a mechanism by which such grants are distributed. The latter problem could be dealt with by establishing explicit norms for disbursements from a capital fund, which should take into account rates of return of the projects, and possible regional development goals. Central regulation and standardization of applications for such a capital fund is needed to prevent rent seeking by localities. Local accountability could be enhanced by turning the grants into loans from central to local government, but in the Chinese context this seems to open yet another avenue for negotiation and renegotiation of repayments. Future disbursements, however, could be made conditional on the repayment of previous loans. Cofinancing requirements on local governments may equally be used to enhance local accountability.

Options for China

China faces challenges in the supply, quality, and financing of infrastructure. In moving toward a market economy, the prospects for meeting these challenges are enhanced. However, to make maximum use of the market mechanism, while maintaining crucial functions for government, a clear division of labor between enterprises and government, and central and local government is necessary for successful provision of infrastructure and infrastructure services.

State-owned enterprises involved in infrastructure supply to enhance their efficiency need more independence from government, and implementation of the "Regulations for Transforming the Operating Mechanisms of State-Owned Enterprises" is a high priority for China's government. Price reform in infrastructure services should make a considerable part of these services accessible for profit-seeking enterprises. Corporatization under a corporate law, adoption of international standards of accounting, and modern governance procedures should enhance the access of state-owned enterprises to the capital market. A competition law should provide equal access to the market for infrastructure services for enterprises of all ownership.

Government should retrench as far as possible from direct involvement in production of infrastructure. Instead, it should concentrate on regulation, standardization, planning, supervision, and—if necessary—subsidization. Institutional homes for the remaining government tasks need to be clarified or developed and strengthened if missing or malfunctioning. Institutions that perform functions that are becoming redundant, such as the enterprise management by line ministries, need a reorientation of their tasks and a reconsideration of their size.

In order to use the market in infrastructure provision, accelerated price reforms should turn many of the sectors involved into commercially viable projects that could be implemented and managed by profit-oriented enterprises with various ownership structures.

Incentives for local government to provide infrastructure should be strengthened. User charges that cover costs would greatly enhance these incentives. A primary tool for this is also to assign local government a tax base that is highly elastic with respect to infrastructure; China's authorities should consider this in the course of fiscal reform. Central government regulations concerning user charges should be reduced, to allow local governments the legal means to adjust charges to local conditions. Interregional cooperation in infrastructure should be enhanced, in order to relieve central government from some of the financial burden. Central government should concentrate on key projects with national impact. It should further regulate local government activities to the extent necessary for the national integration of local infrastructure.

Government legislation should lay the basis for a deepening of the capital market in an orderly way. Incorporation of state-owned enterprises involved in infrastructure would greatly enhance access to the capital market, and would thereby increase the pool of funds available for infrastructure, by means of equity and bonds. Independent state-owned enterprises imply that they themselves should be responsible for their debts, although explicit, carefully handled government guarantees may play a limited role to overcome reputation problems.

The central government clearly has an important role in mobilizing finance for infrastructure, but that role is considerably different from today's role. Rather than raising revenues via taxation and then investing directly in infrastructure, a more decentralized fiscal system would allow the government to restrict its role to using its implicit financial and policy framework guarantee to mobilize private savings, both foreign and domestic. This role would require that the government create a mechanism to tap local and international bond and equity markets, and use the mechanism to channel resources to selected projects carried out by provincial and even private companies. Such a mechanism could take one of several forms: (1) a fund that would take minority equity positions and hold debt instruments issued by enterprises supplying infrastructure with the project, and that would be financed through local and foreign bond issues; (2) a development bank that would have direct loans to enterprises and that could receive (if necessary) regular budget capitalization and interest subsidies, but that would rely primarily on issuing its paper into the domestic market; or (3) a "take-out financing agency" that would operate like the fund, but finance only projects that have completed construction, taking out the financing provided by either commercial banks or the government during the construction phase.

As part of the new financing mechanisms, the fund or development bank could review the project appraisal and, by providing finance, would certify the financial and economic viability of the project. The key principles are that the fund or agency (1) would receive finance on market terms or as line-item transfers from the budget, and *not* be a deposit-taking institution; (2) would make loans on contractual terms only to reformed corporate entities operating in reformed policy regimes; and (3) would offer those terms at market rates except where the government provides interest subsidies specifically designated throughout the budget.

This role is substantially different from those alluded to in the press for the so-called policy bank. The objectives of the latter are to consolidate "policy-based" credits with infrastructure investments as well as those going to loss-making entities elsewhere. Such a policy bank cannot be viable in the market if it inherits a nonperforming portfolio, and must make loans to loss-making or high-risk entities on the basis of judgments made by those outside the policy bank. Finally, it cannot be viable if it subsidizes borrowers by lending at below-market terms and relies excessively on budgetary finance.

If the development bank is (partially) funded from the budget, this should be explicitly budgeted for, and the policy goals of such budgetary funding should be clearly stated. To the extent that the agency is allowed own funding from the capital market, the government should make clear whether this is considered a government obligation. In the latter case, the agency's funding should be explicit in the budget, and its net borrowing requirement should be considered part of the government deficit.

In order to match the financing needs involved in local infrastructure, central government should consider giving local government controlled access to the capital market. Macroeconomic control and efficiency would gain from moving away from the present situation of indirect, uncontrolled access. A development bank could be a means of providing such access.

8

Social Expenditure Assignments in China: Issues and Responses

Zu-Liu Hu*

China has often been cited as an example of success in social development. Over the past four decades, it has achieved remarkable improvements in such important social indicators as life expectancy and adult literacy rate. A newborn Chinese infant in 1991, for example, has a life expectancy of 71 years, compared with 62 years for low-income countries as a whole. More than 95 percent of Chinese children under the age of one are immunized, with the immunization ratio among the highest in the world. By 1991, China had reduced the infant mortality rate to only 38 per 1,000 live births, the same level achieved by middle-income countries. An overwhelming majority of Chinese men and women today can read and write, compared with the still staggeringly high adult illiteracy rates in many low-income countries.

While there are many factors behind China's better-than-average performance, clearly government activity in education and health has played a key role. China's progress owes as much to good social services, including safe drinking water, improved sewage disposal, and other sanitation measures, as to broad immunization coverage and mass campaigns against parasitic diseases. It has much to do with the successful drive to reduce fertility as with the great efforts to provide basic education, nutrition, and preventive health care to the whole population. It reflects a long-term political commitment to social development. China's experience illustrates the critical role of government, especially in low-income countries, in meeting the basic needs of the whole population and promoting social progress.

*International Monetary Fund. Helpful comments from Ehtisham Ahmad, Ke-Young Chu, and Vito Tanzi are gratefully acknowledged.

In spite of its impressive records in social sectors, China faces grave risks and challenges ahead because of three basic problems.

• China's economy is in transition toward a market economy, and the rapid changes have severely strained the existing fiscal system with declining government revenues and rising demands for public resources. Confusion and uncertainty regarding redefining intergovernmental fiscal relations, in particular, may cause neglect and underfunding of social sectors and slow China's progress in social development.

• The distribution of social expenditures has become more skewed, and inequality has emerged as a cause of concern. Fiscal reforms should address the issue of horizontal equity across regions and households.

• There are inefficiencies with existing public programs in financing and provision of education and health, and sectoral reforms are required.

While all these problems must be tackled urgently, the first one, allocating social expenditure responsibilities among various levels of government, seems to be the most pressing. The lack of clear and binding assignment of responsibility may diminish the role of government in education and health sectors, which are precisely the areas where government participation and intervention are indispensable. The restructuring of the intergovernmental fiscal system in China should help to improve rather than undermine the public delivery of essential social services, a goal that is consistent with the economic and social role of government in a decentralized market economy.

Theoretical Considerations and International Experience in Social Expenditure Assignment

Principles of Expenditure Assignment

There is no single rule that dictates social expenditure assignment. Some broad guiding principles ought to be observed, however, in specifying the appropriate role to be played by each level of government in education, health, and housing.[1]

The fundamental questions facing public finance, including social expenditure assignment, are what government does best and what the market does best. These questions are especially important for transitional economies like China's. The government, whether at the central

---

[1]For a general discussion on expenditure assignment, see Chapter 6.

level or at the subnational level, should retire from direct production activities that are best undertaken by firms. Government intervention is justified, however, when "market failures" exist. Education and health services are vital to meet basic needs and improve the productivity of the population. Although, unlike national defense and law and social order, they are not "pure" public goods, education and health services, because of important externalities, cannot be efficiently provided by private markets alone. Government involvement is necessary to remedy market failures such as externalities, moral hazard, incomplete information, and imperfect competition that are commonly associated with social services, most notably, health care. The case for public delivery of housing, however, is much weaker. There are compelling reasons to believe that housing can be more efficiently provided by the private sector.

Another important consideration in social expenditure assignments is horizontal equity across regions and households. In a large, diverse country like China, wide variations in regional and local resource bases exist. Perfect local fiscal autonomy may lead to the underprovision of education and basic health care in poorer regions. Even within the same region, the income gaps among households are widening so rapidly that the access of the poor, especially the rural poor, to basic education and health care is in serious jeopardy. The design of intergovernmental fiscal relations should address the issue of horizontal equity in the distribution of social services. In many cases, intervention by higher level governments, through transfers and subsidies and allocation of grants, is needed.

For social services, such as education and health, however, it is difficult a priori to give clear assignments to either the central or subnational government. The usual "benefits principle," which ties benefits and costs of public services within geographical areas to promote accountability of the responsible government and the cost effectiveness of public spending, can offer some useful albeit limited guidance. The central government usually plays a large role in both education and health because of their externalities. In many countries, education and health are identified as "priorities" of public finance. Central government budgets often allocate a substantial share of total revenues to these "priority" sectors, supplemented with national education and health regulations, plans, and policies. There is scope, however, for decentralization of these social expenditures. Both theory and international experience suggest that much can be gained from an expansion in the responsibility of provincial, municipal, and county governments for these social services. Broadening the involvement of local governments can increase public accountability and responsiveness to local needs and preferences, and improve the quality of education and health care.

International Experience

A cross-country comparison of national and subnational government functions may shed light on the role of government in social sectors as well as on the allocation of social responsibilities between levels of government.

In most countries, ranging from industrial market economies to less-developed countries, government typically plays a very important role in education and health care. Government expenditures in both education and health care on average exceed 5 percent of GDP in industrial countries. Similarly government has had a leading role in education and health in developing countries. Schools are usually owned, administered, and financed by government in most developing countries, with the average percentage of students in public schools exceeding 83 percent at the primary level and 74 percent at the secondary level. Also, in most developing countries, the government accounts for a major share of total health expenditure, although, in contrast to the heavier spending on health in industrial countries, public expenditures on health care are usually less than half of those on education in developing countries.

The fact that government is actively involved in these sectors reflects in part the presence of externalities in these services and, probably more important, the public concern on income redistribution. Private market allocations may not only be inefficient because of the failure to internalize the large social benefits of individuals' education and health status, but also may be inequitable as the poor may be denied access to basic health care and the opportunity for education—the most effective means for escape from poverty and for upward social mobility.

While it is clear that the government should play an important role in social sectors, it is less transparent how social responsibilities should be divided among various levels of government. Table 1 shows the pattern of social expenditure assignment in selected countries. It can be seen that responsibilities in education and health are often shared by at least two tiers of government. The central government in developing countries usually takes principal responsibility in both education and health. By contrast in industrial countries, the degree of decentralization varies across education and health sectors—the role of subnational governments tends to be larger in education, while higher level

Table 1. Social Expenditure Assignment in Selected Countries

	Education			Health		
	Central govt.	State govt.	Local govt.	Central govt.	State govt.	Local govt.
Australia	2	1	3	2	1	3
Canada	3	2	1	3	1	2
Denmark	2	—	1	2	—	1
France	1	—	2	1	—	2
Germany	3	1	2	1	3	2
Luxembourg	1	—	2	1	—	2
Switzerland	3	1	2	1	2	3
United Kingdom	2	—	1	1	—	—
United States	3	2	1	1	2	3
India	2	1	—	2	1	—
Indonesia	1	2	—	1	2	—
Israel	1	—	2	1	—	2
Thailand	1	—	2	1	—	2
Chile	1	—	2	1	—	2
Colombia	1	2	3	1	2	3
Kenya	1	—	2	1	—	2
Malawi	1	—	2	1	—	2
Tunisia	1	—	—	1	—	2

Source: Leach (1970), Levin (1991), and Shah (1991)
Note: 1 = principal responsibility; 2 = secondary responsibility; 3 = minor responsibility; — = marginal or no responsibility.

(central and state) governments usually take principal responsibility in health.

Table 2 indicates how more finely classified functions are allocated between different tiers of subnational governments in selected countries.

In spite of the diversity in the political structures (federal versus unitary) and in the size and population, it seems that among these countries there exists a substantial degree of uniformity about which functions are assigned to local governments (municipality and county). Preschool primary, and secondary education are basically a "local government" service, and vocational and technical training and adult education are provided by both regional (state or province) and local governments, while higher education is usually the responsibility of the regional or central government. It appears that hospitals and personal health services are also the joint responsibility of multitiers of government. Clearly, services such as housing, water supply, and refuse collection and disposal are primarily the functions of local governments.

International expenditure data also display interesting patterns in public spending on education and health care by different levels of

Table 2. Allocation of Social Functions to Subnational Governments in Selected Countries

	Austria	Belgium	Denmark	France	Germany	Ireland	Italy	Luxembourg	Netherlands	Norway	Sweden	Switzerland	Turkey	United Kingdom
Preschool education	R,L	L	L	L	L		R,L							L
Primary and secondary education	R,L	R,L	R,L	L	R,L		R,L				L	R,L		L
Vocational and technical training	R	R,L		R,L			R,L			R,L	L	R,L	R	L
Higher education	R,L				R		R,L					R		L
Adult education	L	L	L	L	R,L		R	L	L	R,L	R,L	R,L	L	L
Hospitals	R,L	R,L	R	L,D	R,L		R,P,L		R,L	R,L	R	R,L	R,L	
Personal health	R,L	L	R,L	L	R,L		R,P,L	L	L	L	R	R	R	
Family welfare services	R,L	R,L	L	L,D	R,L		R,L	L	L	L	L	R,L	L	L
Welfare homes	R,L	L	L	L	L		R,L	L	L	L	L	R,L	R,L	L
Housing	R,L	L		L	R,L	L	R,L	L	R,L	L	L	L	L	L
Refuse collection and disposal	L	L	L	L	L	L	L	L	L	L	L	R,L	L	L
District heating	L	L	L	L	L	L	L		L		L	R,L	L	
Water supply	L	L	L	L	L	L	R,P,L	L	L	R,L	L	R,L	R,L	L

Source: Karran (1988).
Note: R = state, regional government; D = departments in France; L = local government; P = provinces in Italy.

government.[2] Although social expenditures may entirely fall on a particular level of government in some countries (Tunisia and the former Yugoslavia, for example), it is far more common that these expenditures are shared by several levels of government, with some level playing a major role. It appears that there exists considerable variation in the shares of social spending administered by different levels of government across countries. For example, local governments accounted for more than 70 percent of total public expenditures in education in the United States, with the rest being split between the federal government (4 percent) and the state governments (25 percent). In France, the central government administered 75 percent of total government expenditures in education, and local governments spent the other 25 percent. In Germany, however, it is the state governments that administered most of the public expenditures in education (74 percent), followed by local governments (25 percent), while federal government spending contributed only 1 percent.

Likewise, the allocation of public spending on health between levels of government exhibits diversity across countries. Higher-level governments tend to play a larger role in health expenditures than in education. In most countries, central government-administered shares account for more than half of total public spending on health. State governments usually play a secondary role, while, with only a few exceptions, local government expenditures on health are relatively unimportant.

Although the ratios of central government or subnational government expenditures to the total government social expenditures are suggestive of the respective role of each level of government in social sectors, the data cannot provide accurate measures of the true degree of fiscal decentralization because they hide important distinctions between financing, administration, and regulation or control. For instance, the central government may administer only a small portion of total public education expenditures, but it may actually play a large role in financing education by giving grants to provincial and local governments, and it may have substantial control of the education sector because of its power as regulator.

The special role of intergovernmental grants in a multilevel fiscal system is worth mentioning, in particular. There is substantial intergovernmental grant financing of education in Australia, Canada, Switzerland, the United States, and Zimbabwe, but quite little in France, Germany, Luxembourg, and the United Kingdom. Intergovernmental grants cover some 20 percent of total government health expenditures

---

[2]Levin (1991). Data quoted refer to three-year averages for 1980. See also Chapter 6.

in Canada, Luxembourg, and the United States, but very little else-where.[3]

One of the messages from international experience seems to be that an appropriate expenditure assignment should not only be broadly consistent with the economic principles in terms of efficiency criteria but should also fit into the particular social and political structure and institutional framework in a country.

Issues with Current Social Expenditure Assignments

In China, the state traditionally played a central role in the social sectors just as in most economic sectors. Since economic reforms were initiated in 1978, the Chinese economy has become increasingly mar-ket oriented. The central government has retreated from its role as a di-rect producer of goods and services in a formerly command economy and surrendered much of the economic decision-making power to lower-level governments and enterprises. The fiscal system has been considerably decentralized and responsibilities for some public services have been transferred to provincial and local governments.

Since 1978, the share of subnational government (provincial and lower-level governments) expenditures in total government expendi-tures has been rising steadily, reaching 60 percent by 1988 (Table 3), indicating a trend of fiscal decentralization in China. There have been no major shifts in social expenditures between the central government and subnational governments, however. The share of subnational gov-ernment expenditures in the category of CESH (culture, education, science, and health) has been remarkably stable—staying in the neigh-borhood of 88 percent—considering the many drastic changes in revenue assignment that have taken place over the period. Social ex-penditures have been a small portion of total central government ex-penditures, accounting for less than 5 percent of the 1992 central budget (Table 4). They have gradually become the single most impor-tant expenditure responsibility for subnational governments, however, accounting for 30 percent of the total subnational government expen-ditures in 1992. Despite China's efforts to increase budgetary spending on education over the past decade, total government expenditures for CESH still amounted to less than 4 percent of GDP in 1992 (Table 5), an abnormally low ratio by international standards. This ratio, how-ever, understates China's true level of public expenditures in social sec-tors because a bulk of social services is provided by state-owned

---

[3]See Levin (1991).

Table 3. Central and Subnational Shares per Expenditure Category

(In percent)

	1978		1988		1989		1990		1991		1992 (Budget)	
	Central	Local	Central	Local	Central	Local	Central	Local	Central	Local	Central	Local
Total	46.89	53.11	39.17	60.83	36.35	63.65	39.77	60.23	39.47	60.53	44.25	55.75
Capital construction	55.75	44.25	76.73	23.27	73.96	26.04	74.66	25.34	73.59	26.41	78.78	21.22
Working capital	29.31	70.69	70.00	30.00	61.54	38.46	72.73	27.27	70.00	30.00	63.64	36.36
Technological upgrading and research and development	33.33	66.67	31.79	68.21	35.37	64.63	35.71	64.29	33.15	66.85	42.22	57.78
Geological prospecting	30.00	70.00	100.00	—	100.00	—	100.00	—	100.00	—	100.00	—
Industry, transport, and commerce	55.56	44.44	33.33	66.67	28.89	71.11	29.79	70.21	28.85	71.15	30.36	69.64
Agriculture	2.60	97.40	9.43	90.57	8.59	91.41	9.91	90.09	9.09	90.91	9.23	90.77
Culture, education, science, and health	11.50	88.50	12.55	87.45	11.55	88.45	11.65	88.35	11.16	88.84	11.43	88.57
Social relief and welfare	—	100.00	—	100.00	—	100.00	—	100.00	1.47	98.53	1.49	98.51
Defense	95.83	4.17	99.08	0.92	99.20	0.80	99.31	0.69	99.09	0.91	99.19	0.81
Government administration	8.16	91.84	16.32	83.68	15.79	84.21	17.33	82.67	16.84	83.16	17.16	82.84
Government debt service	...	...	100.00	—	100.00	—	100.00	—	100.00	—	100.00	—
Price subsidies	...	...	11.36	88.64	10.19	89.81	10.50	89.50	13.48	86.52	15.18	84.82
Other	47.30	52.70	12.50	87.50	12.94	87.06	12.63	87.37	11.88	88.12	14.73	85.27

Source: Ministry of Finance, China.
Note: Percent of total government expenditures. The local expenditures include the earmarked transfers from the central government.

Table 4. Shares of Expenditure Categories in Total Central and Subnational Expenditures

(In percent)

	1978 Central	1978 Local	1988 Central	1988 Local	1989 Central	1989 Local	1990 Central	1990 Local	1991 Central	1991 Local	1992 (Budget) Central	1992 (Budget) Local
Total	100.00	100.00	100.00	100.00	100.00	100.00	100.00	100.00	100.00	100.00	100.00	100.00
Capital construction	48.37	33.90	45.09	8.81	41.90	8.42	39.48	8.85	35.74	8.36	31.98	6.84
Working capital	3.26	6.95	0.66	0.18	0.72	0.26	0.58	0.14	0.47	0.13	0.38	0.17
Technological upgrading and research and development	4.03	7.12	4.53	6.26	4.71	4.91	4.01	4.76	4.07	5.36	4.17	4.53
Geological prospecting	1.15	2.37	3.02	—	2.99	—	2.62	—	2.54	—	2.30	—
Industry, transport, and commerce	1.92	1.36	1.23	1.58	1.18	1.65	1.02	1.59	1.00	1.61	0.93	1.70
Agriculture	0.38	12.71	1.42	8.75	1.54	9.35	1.60	9.62	1.47	9.58	1.32	10.27
Culture, education, science, and health	2.50	16.95	5.75	25.82	5.79	25.32	5.24	26.26	5.21	27.05	4.83	29.69
Social relief and welfare	—	3.22	—	2.49	—	2.53	—	2.65	0.07	2.92	0.05	2.87
Defense	30.90	1.19	20.38	0.12	22.53	0.10	20.98	0.10	21.84	0.13	20.19	0.13
Government administration	0.77	7.63	3.68	12.15	4.07	12.40	4.15	13.08	4.28	13.76	3.78	14.50
Government debt service	—	—	7.26	—	6.52	—	13.84	—	16.43	—	23.59	—
Price subsidies	—	—	3.40	17.07	3.44	17.31	2.91	16.40	3.34	13.98	2.80	12.41
Other	6.72	6.61	3.58	16.16	4.62	17.73	3.57	16.31	3.54	17.12	3.68	16.89

Source: Ministry of Finance, China.

Note: Percent of total central or local expenditures. The local expenditures include the earmarked transfers from the central government.

Table 5. Central and Subnational Expenditures as a Percentage of GNP

	1978		1988		1989		1990		1991		1992 (Budget)	
	Central	Local	Central	Local	Central	Local	Central	Local	Central	Local	Central	Local
Total	14.52	16.44	7.58	11.77	7.00	12.26	7.89	11.95	8.04	12.33	9.11	11.48
Capital construction	7.02	5.57	3.42	1.04	2.93	1.03	3.11	1.06	2.87	1.03	2.91	0.78
Working capital	0.47	1.14	0.05	0.02	0.05	0.03	0.05	0.02	0.04	0.02	0.03	0.02
Technological upgrading and research and development	0.59	1.17	0.34	0.74	0.33	0.60	0.32	0.57	0.33	0.66	0.38	0.52
Geological prospecting	0.17	0.39	0.23	—	0.21	—	0.21	—	0.20	—	0.21	—
Industry, transport, and commerce	0.28	0.22	0.09	0.19	0.08	0.20	0.08	0.19	0.08	0.20	0.08	0.19
Agriculture	0.06	2.09	0.11	1.03	0.11	1.15	0.13	1.15	0.12	1.18	0.12	1.18
Culture, education, science, and health	0.36	2.79	0.44	3.04	0.41	3.10	0.41	3.14	0.42	3.34	0.44	3.41
Social relief and welfare	—	0.53	—	0.29	—	0.31	—	0.32	0.01	0.36	—	0.33
Defense	4.49	0.20	1.54	0.01	1.58	0.01	1.66	0.01	1.76	0.02	1.84	0.01
Government administration	0.11	1.25	0.28	1.43	0.29	1.52	0.33	1.56	0.34	1.70	0.34	1.66
Government debt service	—	—	0.55	—	0.46	—	1.09	—	1.32	—	2.15	—
Price subsidies	—	—	0.26	2.01	0.24	2.12	0.23	1.96	0.27	1.72	0.25	1.42
Other	0.98	1.09	0.27	1.90	0.32	2.17	0.28	1.95	0.28	2.11	0.33	1.94
Memorandum item												
GNP (in billions of yuan)	358.80		1,398.40		1,578.90		1,740.00		1,861.80		2,001.40	

Source: Ministry of Finance, China.
Note: The local expenditures include the earmarked transfers from the central government.

enterprises. Much of the recent growth in budgetary CESH expenditures has come from subnational governments.

Although expenditure data suggest that, compared with many developing countries, subnational governments in China play a greater role in social sectors, particularly in administration and financing, the central government nevertheless has substantial power in regulation and in formulating national policies. In education, for example, the central government, through the State Education Commission, sets national standards for primary and secondary education and administers the national university entrance examination system. Provinces must also follow the central government mandate to achieve the goal of universalization of nine years of basic education. In addition, the central government affects the financing of education at the provincial levels through allocating earmarked grants. Indeed, tight central supervision and application of uniform standards nationwide in particular may help to explain the relatively high quality of primary and secondary education in China.

Further breakdown of subnational government expenditures at the provincial and local level (municipal and county) is difficult because of lack of data, but Hubei Province may provide a good example. Table 6 illustrates how expenditures are divided at different tiers of subnational governments in Hubei Province. Of the Y 8.2 billion expenditures in 1990, about 26 percent was spent at the provincial level, down from 30 percent in 1981. Capital construction expenditures largely remained at the provincial level, which still accounted for 85 percent. Social expenditures, however, were concentrated in local governments—the municipalities, counties, and townships, which together accounted for 77 percent of the total. Townships, at the lowest level of the government structure, play an especially important role in social sectors. About 30 percent of social expenditures in Hubei Province was spent at the township level in 1990.

Examining the current fiscal system also reveals that subnational governments to a large degree depend on self-financing in funding social responsibilities and that the role of intergovernmental grants is relatively unimportant in determining social expenditures of subnational governments. In Hubei Province, for example, earmarked grants from the central government accounted for less than 2 percent of total social expenditures in 1990 (Table 7).

Some of the features in China's intergovernmental fiscal relations, especially the delegation and devolution of fiscal responsibilities for social sectors to lower-level governments, appear to be consistent with the general principles of expenditure assignment. Fiscal decentralization has given provinces and lower-level governments powerful incen-

Table 6. Hubei Province: Expenditure by Level of Government

	In Millions of Yuan					As a Percent of Total				
	Total	Capital construction	Technological upgrading	Education, culture, health	Other	Total	Capital construction	Technological upgrading	Education, culture, health	Other
1981										
Total	2,360	286	68	737	1,269	100.0	12.1	2.9	31.2	53.8
Province	706	286	52	76	292	29.9	100.0	76.5	10.3	23.0
Municipalities	589	...	7	187	395	25.0	0.0	10.3	25.4	31.1
Counties	1,065	...	9	474	582	45.1	—	13.2	64.5	45.9
1985										
Total	4,359	438	182	1,170	2,569	100.0	10.0	4.2	26.8	58.9
Province	1,556	391	84	155	926	35.7	89.3	46.2	13.2	36.0
Municipalities	1,211	48	43	327	793	27.8	11.0	23.6	27.9	30.9
Counties	1,593	...	55	688	850	36.5	—	30.2	58.8	33.1
1990										
Total	8,284	556	367	1,987	5,374	100.0	6.7	4.4	24.0	64.9
Province	2,188	472	86	249	1,381	26.4	84.9	23.4	12.5	25.7
Municipalities	2,506	84	140	543	1,739	30.3	15.1	38.1	27.3	32.4
Counties	2,506	...	141	589	1,776	30.3	—	38.4	29.6	33.0
Townships	1,084	...	...	605	479	13.1	—	—	30.4	8.9

Source: Hubei Finance Bureau, Wuhan, China. The fiscal system has recognized the township level since 1986. Figures include Wuhan City.
Note: Figures may not add because of rounding.

Table 7. Hubei Province Budgetary Expenditures and Central Earmarked Grants, 1990
(In millions of yuan)

	Total Expenditures	Central Government Earmarked Grants	Grants as Percent of Total
Capital construction	556	60	10.8
Technological upgrading	367	10	2.7
Agricultural support	831	89	10.7
Education, science, health	2,035	37	1.8
Urban maintenance	366	5	1.4
Administration	1,147	59	5.1
Price subsidy	1,613	947	58.7
Other	1,369	203	14.8
Total	8,284	1,410	17.0

Source: Hubei Finance Bureau, Wuhan, China.
Note: The figures include Wuhan City.

tives and increasing autonomy to manage local public finances and hence produced substantial efficiency gains. Since fiscal decentralization is somewhat poorly planned and implemented piecemeal, however, it has also created many problems. Specifically, the Chinese authorities ought to address a number of issues outlined below.

Define Expenditure Assignments

To date, China has failed to work out a law that clearly defines expenditure responsibilities for different levels of government. Existing expenditure assignments are murky, and often, motivated by political expediency, shift between levels of government in ad hoc ways. The central government may shift its own expenditure responsibilities to provincial governments in times of difficulty (price subsidies and state-owned enterprises subsidies, for example), and provincial governments may use their broader responsibilities to bargain for a larger share of revenue. Intergovernmental bargaining has weakened budgetary planning and control and contributed to the instability of China's fiscal system. Without first reaching decisions on expenditure assignment, the Chinese authorities have found it difficult to reform tax assignment rules and revenue-sharing mechanisms between the central and provincial governments.

Expenditure assignments between the provincial government and lower-level authorities, such as municipal and county, are even more vague. Local governments are often forced to take the responsibility that should be undertaken by higher-level government, accentuating the mismatch between local revenue and local expenditure responsibility. The lack of specificity and the unpredictability built into the current system of expenditure assignments have given rise to budgetary uncertainty for the central government and made fiscal planning an impossible task for provincial and local authorities, hence adversely affecting the supply of public goods and services in both quantity and quality.

Relieve Social Burden of Enterprises

Historically, state-owned enterprises have been undertaking many social responsibilities such as day care, schools, hospitals, housing, sports, and theater, most of which would belong to the public sector in a market economy. With increasing competition from rural township enterprises, foreign joint ventures, and other private enterprises, state-owned enterprises—many of them incurring losses—have difficulty financing social services for their employees and the local community. An important task of both fiscal reform and restructuring state-owned enterprises is to relieve enterprises' social burden through transferring their social expenditure responsibilities from the enterprise sector to the appropriate level of government.

Equalize Social Services Across Provinces

Horizontal inequity has increasingly become a problem in China as market-oriented economic reforms proceed. The current fiscal system has produced an inequitable distribution of social services across both regions and households. Poorer provinces tend to spend much larger shares of their fiscal revenues on primary and secondary education, but still have considerably lower per capita expenditures relative to the national average. In 1990, per capita expenditures on CESH in Beijing, Shanghai, Tianjin, and Tibet well exceeded Y 100, while those in poorer provinces, such as Anhui, Henan, Sichuan, and Guizhou, were less than Y 35 (Table 8).

The inequality between urban residents and rural peasants is especially striking. For the past decade, government spending per capita on health care has been five times higher for urban residents than for rural residents. Most of the budgetary subsidies on education and health care have gone to employees of the urban state-owned sector. Peasants, who account for 80 percent of population in China, are not covered by any medical insurance plans. The rural poor in some areas often lack

Table 8. Main Items of Expenditures per Capita by Provinces
(In yuan)

	Capital Construction		Culture, Education, Health			Welfare	
	1987	1990	1978	1987	1990	1987	1990
Total province	14.90	15.41	10.4	31.29	46.03	3.43	4.77
Beijing	98.13	109.21	28.7	80.88	147.88	9.56	14.73
Tianjin	62.58	48.42	24.3	83.63	106.90	5.54	7.58
Hebei	6.83	5.97	9.5	26.22	40.30	3.85	5.68
Shanxi	22.67	14.52	11.8	36.03	52.50	4.82	6.17
Inner Mongolia	26.19	22.84	9.8	48.94	67.18	5.37	6.52
Liaoning	28.25	21.53	15.6	42.71	65.21	4.95	6.88
Jilin	15.60	14.14	16.0	45.65	62.51	6.10	6.24
Heilongjian	14.81	15.92	13.8	37.70	52.50	3.83	4.63
Shanghai	80.24	104.49	27.8	88.00	128.42	5.04	5.39
Jiangsu	9.31	8.42	8.5	28.51	42.43	3.39	4.95
Zhejiang	10.40	9.21	9.1	32.89	51.08	3.08	5.13
Anhui	5.96	6.03	8.3	20.44	29.41	2.51	3.63
Fujian	17.74	26.41	11.4	34.05	54.49	3.42	5.10
Jiangxi	9.42	8.74	9.2	25.63	35.49	3.40	4.30
Shandong	6.14	9.20	8.6	26.73	40.37	3.88	5.58
Henan	6.78	6.29	8.2	20.18	27.51	2.90	2.87
Hubei	12.13	10.22	10.1	26.64	36.53	2.97	4.01
Hunan	8.03	9.14	8.4	25.68	35.77	2.68	4.16
Guangdong	23.47	31.47	10.4	35.55	55.66	2.89	3.66
Guangxi	10.19	8.59	9.7	29.51	41.45	2.31	2.70
Hainan	...	52.49	...	...	65.61	...	4.98
Sichuan	9.13	9.27	7.8	22.29	33.69	2.45	3.42
Guizhou	11.39	13.89	8.5	25.22	34.27	3.03	3.82
Yunnan	20.26	24.28	8.3	34.15	55.05	3.59	9.92
Tibet	57.21	66.22	...	111.06	124.77	10.10	16.22
Shaanxi	11.82	10.07	11.4	30.82	43.70	3.14	4.43
Gansu	20.60	17.12	11.2	32.75	46.65	3.64	4.12
Qinghai	44.63	32.59	24.3	63.32	80.36	5.14	6.47
Ningxia	46.44	31.06	22.2	59.54	73.62	4.14	4.47
Xinjiang	35.81	32.44	18.2	55.69	79.27	3.44	3.79
Mean	25.20	26.00		42.40	60.40	4.20	5.70
Standard deviation	23.10	26.10		22.60	30.10	1.80	3.00
Coeff. of variation	0.92	1.00		0.53	0.50	0.44	0.52

Source: China Finance Statistics; *China Statistical Yearbook* (various issues).

access to even basic health services, and rural schools—especially those in poorer regions—are grossly underfunded.

As the resources in the revenue-sharing system stagnated, the central government allowed the redistributive element of the fiscal system to weaken, at times when diverging economic conditions would require more equalization among regions. Fiscal redistribution now takes place mainly through ad hoc, earmarked grants, often poorly targeted and too small to meet basic needs in the poorer regions.

Reduce Risk of Crowding Out Social Expenditures

Facing tight budget constraints and the competition for faster regional growth, local governments are often compelled to shift their spending priorities to industrial projects that can potentially generate fiscal revenue and enlarge local resource capacity. The current fiscal system gives disincentives for local governments to fund social sectors, where government participation is critical. More of the limited local financial resources are allocated to local industrial investment, development zones, and physical infrastructure, such as roads, power stations, communication systems, and so on, at the expense of education and health care, whose benefits accrue only slowly and cannot be reaped exclusively by the local economy. Fiscal decentralization may result in underfinancing of social sectors, particularly in the revenue-stricken poor regions.

Directions for Reforming Social Expenditure Assignment

The reform of intergovernmental fiscal relations should enhance the role of government in the provision of social services. Public finance should continue to set education and basic health care as top spending priorities so that China's remarkable progress in human and social development can be sustained. China needs a healthy, well-educated, and skilled labor force to maintain its productivity growth and external competitiveness. Human capital investment is a key variable that determines long-run economic growth, as demonstrated by China's own and its East Asian neighbors' experience. Since government activity in education and health is crucial for human capital formation, it needs to be assessed as an essential part of the overall set of government responsibilities.

More specifically, the reform of social expenditure assignment in China should focus on the areas described below.

Decentralize Social Services. The decentralization of education and health systems now evolving in China should be improved and consolidated. First, responsibilities for financing, providing, and regulating social services can be separated and properly divided among different levels of government. Second, assignment of expenditure responsibilities for each level of government should be made more specific, more stable, and more transparent. It should be finalized in the form of laws and regulations that govern intergovernmental fiscal relations. The central government should retain substantial power in the regulation and supervision of education and health-care sectors, to ensure conformity with national goals and standards. Transferring administrative and spending responsibility for primary and secondary education and basic health care from the central government to provincial and lower-level governments, however, will likely lead to substantial efficiency gains.

Reduce Disparity in Social Services. The new intergovernmental fiscal system should aim at reducing the wide disparity in social expendi-tures across regions and the coverage of social services for urban and rural families. The central government and provincial governments should explore various policy instruments to achieve horizontal equity in education and health care.

Improve Allocative Efficiency. The current allocation of public funds within social sectors is biased. It favors higher education and urban schools, and too much health spending goes to urban hospitals and curative health care. The new expenditure assignments should enable the responsible government to shift more resources to primary and secondary education, to increase subsidies to rural schools, and to refocus on basic preventive health care, especially in poor rural areas.

Mobilize Financial Resources. The education and health care sectors can improve efficiency and achieve cost recovery through user charges and other benefit-related fees for primary and secondary education in urban and rich regions, as well as most of the curative health-care services and higher education. Applying charges can provide incentives for efficiency in the delivery and consumption of social services, as well as increase revenue.

Expand Role of Private Sector. While the public sector will probably have to remain the dominant supplier of education and health care, China should encourage private provision of these services. Particularly in health care, the scope for private sector participation is large. The government should continue to expand basic health care with greater emphasis on access for the poor and take responsibility for health services that have a public-good character (e.g., clean air and water safety) or externalities (e.g., immunization programs), while allowing the private sector to play a larger role in providing curative care services. Most important, the provision of housing should cease to be a responsibility of the state-owned enterprises or government agencies. The authorities should push forward housing reform by encouraging private home ownership and development of housing market.

Policy Recommendations

The following policies are recommended.

- The Chinese authorities should continue setting education and health care as top priorities of public finances, while the government should further withdraw from direct economic activities that should be left to the market. Housing, which can be efficiently produced and provided by the market, should no longer remain a responsibility of the public sector, except for some form of necessary intervention on equity grounds. At the same time, the government should assume responsibility for providing social services delivered previously by enterprises. Social functions of state-owned enterprises can be transferred to local governments—municipalities and counties—since local governments are in closer touch with local conditions and needs and can thus provide the right amount of services to residents in their jurisdictions at lower costs.
- In the new intergovernmental fiscal system, the central government should have the primary responsibility for the legislation and supervision of education and health care, for formulating general policies and guidelines (universalization of basic education, vaccination for children, family planning, and so on), and for setting national education and health-care standards (e.g., curriculum design, central inspection, and national examination), while provincial governments and lower-level governments should play the principal role in the administration and financing of basic public education and public health care.
- The central government can continue undertaking responsibility for administering and financing national universities, and for supporting basic medical research programs vital to public health. It can share with provincial governments the responsibility for information and control of contagious diseases and for immunization. Provincial, and especially lower-level, governments such as municipalities and counties can be given primary responsibility for the financing and provision of primary and secondary education. Safe water supply, sanitation, sewage, and other local services concerning public health should be financed and provided primarily by local governments at municipal, county, or township level.

- Increase diversification in China's education and health sectors. In particular, expand the role of the private sector in education and health care services. Encourage the establishment of privately run schools and hospitals and foster competition between the private sector and public schools and public hospitals. Review and study alternatives for the development of national health insurance systems, including both public and private, market-related, decentralized approaches, and centrally or provincially funded and coordinated "universal health insurance systems."
- Improve the cost effectiveness of social services. This would be done by increasing the role of tuition and fees for public schools in rich regions and urban areas and applying user charges to curative care services, while preventive care, including prenatal care and immunization, would continue to be provided free of charge. Most social expenditures at the local government level should be financed out of "own revenues" to increase the accountability of local governments and encourage cost effectiveness of public services. To this end, revenue assignment should follow expenditure assignment so that local governments would have adequate resources to finance their social responsibilities.
- Establish a sound system of intergovernmental transfers and grants. Intergovernmental grants are an important instrument to redress horizontal inequality in social expenditures. Both matching and equalization grants, allocated from central and provincial to lower levels of government, are likely to be needed to rationalize intergovernmental fiscal relations.

References

Agarwala, R., "China: Reforming Intergovernmental Fiscal Relations" (Washington: 1992).

Bahl, R., and C. Wallich, "Intergovernmental Fiscal Relations in China" (Washington: World Bank, 1992).

International Monetary Fund, Government Financial Statistics Yearbook (Washington, International Monetary Fund, 1992).

Karran, T., "Local Taxing and Local Spending: International Comparisons," in Local Government Finance: International Perspectives, ed. by R. Paddison and S. Bailey (London: Routledge, 1988).

Leach, R., American Federalism (New York: Norton, 1970).

Levin, J., "Measuring the Role of Subnational Governments," IMF Working Paper, WP/91/8 (Washington: International Monetary Fund, 1991).

Oates, W., Studies in Fiscal Federalism, Edward Elgar.

Shah, A., "Perspectives on the Design of Intergovernmental Fiscal Relations," World Bank, WPS 726 (Washington: World Bank, 1991).

Wallich, C., " Fiscal Decentralization: Intergovernmental Relations in Russia" (Washington: World Bank, 1992).

World Bank, *China: Revenue Mobilization and Tax Policy* (Washington, 1989).

——, *China: Provincial Education Planning and Finance—Sector Study* (Washington, 1991).

——, *China: Long-Term Issues and Options in the Health Transition* (Washington, 1992).

——, *China: Budgetary Policy and Intergovernmental Fiscal Relations* (Washington, 1993).

Revenue Assignments—
Tax Policy and Administration

9

Reform and the Market Economy and Tax in China

Xu Shanda and Ma Lin*

China started to reform its old tax system under the traditional planning economic mode in 1988. Since then, it has undergone a process of formulating reforms, putting them into operation, and making constant efforts to perfect them. A complex tax system is the result, with turnover taxes and income taxes as the main taxes, supplemented by other taxes. For the past dozen years or so, the system basically provided for needs of the development of the economy and the reform of the economic system. In 1992, however, the authorities decided that a socialist market economic system should be established. Accordingly, the tax system would also need further reform and adjustment in light of the requirements of the market economy.

Role of Taxation in a Socialist Market Economy

Under a socialist market economy, economic operations are organized via the market mechanism, and the market plays a basic role in resource distribution. Taxation is a means by which the state participates in the redistribution of income, raises public revenue, and forms a macroeconomic lever directly controlled by the state to regulate social production at all stages. No other administrative measures and economic tools can replace taxation. With the transition from a planned economy to a market one, the former heavy reliance on regulation, through administrative orders and mandatory production plans, will be reduced substantially, as will the role of administrative

---

*State Administration of Taxation, China.

137

pricing tools. The state, however, will continue to play a role in the overall balance of the economy, industrial restructuring, the maintenance of an equitable competitive environment, and the alleviation of unequal social distribution. Thus, taxation will undoubtedly become one of the most important macroeconomic tools of the state in a socialist market economy, given its legal basis and regulation functions. Taxation, in this context, would guarantee the stabilization functions of the market economy, promote the formation and perfection of allocative market mechanisms, regulate social redistribution, and limit the negative externalities generated by the market.

The effective functioning of taxation in the market economy requires the following basic conditions:

- All stages and the whole process of social reproduction, including production, distribution, exchange and consumption, and all economic activities, must be directly or indirectly placed within the market relationship. The market is the fundamental operational mechanism regulating the whole social economy, pushing the flow of productive elements and guiding the distribution of resources.
- All enterprises must be given autonomy to run their own businesses, shoulder the obligations of paying taxes in accordance with law, and account for their own profits and losses. Separate producers and managers of commodities and financial transactions form the main body of the market.
- The government must not directly interfere with the day-to-day affairs of production and management of enterprises, but rather regulate and standardize the operational activities of enterprises via financial, taxation, price, and banking policies.
- All business operations must be conducted in accordance with the provisions of laws and regulations. The entire operation of the economy must be placed on a comprehensive legal basis.

The reform of China's tax system must conform to the basic characteristics and rules of the market economy. The market is uniform, therefore the tax legislation must be unified; the market is open, therefore the tax structure and tax administration must be adaptable to the needs of opening up the economy and be aligned with the common international taxation norms; the market is competitive, therefore taxation policy must reflect the principle of equitable tax burden; the market operates in conformity to objective economic rules, therefore taxation should play a greater role in strengthening macroregulation and promoting microeconomic incentives.

It should be noted that, despite the outstanding achievements China has attained in restructuring its tax system over the past few years, the current system cannot entirely cater to the needs of the market mechanism, neither structurally nor functionally. A more fundamental tax reform is needed without delay.

Basic Principles Governing Tax Reform

Viewed from the practice of China, and the experiences of other countries, the construction and reform of a taxation system under the condition of a market economy must use the following basic principles.

Principle of Effectiveness

A scientific (or nonnegotiated) taxation system is the basis on which taxation can correctly and effectively play its intended role. The orientation of tax reform, therefore, must conform to the requirements of the development of a market economy and forge a tax system that can really help the effective operation of the economy; meanwhile, the tax administration system should also raise efficiency and reduce administrative cost.

Principle of Equity

Taxation should treat all taxpayers equally, in the sense of horizontal equity and vertical equity. The former implies that taxpayers with equal economic ability (ability to pay taxes) must pay the same amount of tax, that is, to treat people of similar conditions equally. The latter implies different economic capacities of taxpayers also be taken into account by the tax system.

Principle of Standardization

The nature of taxation calls for standardization of the tax system. At the same time, standardization is an important condition for the enforcement of tax laws and the realization of equal tax burdens. The design of the overall tax system, the determination of various tax elements, and the methods of tax collection and administration, therefore, must all be considered from this starting point. The proposed tax system will be unified and integrated, thus avoiding arbitrariness, and will respect international norms, as well as China's specific characteristics. The features must, finally, be reflected in the respective tax legislation.

Principle of Stabilizing the Economy

Taxation is a lever used by the government to regulate the economy, specifically to maintain full employment and stable relative prices. When the economy is approaching full employment and is experiencing inflation, tax rates can be raised to reduce demand and alleviate the pressure of inflation; when the growth of economy is slowing down and the unemployment rate is rising, the tax rates can be lowered to curb the trend of economic depression.

Principle of Neutrality

Under market economic conditions, profits will guide investment and the market will play a leading role in resource allocation. Therefore, taxation should be as economically neutral as possible; that is, it should not interfere with or distort the effective operation of market mechanisms.

Main Problems of Existing Chinese Tax System

Although outstanding achievements have been reached, the prevailing Chinese tax system leaves much room for improvement in view of keeping abreast of the development of the market economy. It is necessary and urgent to further the reform of China's tax system.

The main manifestations of disharmony between China's present tax system and the market economy are as follows:

- Through the gradual evolution of economic structural reform, constrained by historical conditions and policy choices, China has established an enterprise income tax system, whereby enterprises of different types apply different categories of taxes with different tax rates and preferential treatments, resulting in unequal tax burdens. This pattern is detrimental to enterprise restructuring and fair competition.
- There are high nominal tax rates but low actual tax burdens. In the state-owned enterprise, the nominal tax rate is 55 percent. The actual tax burden, however, is far less than this figure, because of the treatment of the repayment of loans as a before-tax charge (Chapter 12). Moreover, the management contract responsibility reduces the effective tax burden. Similarly, with turnover taxes and other taxes, the tax bases are incomplete and various kinds of tax preferential treatments exist. Thus, there is a much lower actual tax burden than the rate structure would imply.

- There is irregular and indeterminate distribution of functions between the state and the state-owned enterprises. The state's functions in distribution, as the manager of the society and the owner of the state's properties, are not duly reflected in the tax system.
- The scope and depth of regulation by taxation are not in line with the requirement that all productive elements should enter into the market. The regulating functions played by taxation are very weak in such areas as land values, individual incomes, and capital market gains. The structure of tax revenues should reflect changes in the sources of income as the market economy expands.
- A complete local tax system is yet to be established. Revenues raised by local taxes are very limited. The division of tax administrative power is not very rational, which impedes the smooth transition to a system whereby the central government and the local governments raise their own revenue through different taxes.
- The current turnover tax features too many rates and steep rate brackets. This is because the turnover tax is designed to alleviate the sharp differences in profit margins of enterprises, resulting from the controlled price system. Presently, however, most commodity prices have been freed. Thus, a neutral indirect tax system should be established in accordance with the requirement of the market mechanism.
- The fact that domestic enterprises and foreign-funded enterprises are under the jurisdiction of two separate tax legislations causes a contradiction that is becoming more and more acute.

Proposed Reform of Tax System

The decision to establish a socialist market economy has brought forth a series of issues to be solved. It is our view that the guiding principles for designing the tax reform should be as follows: unify tax laws; balance the tax burden; simplify the tax system; rationalize the division of tax jurisdictions; standardize the pattern of allocation; and put allocational relationships in order. The principles of enlarging tax bases, rationalizing tax burdens, reducing tax incentives, and enhancing penalties should also be followed.

Tax Structure

China is a developing country with low productivity and relatively low personal incomes. Thus, direct taxes are unlikely to be the main revenue source in the foreseeable future. Based on the actual conditions in China, the selection of the main tax instruments must satisfy the dual requirements of state finance and economic regulation. In the social reproduction process, production and circulation are two stages whereby the national income is created and realized, respectively. Extensive and easy-to-control tax sources are concentrated there. Taxes levied on these stages can guarantee the steady growth of tax revenue and, effectively, play the function of regulating production, circulation, distribution, and consumption. Furthermore, the stage of allocation of national income mainly relates to enterprise net income, that is, the enterprises' profits. The tax source is thus relatively concentrated. Taxes levied at this stage can also play a certain regulatory function, particularly with regard to allocation. Therefore, starting from China's status quo, it is appropriate to rely on indirect taxes on the sales of commodities, at the production and distribution stages, and the enterprise income tax as the main taxes of the country's tax system. In addition, some supplementary taxes will also be enacted, so that the function of taxation will exist in all sectors.

Currently, the revenue from indirect taxes (value-added tax, product tax, business tax, and the consolidated industrial and commercial tax) exceeds two thirds of the total tax revenue (excluding customs duty). Such a big proportion presents some difficulty for tax reform. The short-term tax reform should first of all consider the adjustment of the revenue structure. Given the particular development level of China's national economy, and the specific conditions of its economic system, however, indirect tax revenue will continue to make up the better part of the total tax revenue for a relatively long period of time. Indirect taxes and enterprises' income tax will be the main taxes complemented by other smaller taxes.

Reform of Enterprise Income Tax

The immediate target of the enterprise income tax reform is to unify the domestic enterprise income tax. The separate domestic enterprise income tax and the income tax of enterprises with foreign investment (joint ventures) and foreign enterprise will be unified to form a uniform "Enterprise Income Tax Law of the People's Republic of China" applicable to all enterprises. The establishment of a unified and standardized domestic enterprise income tax system will not only eliminate an obvious obstacle to the transformation of enterprises' operating mechanisms, so as to help push the enterprises to the market and create a fair competition environment, but also may set right the allocational relationship between the state and the enterprises.

The main ideas on unifying the domestic enterprise income tax are as follows:

- Unify the current State-Owned Enterprise Income Tax, the Collective Enterprise Income Tax, and the Private Enterprise Income Tax. Phase out the Adjustment Tax for State-Owned Enterprises.
- Reduce the income tax rates for enterprises to apply a uniform 33 percent flat rate. Appropriate measures will be adopted within a certain period of time to take care of small enterprises (see Chapter 12). Unify and standardize the items deductible and the corresponding limit. To avoid erosion of the tax base, deduction before tax must follow the stipulations of the tax law.
- As a supporting measure to the unification of domestic enterprise income taxes, the present practice of the repayment of loans as tax deductible items will be changed to conform with international practice, whereby loans have to be repaid from after-tax resources. With the introduction of this system, the key energy and communication construction fund and the budgetary regulating fund appropriated after tax should also be eliminated.
- The state, as the owner of the state-owned enterprises, has the right to share the after-tax profit of the enterprises. Considering the actual conditions of the enterprises, however, most enterprises, except a very few, will be allowed to keep all their after-tax profits for a certain number of years.

Unifying the domestic enterprise income tax is of great significance to the deepening of the economic structural reform. It will touch upon a series of reforms in relation to the enterprise system, including the depreciation system, the investment system, the financial and accounting system, the wage and bonus system, and the employee's social security system. The reform of the enterprise income tax system and these reforms are constraints, but also influence and promote each other. With the aforesaid reform measures being gradually put into place, the transformation of operating mechanisms of enterprises will be assured.

Changing the possibility of loan repayment before tax into an after-tax charge is a key point of unifying the domestic enterprise income tax. Simply put, loan repayments before tax were associated with the old system, whereby all profits were remitted to the state, and all expenditures of the enterprises were allocated by the state. The main manifestation areas follow. First, investment loans borrowed by enterprises are mainly guaranteed by the state's tax revenue. Enterprises and banks both take quite small risks. This kind of no-risk investment mechanism is likely to result in an unreasonable and inefficient investment structure. Second, inappropriate investment signals can lead to excessive overall outlays, detrimental to the macroeconomic control of the state. Third, the income tax base of enterprises is seriously eroded, resulting in a gap between the nominal tax rate and the actual tax paid. The reforms will support the steady growth of the state's revenues. By the introduction of repayment of loans after tax, a risk-taking mechanism will be built up in the investment system of enterprises. This is conducive to improvements in investment efficiency, and in the economic performance of the state-owned enterprises. It is also helpful from the view of enterprises building up the mechanisms of self-constraint and self-development. This is a crucial link to encourage enterprises to change their operating mechanisms. Without making enterprises responsible for investment risks, the transformation of enterprises' operating mechanisms would not be feasible.

Reform of Indirect Taxes

The reform of the turnover tax is targeted at establishing a system whereby the *value-added tax* (VAT), the *product tax*, and the *excise tax* co-exist and a two-tiered regulatory function is formed. Specifically, the VAT will be used in the production and circulation sectors of commodity for general regulatory purposes, while the product tax will be used for special regulatory purposes, applicable only to a few selected consumption goods such as cigarettes, alcohol, gasoline, and cars. In addition, a business tax will be imposed on the tertiary industries, except commercial wholesale and retail businesses.

When China was beginning to introduce the VAT, there was a view that it could be levied on only the manufacturing stage with the purpose of eliminating cascading effects of taxation. Trial experimentation of the tax over the past dozen years, however, has shown that there has been a superficial introduction of the computation methods of the value-added tax, while the requirements of a *wide base* and *simple rates*, which are needed by the nature of the tax, have been overlooked. This negligence plus a controlled price system have combined to cause the problem of complicated computational processes and distorted deductions.

The future reform will follow the common international practices, determine a standardized principle, and make the value-added tax cover all stages of production and distribution of commodities, while at the same time simplifying the rate structure. Only in this way can the full function of this tax be brought into play. This is because first, only when the tax is extended to all stages of production and distribution can the system of deducting VAT, based on the tax stated on invoices, be established. The current problem of deducting the tax based on purchasing cost does not reflect the true tax element, and usually results in tax leakages. Thus, a check-and-balance mechanism among taxpayers themselves will be established. Second, the computation methods will be greatly simplified, so that tax compliance and tax administration will become more convenient. Third, the chronic problem of distinguishing wholesale and retail businesses will be tackled by setting the standard rate of VAT at a higher level than the tax burden on the retail stage.

Specific ideas on turnover tax reform are as follows:

- *Extend the coverage of VAT.* As the first step, VAT will be imposed on all manufacturing sectors, and then, during the second step, the tax will extend to the retail stage.
- *Simplify the VAT tax rates.* The rate structure will be one standard rate and another reduced rate.
- *Simplify the computation and collection methods of VAT.* Input VAT will be credited against output VAT, and the balance will be paid by the taxpayer by means of invoices on which the tax amount is separately listed.
- *Calculate VAT on the basis of the sales prices*, excluding VAT.
- *Enact the excise tax*, which will play a special regulatory role. After the merging of VAT tax rates, a considerable number of products will experience a drop in the tax burden. In order to maintain the overall scale of fiscal revenue, the excise tax can be levied on a few selected consumption goods *after* subjecting them to a general levy of the valued-added tax. The coverage of the excise tax could include some high grade and luxury consumption goods.
- *Adjust tax rates* in accordance with the industrial policy of China and the actual condition of the development of the tertiary industry. The *business tax* mainly plays its function in the tertiary industry sector.

On the premises of improving the indirect tax system, and the unification of the domestic and foreign-funded enterprise income tax, some taxpayers may experience an increased tax burden. Some transitory preferential methods will be conferred within a prescribed period of time.

Reform of Individual Income Tax

Equitable allocation of income is one of the important social targets a socialist country seeks to attain. The market, however, is not able by itself to realize this objective. Therefore, appropriate income and tax policies are devised by the state to maintain the impartiality of allocation and distribution.

At present, the three taxes charged on natural persons, namely, the individual income tax, the individual income regulatory tax, and the income tax on individual businessmen exist in parallel. This practice lacks legality, and there is an absence of standardization of legislation and policy integrity. Thus, it causes some contradictions. With a view to implementing effective macrocontrol, by means of taxation, in the field of allocation, a new individual income tax system will be established in the near term. This will suit the allocation pattern of distribution according to work, acknowledging reasonable differences in individual income, but also to perform needed income redistribution functions. The specific ideas are as follows:

- A unified "Individual Income Tax Law of the People's Republic of China" is to be formed to consolidate the current individual income tax, individual income regulatory tax, and income tax on individual businessmen of cities and towns.
- With reference to the common international practices, expand the scope of levy of the individual income tax. The individual's income from business operation will be subject to this tax.
- The individual income tax will use progressive tax rates. Experiences of foreign countries will be assimilated in connection with the actual conditions of our country when setting up an appropriate level tax burden.
- The individual income tax will adopt different allowable deductions with respect to Chinese citizens and foreigners.

Reform of Local Taxes

With the furtherance of the economic structural reform, the shortcomings of the current contracted financial system started to surface. The relationship between the central government and the local government needs urgent adjustment. The direction of reform is to implement a separate tax jurisdiction system. Proposed tax reforms must suit the implementation of this system.

Establish Local Tax System

Those taxes that have less significant macroregulation functions but are closely linked with the development of the local economy and are also convenient for the local government to administer will be assigned to the local government as their fixed revenue basis. Tentatively, in addition to the present local taxes, the business tax will be basically within the jurisdiction of the local government. Second, the scope of the resource tax will be for local government revenue. Third, taxes levied on property and land will be local taxes.

Expand Scale of Local Tax Revenue

It is important to raise considerably the proportion of local tax revenue in relation to the total tax revenue so that the local governments can cover most of their expenditures through their own resources.

Macrocontrol

On the premise of concentrating necessary macrocontrol with the central government, tax administration responsibilities must be clearly defined. The present chaos of the tax administration must be changed. Tax jurisdiction powers over taxes that have been assigned as fixed local government revenue should be mostly delegated to the local government.

Legislation

Tax legislation power over local taxes can be appropriately delegated to the legislative organs of the province, autonomous regions, and municipalities directly under the State Council, except those that require unified implementation across the country.

Reform Local Tax Structure

At present, China has a complicated, compound tax system with overlapping responsibilities, and local tax assignments are not very reasonable. Some local taxes should be merged or abolished; some should be restructured and perfected; and a few new taxes should be enacted. Specifically, the market trade tax, the livestock transaction tax, the bonus tax, the wages and salaries adjustment tax, and the oil consumption special tax will be abolished; the salt tax will be merged into the resource tax, and the special consumption tax into the excise tax. In addition, it should be possible to replace the urban land and house tax, and the vehicle and vessel license tax, with a unified house property tax and vehicle and vessel use tax; introduce at an appropriate time the land gains tax, the security transaction tax and the inheritance tax; delegate the feast tax and the slaughter tax to local governments; and reform and adjust the urban maintenance and construction tax, and the city and township land use tax.

Measures Supporting Reform of Tax System

A number of measures are needed to initiate the tax reforms discussed above. These are briefly summarized as follows:

Reform of Tax Administration System

The current tax administration system of China was formulated in 1977. Constrained by the then-planned economy, this system focused on the division of administrative powers. Since then, China's tax system has undergone large adjustments. Furthermore, great changes have also taken place with respect to the state's economic structure and situation. Under such conditions, the present tax administrative system must be reformed in parallel. The general principle for such reform is to tie together tax jurisdictional power and responsibility of tax revenue. Taxes that are central government revenues, or shared revenues between the central and the local governments, should be under the jurisdiction of the central government. Taxes that will go to local coffers should be under the jurisdiction of local governments.

Tax Legislation Work

At present, of all the tax legislation in China, only the following are promulgated by the National People's Congress and enjoy the status of law: "Income Tax Law for the Enterprises with Foreign Investment and Foreign Enterprises", "Individual Income Tax Law," and the procedure law "Tax Collection and Administration Law." Most other taxes have yet to be formally legislated. Some have only the status of provisional rules, of which some even do not have implementation regulations; still others have been implemented in the form of draft regulations for quite a number of years. To establish a modern market economy, it is not only necessary that the legislative work must be carried out in parallel with tax reform but also that tax legislation must become a guarantee to tax reform. Therefore, tax legislation work must be strengthened. At every step of the tax reform, tax legislation work must also be fulfilled in accordance with legal procedures, to realize the target of placing taxation on a legal and standard basis in the market economy environment.

Reinforcing Tax Administration

In parallel with the tax system reform, the reform of tax administration should also be furthered and deepened. Thus, the present backward tax administrative system should be thoroughly overhauled and a scientifically based, rigorous, and highly effective tax administration system be established.

The strategy for tax administration reform is as follows. First, popularize the self-assessment and self-filing system. It must be made clear to taxpayers that filing their tax returns is the primary link for fulfilling their tax-paying obligations. Establishing the taxpayer self-filing system is conducive to the formation of a check-and-balance mechanism among taxpayers themselves and helpful in strengthening their consciousness of tax compliance. It is foundation-laying work for the effective management of the tax administration. Once the system is established, those who do not file their tax returns within the prescribed time limit will be subject to economic penalties. Those who make false declarations will be treated as tax evaders and severely punished in accordance with law.

Second, actively introduce the tax agent system. International practice should be followed so that nongovernmental agencies, such as accounting firms, law firms, and tax consultancy firms, can be trusted with the task of helping taxpayers perform tax-paying procedures. Tax agent services will be an indispensable and important link in the entire tax administration system, forming a three-part, check-and-balance mechanism between taxpayers, tax agents, and tax authorities.

Third, expedite the process of tax administration computerization. International experience has proved that computerization is the surest way to establish a scientific, rigorous, and effective tax administration system that is also less costly. Because China has many sparsely populated areas, small-scale taxpayers, and the foundation of computerization is relatively weak, it might be wise to start with the cities, and first computerize the administration of the major taxes, and then gradually form a nationwide, criss-crossing tax administration computer network.

Fourth, establish a rigorous tax inspection system. After the establishment of a general taxpayer self-filing system and a full-fledged tax agent service sector in place, the tax administration can shift its main resources into day-to-day, priority tax inspection, forming a three-part tax administrative pattern of tax declaration, tax agenda, and tax audit. This system will be enforced by heavy punishment for tax evasion and tax leakage.

With the above measures, China will have a tax administration system whereby tax legislation, tax administration, tax audit, lawsuit and administrative reconsideration will co-function, and form a check-and-balance pattern. The system will better serve the development of a socialist market economy.

Tax collection and administration is, in essence, a process of law enforcement. Therefore, to establish a tax system that meets the needs of the development of a market economy, tax administration work must be strengthened. To strengthen tax administration, the principle of rule by law and its strict enforcement must be adhered to. The priority of the tax administration should be to discover and punish acts of tax evasion and tax leakage. The principle of severe punishment should also be reflected to enhance the deterrent effect of tax law. Through strict enforcement, the market transaction activities can be disciplined and the market order straightened up, all abnormal competition and action in violation of the market order will be checked, so that tax laws and tax policies can be implemented smoothly.

Striving to set right the allocational relationship of tax revenue and perfect the tax system in the next few years is of great significance to the development of the market economy. Tax reform is a key tool of macroeconomic policy and entails a series of reallocations and readjustments that will be of economic benefit to various sectors. Therefore, strong leadership is necessary, as well as popular support for the reform of the macro control system. In designing the reform scheme, extensive investigation must be carried out, meticulous forecasting and verification must be conducted, opinions of different departments and economic sectors need to be elicited, and international experiences will be conscientiously studied and assimilated. Through the aforesaid reforms, the tax system of China will be more streamlined, rational, and efficient.

10

Unifying the Enterprise Income Tax and Reforming Profit Distribution Between Government and State-Owned Enterprises

Shi Yaobin*

China will establish a socialist market economic system, as has been clearly stated during the Fourteenth Congress of the Communist Party of China. This is a fundamental change, requiring comprehensive and substantial reform of the overall economic system. As an important component of the overall distribution system, the system of profit distribution between the government and state-owned enterprises (SOEs) needs a thorough reassessment.

Historical Background

Since the founding of the People's Republic of China in 1949, the system of profit distribution between the government and the state-owned enterprises has experienced various changes. Despite the variety, however, two stages can be identified: pre-1978 (i.e., before the Third Plenary Session of the Eleventh Congress of the Communist Party of China) and 1978 to the present.

Reforms Before 1978

Before 1978, the distribution relationship between the government and the state-owned enterprises was basically a unified system of reve-

---

*Ministry of Finance, China.

nue and expenditure. The enterprises were subject to 100 percent profits tax—that is, realized profit was handed to the government—but were free from income tax. This system was determined by the then highly centralized planning system. Of course, owing to circumstances and different stages of economic development and political environments, the unified system of the revenue and expenditure took various forms.

During the economic recovery period (1950–52), all profit realized by the state-owned enterprises was handed over to the government, and the enterprises had no own financial resources at all. During the first five-year plan period (1952–57), the Enterprise Incentive Fund and the Extraplan Profit-Sharing System were introduced. Resources retained by the industrial enterprises accounted for 3.6 percent of their total realized profit. During the period of the "Great Leap Forward" (1958–59), in order to further mobilize the incentives of the local governments, the enterprises, and administrative agencies, the profit retention system was introduced, and some of the profits were partly retained by the enterprises. With this system in place, the autonomous financial resources of the enterprises and administrative agencies were further expanded. Profits retained by the industrial state-owned enterprises amounted to 10.2 percent of total realized profits. During the three-year period 1960–62, the profit retention system was abolished and the Enterprise Incentive Fund was renewed. During the Cultural Revolution (1966–76), the Employees' Welfare Fund System replaced the Enterprise Incentive Fund, the actual result being that almost all the realized profit was appropriated by the government.

In sum, under the highly centralized planned economic system before 1978, the own financial resources of state-owned enterprises were very limited. Even these limited autonomous financial resources could not be actually utilized by the enterprises, because of the policy stance, which seriously depressed the initiative of the enterprises and employees, and which in turn hampered production.

Reforms After 1978

The reforms after 1978 can be roughly divided into three stages: (1) from 1978 to 1982, experimenting with the enterprise fund system, and reintroducing the profit retention system; (2) from 1983 to 1986, the transformation from profit delivery to tax payment by the state-owned enterprises; and (3) from 1987 to the present, various forms of the contract management responsibility system were promoted widely and comprehensively, and experimentation with the separation of tax from profit was tried.

From 1978 to 1982

In 1978, the Government began to experiment with the enterprise fund system. With this system in effect, provided the enterprise fulfilled all the eight annual planning indicators stipulated by the government (i.e., output, variety, quality, cost, profit and labor productivity, and so on), it could allocate, out of profits, to the enterprise fund an amount equivalent to 5 percent of the total payroll. Failure to fulfill one indicator would mean a certain decrease in retained profits. The enterprise fund could be used for the employees' welfare and bonuses. In 1979, to further expand the financial capacity of the enterprises, the State Council promulgated "Stipulations on the SOE's Profit Retention," followed by specific stipulations concerned issued jointly by the Ministry of Finance, the (then) Economic Commission, and the People's Bank of China. According to these stipulations, a pilot enterprise could retain a certain share of the realized profit, according to the ratio approved by the government, which would be used to establish the production development fund, the employees' welfare fund, and the employees' incentive fund. In 1981, based on the lessons gained from the pilot enterprises, another document was issued jointly by the Ministry of Finance and the Economic Commission entitled "Stipulations on the Method of the Profit Retention and Profit-Loss Contract by the Industrial and Transport SOEs," which introduced many kinds of profit-retention and profit-loss contract methods.

As for profit retention, the major forms were "base-number profit retention plus incremental profit retention," and "contracting subsidy for loss and sharing or retaining the loss deduction." During this period, profit retention by the industrial state-owned enterprises reached, on average, 22.3 percent of the total realized profits.

From 1983 to 1986

To generate experience and smoothly promote the profit-cum-tax reform, the reform was first tried in more than 600 state-owned enterprises in 1980. Several years of experimenting gained quite a large body of experience, and the outstanding effects achieved led to consensus on the reform. In this context, the State Council decided in January 1983 and October 1984 to carry out, in two steps, the overall profit-cum-tax reforms of the state-owned enterprises.

The major objective of the first step was to replace the profit delivery by income tax at the rate of 55 percent. Profits, after deducting income tax, would be further distributed in many forms between the government and the enterprise: one part would be left to the enterprise in accordance with the ratio approved by the government; the remainder would be subject to a number of taxes, such as the regulation tax, and contract provisions—such as the progressive increase contract, and fixed number contract. A progressive profit tax, with eight rates, was levied on the small enterprises. For a few enterprises with exceptionally large profits, the government would usually charge an additional contract fee. In enterprises with relatively small profits or losses, however, a profit-loss contract was specified.

The main objective of the second step of the profit-cum-tax reform was to levy an enterprise income tax and a regulation tax on the enterprises, and all posttax profits would be retained by the enterprises. The enterprise income tax was levied on large and mid-sized enterprises at a rate of 55 percent. The regulation tax would be levied on these enterprises if their posttax profit was greater than their previously retained profit. The regulation tax rate was determined case by case, and while it was a tax in name, it was a de facto profit adjustment. Enterprises were permitted to repay the fixed investment loans with the pretax profits, and to allocate a portion of the posttax profit to the employees' welfare fund and the employees' incentive fund. During this period, the profit retention by the industrial state-owned enterprises was 22.4 percent of the realized profit.

The profit-cum-tax reform differed from the practice of delivering profits by the enterprises to the government, and for the first time introduced the income tax into the distribution relationship between the government and the enterprises. In this sense, this reform had epoch-making significance and lasting influence. The reform had the following effects: (1) there was reduced bargaining about the base number and ratio of profits for distribution; (2) the distribution structure between the government and the state-owned enterprises became more rational; (3) there was a large increase in retained profits by the enterprises—in 1986, the profits retained by the industrial state-owned enterprises amounted to Y 26.5 billion, being Y 14.6 billion more than those in 1982, an increase of 123 percent, the share of the profits retained to total enterprise profits increased from 20 percent in 1982 to 41 percent in 1986; and (4) there was an enhanced enterprise capacity for restructuring, accumulation, and development.

The reform strengthened the enterprises' capacity for technological transformation and accumulation in two aspects. First, by allowing the enterprises to repay investment loans with the pretax profits, there was an incentive for enterprises to invest. On the other hand, banks, being assured repayment out of pretax profits, had incentives to lend to the enterprises. From 1983 to 1986, the fixed investment loans to the industrial enterprises jumped to Y 123.1 billion from

Y 54.3 billion, increasing by 127 percent, with an annual average growth rate of 31 percent.

From 1987 to the Present

In December 1986, State Council "Stipulations on Deepening the Enterprise Reform and Enhancing the Enterprise Vitality," promoted the contract management responsibility system to all the state-owned enterprises. The major goal of the responsibility system was to establish a contract for the entire realized profits of the enterprises. It was important to "fix the base amount (of the contract)," to ensure a share for the government, allowing enterprises to retain a larger share of excess profits, but shifting responsibility for losses to enterprises. Forms of contracts included, inter alia, the indexed contract, an increasing share contract, a nominally fixed contract, a contracted subsidy to enterprises, contracts linked to technological renovation, payroll, asset management, and so on.

The contract system was conducted for two rounds (for most of the enterprises). The first ran from 1987 to 1990. Compared with the two-step profit cum tax, the contract system created a more favorable environment for enterprises, allowing them greater profits—generating enterprise enthusiasm for the system. By 1990, the enterprises practicing the contract system accounted for 84 percent of all the state-owned enterprises. During the first round of the contract system, from 1987 to 1990, the retention by the industrial enterprises accounted for 43 percent of the total realized profits. In order to ensure policy continuity, the second round of the contract system was based on marginal adjustments. This round of contracts, however, proceeded far less smoothly than the first. Enterprises showed a general lack of initiative and confidence. This was, in part, due to the external economic environment, and the need to restrict credit to control inflationary trends. Enterprises continued to have an incentive to borrow. In 1991, despite administrative intervention, enterprises practicing the contract system accounted for 77 percent of all the state-owned enterprises, only 7 percent less than the previous year.

Two basic conclusions can be drawn from the historical changes and transformations of the distribution relationship between the government and enterprises in China. First, since 1949, the general trend of the profit distribution system of the state-owned enterprise has been characterized by a gradual expansion of the enterprises' autonomous financial resources and capacity, with the government's share of profits gradually decreasing, and the share of enterprise retention increasing. Before 1978, the share of enterprise retention in realized profits was

4.5 percent on average. During the period 1979–81, the profit retention by the industrial enterprises in successive years was 22 percent,
33 percent, and 43 percent, respectively.

Second, the distribution relationship between the government and
the state-owned enterprises shifted from simply emphasizing tax reduction and profit concession to establishing a scientific and rational
distribution system. While tax and profit exemptions played an important role in mobilizing the initiatives of the enterprises in various historical periods, and therefore promoting the production development
of the enterprises, these practices failed to address, in a fundamental
way, the incentive issues relating to the enterprises. Although the autonomous financial resources of an enterprise do have an impact on
investment potential (especially when the autonomous financial resource base is small), the reformed operating mechanisms and the creation of a fair and rational competitive external environment, such as
taxation, pricing, and market discipline, are crucial for enterprise incentives. Therefore, the reforms should be aimed at generating proper
incentives for enterprises for efficient economic development.

Current Problems in the Profit Distribution System

The contract-based system has achieved much in rural reforms, which
promoted rapid development of the rural economy. But the contract-
based system implemented in state-owned enterprises differs from the
rural contract system on two accounts. First, the enterprises contract an
assignment of the income tax to the government; second, the enterprise
contract system is based on enterprises that have large-scale production.
These two basic points lead to different results. At the preliminary stage
of implementing the contract system in current enterprises, it had positive effect on incentives for increased enterprise production. However,
along with further reform and evolution of economic activity, problems
have gradually emerged. While the contract-based enterprise system led
to assured revenues during periods of low growth, enterprises faced
losses when contracts exceeded profits. In periods of rising profits, however, the government's share of profits has declined.

Varying Tax Rates

Different enterprise income tax rates, applied according to the different ownership classification of enterprises, have resulted in unfair market competition. The income tax rate for large and medium-sized
enterprises was 55 percent, with an additional adjustment tax. In the

eight-slab, progressive tax rate above contracts, the highest rate was 55 percent, and the lowest 10 percent. Private firms face a 35 percent tax rate, which was 30 percent for foreign-funded firms, together with an additional 3 percent local tax. In coastal areas, the rate was 24 percent, plus a 3 percent local tax. In special economic zones and economic and technology development areas, the rate was 15 percent, plus a 3 percent local tax. Moreover, tax-accounting standards vary according to ownership, and this was also unfavorable for fair competition. While there were about ten items considered as pretax expenditures, the main item that enterprises could deduct was loan repayments for fixed asset investments. Township and collectively owned firms could deduct 60 percent of profits for the above-mentioned purpose, but other types of firms were not permitted the same benefit. Cost expenditure standards varied greatly; for example, foreign-funded firms, Sino-foreign joint ventures, and Sino-foreign cooperative firms could withdraw bad debt provisions as a bonus, but domestic enterprises and collectively owned firms were not allowed to do so. There were no unified standards for business fees.

Disparity in Tax Collection and Tax Burdens

The state-owned enterprises' nominal tax rate was 55 percent. However, in the implementation of the profit contract system, which mixes profits and taxes, the government negotiated different contracts with each firm, and the profit and tax rates differed from one firm to another. Effectively, with this system, the income tax ceased to exist, although a nominal tax rate remained. In the early 1990s, the average real tax rate for enterprises was about 30 percent; the tax rate for about 20 percent of enterprises was 5 percent; in some large and medium-sized enterprises, the rate even reached as high as 50–70 percent. According to the regional distribution, in some provinces, the tax rate was about 10–20 percent, whereas in other provinces, the rate reached 40–50 percent. There were also additional cases of policy-based tax exemptions for other types of firms.

Constraints on Enterprise Restructuring

Reforms over the past ten years of the contract system increased retention funds for enterprises. However, this was at the expense of revenues at a period of budgetary stringency and extensive infrastructure needs. A response by the state was to withdraw directly 1 percent of enterprises' net revenues for technology and new product development, after contracts and income tax payments.

The relationships between the state and enterprises often changed, and as a result, enterprises had an incentive to generate nominal losses to minimize contracted payments to the state. This had an unfavorable influence on the further development potential of enterprises. There was little provision for maintenance expenditure for equipment, or resources for replacement of machinery or investment. For some firms, payment of contracted amounts could not be supported by actual profits incurred, thus resulting in cumulative losses, and a draw-down of state-owned assets.

Inappropriate Investments

The system weakened the sense of responsibility of enterprise managers, which generated an uncontrolled expansion of fixed assets investment. In 1992, borrowing for fixed assets investment, in domestic enterprises, was more than Y 450 billion, in 1995, the existing loans for firms' fixed assets investment are expected to reach Y 1,100 billion (using the average growth rate of investment between 1986–91). Such a heavy burden not only influences the development of firms but also places a negative constraint on the sustainable growth of the economy. If allowed to continue unchecked, the resulting debt will form a heavy burden for the national budget. It is thus essential to curtail the adverse incentives generated by the system of treating loan repayments as part of pretax profits.

Enterprise Behavior

The economic structure was not conducive for enterprise response to the market, such as price signals. Since the reforms have been implemented, China has undertaken major price reforms, with liberalized prices for many products, and price signals should play a significant role in economic restructuring. However, the enterprise profit contract responsibility system remains a major obstacle to a more market-oriented system.

In general, the contract profit distribution system has generated more problems than benefits for enterprises. The problems restrict efficient functioning of the market mechanism.

Results of Experiments Since 1988

Further reforms of the profit distribution system of state-owned enterprises are to be based on "Two Standards" (that is, the "Accounting

Standards" and the "General Regulations on Enterprises Finance and Accounts"). In effect, enterprises would pay to the government income taxes and dividends, and the loan repayment mechanism described above would be reformed. First, enterprises will pay the state income tax, from their realized profits, according to the legal tax rates. Second, the pretax loan repayment will be abolished. The state could provide some direct support to firms, after considering their current situation, prospects, and industrial policy goals. The Construction Fund, for key energy and transportation projects and for depreciation of enterprises' fixed assets, and the Budgetary Adjustment Fund would be abolished.

Pilot reforms in enterprises, known as "separation of tax from profit," have achieved certain successes. Since 1988, in Chongqing and Xiamen, 4,000 enterprises have experimented with the new system. Although there is room for further improvement of experimental methods, the experiments have shown several things.

First, a rational tax burden has been achieved, together with the principle of sharing both interest and risk between the government and enterprises, along with a reasonable stability of enterprises' profit distribution. Between 1990 and 92, in experimental enterprises, on average, 32.2 percent of profits was paid in taxes to the government, profits retained accounted for 38.8 percent, and loan repayments amounted to 29.0 percent of total profit. This pattern remained stable during the period. But, in other enterprises in the two cities, the profit distribution structure varied greatly. For example, between 1987 and 92, the top effective income tax transfer by state-owned enterprises to the state varied from 39 percent (in 1987) to 27 percent (in 1988 and 1992). The stability of the tax payments by the experimenting firms was noticeable.

Second, the reform has put the stabilization role of income tax into full play. Under the contract system, with a "fixed profit and tax base assignment," during the high growth period (1988–92), the state revenue ratio declined, while enterprise retention rate increased. During the economic recession (in 1990), state revenues increased while the enterprise profit retention rate declined. This pattern countered the stabilization needs, by enhancing profits during a boom, and contracting profits during the recession; it thus exacerbated cyclical swings. The scenario is different in the experimental firms: during the economic downturn in 1990, the proportion of profits paid in income taxes was 33.6 percent, with a 40.2 percent profit retention ratio of total profit. The profit retention rate was 7 percent higher than in the firms that had not implemented the new system and was thus favorable for economic recovery. During the expansionary period, the retention rate in experimental enterprises was 2 percent lower than in those not implementing the new system. Thus the new system would help to curtail economic overheating in expansionary periods, as well as to cushion economic downturns—forming an automatic stabilizer for macroeconomic policy purposes.

Third, the borrowing pattern of experimenting enterprises has been consistent with the growth of production. In 1992, borrowing by pilot enterprises grew by 14 percent, which is higher than the growth rate of firms that had not implemented the new system, but lower than the growth rate of sales (59.0 percent). The new rules concerning loan repayment have curbed the unbridled expansion of fixed investments and encouraged an emphasis on investment efficiency.

Fourth, the speed of loan repayment has been accelerated. In 1992, the loan repayment rate of "experimenting firms" was higher than that in firms not implementing the new system.

And finally, the technology renovation capacity and the potential development of the firms have been increased in the pilot firms. The experimental enterprises face lower effective tax rates, with the abolition of the "Two Funds" policies, increasing their financial autonomy, loan repayment speed, and efficiency.

Unifying the Enterprise Income Tax Rate

The enterprise income tax (EIT) rate was unified to 33 percent in 1994. However, considering the low economic efficiency and low level of profits in some enterprises, two additional levels of tax rates were set as transitional measures—a rate of 18 percent applied to firms with an annual taxable profit below Y 30,000 and 27 percent for firms with taxable profits between Y 30,000 and Y 100,000. The regulation tax was abandoned.

The 33 percent standard EIT rate was set by taking into consideration the following factors. First, the new EIT rate is lower than the ratio of enterprises' current (paid-in) profit rate. The current paid-in profits include payments for enterprises' income tax payments and the profit delivery. From 1990 to 1992, the paid-in profit rate (including payments for "Two Funds" from retained earnings) for profitable enterprises was 45.6 percent, 43.3 percent, and 35.6 percent in each year respectively, with a period average of 41.5 percent.

Second, the new EIT rate is close to the international average. According to statistics for 91 countries, the average EIT rate is 33.8 percent, 33.0 percent for developed countries, and 34.7 percent for developing countries.

Third, the unified EIT rate of 33 percent is the same as the current tax rate for joint ventures, and is around the level of the average tax rate for collectively owned enterprises and privately owned businesses. At present, the 33 percent tax rate is applied to Sino-foreign ventures, according to the "Income Tax Law for Foreign Investment Joint Ventures and Foreign Enterprises within the P.R.C.": an eight-level progressive tax rate is used for collectively owned enterprises, with an average rate of about 30 percent; and 35 percent for privately owned businesses. In this context, the unified tax rate will not add an additional burden to the nonprivate sector.

Fourth, the new EIT rate will assure relatively stable state revenues. The fiscal function of the government and the ongoing difficult financial situation have made it clear that state revenue should not be adversely affected by the reform, and therefore, the EIT rate should not be set too low.

Fifth, the setting of a two-level concessionary tax rate is a transitional and temporary measure for those enterprises with annual taxable profits below Y 100,000, in parallel with the prevailing 33 percent unified rate. The rationale for temporarily setting concessionary tax rates is that, first, some enterprises may have difficulty in surviving the reforms; second, because of the current low level of paid-in profit of these enterprises, the concessionary tax rate will not have much effect on fiscal revenue.

Reforming the EIT Base

The new rule for borrowing for enterprises' investments is that interest and amortization payments shall be repaid from enterprises' retained earnings, rather than being deducted from before-tax profits.[1] This regulation changes the practice of loan repayment and is based on two reasons. First, the purpose of enterprise borrowing for investment is to obtain future gains, and in this connection, the repayment of borrowing should come from enterprises' retained earnings. The previous practice of treating loan payments as a before-tax item is financed, in fact, by reduced fiscal revenues—thus enterprises borrow money and enjoy investment gains, whereas the state shoulders the burden of repayment. This separation of responsibility for rights and profits is not justified. Second, the policy of repayment before tax leads to overborrowing for fixed asset investment, which could adversely affect the sustainable growth path of the economy.

---

[1]According to regulations, increasing depreciation and interest on loans for fixed asset investment, as well as bonuses and expenditures on research and development, should also be treated as posttax items of expenditures.

The state will take various measures to collect gains from investment in state assets. The main practices include dividend sharing for share-holding enterprises, profit sharing for joint ventures, and profit alloca-tion, after tax, for purely state-funded enterprises. Taking into account the difficulties facing the enterprises, as well as the industrial policies, and the need for enterprise technology transformation, temporary measures are applied, such as allowing those purely state-funded enter-prises, registered before 1993, to keep after-tax profits, and tax holidays (or reduced rates) for some enterprises with low profitability.

Actually, the state can take various measures to collect investment gains from state-owned assets. Investment in state-owned assets mainly benefits state-funded enterprises and the joint entities, which comprise state and other forms of assets holdings. In the category of direct state investment, investment benefits can be collected directly, according to the decisions made by the enterprises' Board of Directors. If enterprises make the investment, they will obtain the investment benefits, first from joint entities, and then shared with the state. In general, for joint entities, the ways to collect investment benefits are simple, as asset ownership is clear. "The General Applicable Financial Principle" cites explicitly that the distribution order of profits after tax is as follows: (1) losses from confiscated assets, fines for delaying pay-ments, and penalties for violating regulations of tax law; (2) previous losses; (3) provident funds; (4) mutual benefit funds; and (5) profit dis-tribution among investors. In this way, provident funds can ensure en-terprises' interests; mutual benefit funds guarantee the interests of enterprise management and employees; and profit distribution as divi-dends to investors will ensure the interest of the state as the owner. Of course, the amount of investment benefits that can be collected by the state will depend on factors as to whether the production of enter-prises is in line with state industrial policies, the potential of the enter-prises, and so on.

Abolishing the "Two Funds"

The rationale for abolishing the "Two Funds"—the Construction Funds for energy and transportation and the Budget Adjustment Fund—is to abandon a nonstandard practice, increase enterprises' fi-nancial capacity, and accelerate the reform pace of enterprises' profit distribution system. The Two Funds were set up under specific histori-cal circumstances, when the state underwent extreme financial diffi-culties and a severe shortage of construction funds for key energy and transportation projects. The practice helped to accumulate a greater amount of funds to support state key projects and to contribute to the budget balance. Collecting the Two Funds, however, is not a standard practice in itself, which makes the enterprises' profit distribution system even more abnormal. Thus the Two Funds will be abandoned, as a reform measure, to standardize the enterprises' profit distribution system. The increased financial capacity will be used to repay past borrowings.

Past Borrowings

Most of the old enterprise loans are required to be paid back in full. Should enterprises have real difficulty in repaying the loans, repayment periods can be extended, subject to examination by banks. The approved bad debt could be reversed with banks' bad-debt provisions, according to relevant regulations. At the same time, the bad-debt provision ratio should be raised. Most enterprises have improved their repayment capacity through the reform. Therefore, although the enterprises' profit distribution system changes the current enterprises' repayment practices, it significantly strengthens enterprises' repayment capacity, rather than having an adverse effect on the firms.

Preferential EIT for Joint Ventures and Special Economic Zones

These preferential arrangements will remain unchanged for the duration of the stipulated agreements.

11

Basic Issues of Decentralization and Tax Assignment

Vito Tanzi*

This chapter deals with an issue normally referred to as the tax assignment problem. A government is responsible for performing various functions. It needs to raise tax revenue in order to finance the functions that require spending. It may be monolithic or unitary, in which case all responsibilities are carried out at one level, or it may be decentralized, whereby some responsibilities are carried out by the top level, that is, the national government, and some by lower levels, normally local jurisdictions. When responsibilities are decentralized, it is necessary to assign resources to the lower levels. This chapter discusses the way in which various taxes can be allocated to different jurisdictions. It also discusses briefly some international experiences and comments on Chinese tax development.

Governments must perform some basic functions, which economic literature has generally classified in three broad categories. First is resource allocation: that is, the need to allocate resources in ways that improve the welfare of a country. In a market economy, the assumption is that the private sector carries out much of the allocation of resources but, given the presence of externalities and public goods, the government is still required to perform some important allocative functions.

Second is the redistribution of income. Once again, the market allocates resources and, through its allocation of resources, generates a certain distribution of the total income among the citizens. Most societies, however, have expected the government to play some role in this area. In particular, the government, in order to support a higher

---

*International Monetary Fund.

standard of living of poor individuals, has been required to tax proportionately more the income of richer individuals than that of lower-income persons. These poorer individuals often belong to particular categories, such as the disabled, the young, the old, those unable to earn an income because of poor health, the unemployed, or those who live in depressed or poor regions. There has always been a concern that the redistributive role of the government should not carry with it a high cost in terms of the efficiency of the economy by reducing incentives to work, save, and invest or by creating an inefficient government bureaucracy.

The third important function of the government is stabilization of the economy. Most economies experience periods of economic instability. This instability may be reflected in the behavior of prices, of output, of the balance of payments, or in some other ways. When economic conditions diverge significantly from the desired objectives, the government is often required to promote policies aimed at stabilization.

The government tries to perform the above-mentioned functions by using various instruments such as (1) taxes; (2) spending programs; (3) regulations; and (4) other policies, such as monetary and credit policy, exchange rate policy, and so forth. The activities of the government aimed at performing the above-described functions can be organized (1) in a completely centralized way, that is, through a unitary form of government; (2) in a completely decentralized way, that is, through the activities of local jurisdictions; or (3) through a central government that coordinates and complements the activities carried out by local jurisdictions. In some cases, these local jurisdictions can be more properly called local "governments," especially when their existence is guaranteed by the constitution of the country. In fact, it may even precede the existence of the national government, as is the case in the United States and Germany.

These three alternative organizations of the public sector have implications for public financing and the way the government performs its function. Experts who have studied these problems have generally agreed that complete centralization (whereby a powerful unitary government has responsibility for all the public finance functions, that is, for all the spending and taxing in a country) may be accompanied by some significant costs. Some of these costs may be associated with the fact that such an organization leads to little experimentation and little innovation. The way of doing things determined by the national government can perpetuate itself and become rigid and anachronistic when there is no pressure to innovate. With many smaller jurisdictions competing for resources, innovation is likely to take place even as errors are made. The benefits derived from innovating will often compensate for the errors made. Experts agree also that when tastes and attitudes differ from region to region, as would likely be the case in a large country or in a country with different ethnic and cultural groups, centralization brings about inefficiency as it forces every region to "consume" the same mixture of taxes and public spending. For example, an area might like to spend more for cultural activities, while another might like to spend more for roads. But both would be forced to adjust to the pattern imposed by the national government thus reducing the welfare of their citizens.

A third problem associated with complete centralization may arise when some taxes and some spending programs experience diseconomies of scale. Because they are carried out at a national level, some programs may become inefficiently large and thus lead to organizational problems. Also, bureaucratic inefficiencies and rent-seeking activities can become important in large institutions or programs. Furthermore, central governments may have less direct information on local needs and preferences than local jurisdictions.

By the same token, total decentralization brings with it some inefficiencies that, for particular functions, can be larger than those connected with complete centralization. For example, the pursuit of a stabilization policy for the whole country becomes very difficult because each one of the jurisdictions will not have an interest in pursuing the necessary policies. The reason is that the benefits derived from these policies will be diffused among all the jurisdictions and will thus benefit only marginally the local jurisdiction that implements the stabilization policies. In other words, the spillover effects from policy actions will be large.

Experience among countries shows that when governments become very decentralized, the government loses its ability to pursue efficient stabilization policies. Examples from Brazil, Argentina, Nigeria, and some other countries support the view that excessive decentralization is likely to make the pursuit of stabilization more difficult.

Excessive decentralization also reduces the ability of the government to pursue redistributive policy. Highly decentralized governments have little interest in pursuing redistributive policy because generous spending policies aimed at helping their poor would become very expensive because they would attract the poor from other jurisdictions. Thus, the jurisdiction that promoted these policies would end up carrying a high cost by helping the poor of other jurisdictions. By the same token, highly progressive tax policies would push the rich out of the jurisdiction and would thus reduce its tax base.

Excessive decentralization would also make it more difficult for the country to allocate the right amount of resources to the production of national (i.e., countrywide) public goods, because the national government would not have the means to do so and the local governments would not have the interest to finance these expenditures because the benefit to each of them from these policies would be small. There would be an incentive for each jurisdiction to argue that it derives little benefit from the national public goods and therefore the burden of financing those goods should be shifted to those who do benefit. This is the classic free-rider problem.

Public finance experts generally prefer to have a central government that takes over nationwide responsibilities, such as stabilization, redistribution, and generation of national public goods, but leaves local jurisdictions free to carry out government functions of particular interest to the individuals who live in those jurisdictions. The less spillover the policies generate outside the jurisdiction, the more they should be the responsibility of the jurisdiction. In this way the pattern of taxes and spending can be tailored to local preferences. This would increase the welfare of all the citizens.

Tax Assignment Policies

The basic question that arises then is the assignment of spending and taxing responsibilities between the national government and the local jurisdictions. The question has often been discussed separately for *taxing* and for *spending* assignments. In other words, which taxes should be assigned to the different levels of government and which spending responsibilities? It must be recognized, however, that some simultaneity exists in making that kind of decision, because the easier it is to assign taxes to local jurisdictions, the more justified it is to assign expenditure responsibilities to them. It is important not to create an imbalance between expenditure responsibilities and the means available to local jurisdictions to carry them out including own-tax resources, proceeds of shared taxes, and transfer from other levels of government—as discussed below.

If decisions about the delegation of spending responsibilities to the local jurisdictions have been made, the basic issue is how to provide them with the means to finance them. It is generally agreed that local jurisdictions should not be allowed to engage in deficit financing and should be required to balance their budgets annually. In other words, they should cover their expenditures out of current revenues, except for exceptional circumstances related to large and productive capital projects when some borrowing might be allowed. There must therefore be a hard budget constraint applied to local jurisdictions so that their budgets are actually balanced not only ex ante, or on a provisional basis, but also ex post. The budgets must also be balanced without recourse to gimmicks, such as buildup of arrears, anticipation of taxes, extrabudgetary accounts, and the like.

The assignment of funds to local jurisdictions can follow several options. The first, and probably least attractive, option is to assign all tax bases to the local jurisdictions and ask them to transfer upward to the national government some of the revenue so the national government can meet its spending responsibilities. This option is clearly unattractive and welfare-reducing for a variety of reasons. It is not consistent with a national policy aimed at redistributing income through the use of the tax system. It is not consistent with a policy that assigns to the public sector the role of stabilizing the economy and that depends on the use of the tax system to help achieve this objective. It may not be consistent with the lowest possible way of raising public resources, because it inevitably excessively fragments the tax system. And, finally, it may provide the wrong incentives to the local jurisdictions if they know that part of the taxes they collect will be shared with the national government. There is evidence from some countries that this policy leads to inefficient tax administration.

The second option is for the national government to collect all taxes and to transfer some of these funds to the local jurisdictions so they may finance their own spending responsibilities. The transfer of funds to the local jurisdictions can be done through earmarking and thus sharing of total tax revenue or through earmarking and sharing of specific taxes. The first alternative is clearly superior to the second because it gives the local governments a more stable revenue source and gives the national government more freedom in pursuing tax policy options.

There are several problems with the option of transferring from the national authorities all the revenue of the local jurisdictions. First of all, by breaking the nexus between decisions to collect tax revenue and decisions to spend that revenue, the concept of the tax price for public spending (that is, the idea that spending decisions carry a specific cost expressed through the taxes paid) is broken at the local level. Local officials and local taxpayers may not connect the benefits they derive from public spending with the taxes paid. They may, thus, not exercise the required restraining function on expenditure, and taxpayers will be less willing to support the tax effort. Also, no attempt will be made at the margin to bring the benefit from the last unit of money spent in line with the cost of the last unit of money collected in taxes, as would be required by an optimal size of public sector.[1]

A third alternative is the more customary one of assigning to the local jurisdictions *some* taxing power and of complementing, if necessary, the revenue raised locally with some transfers from the national government. The taxing power provided to the local jurisdictions can be given by (1) assigning to them the exclusive use of some tax bases; (2) allowing them to share some bases with the national government; and (3) allowing the local governments to piggyback on some national taxes, for example, by asking the national government to charge higher rates on sales taxes and to transfer the additional revenue to the local government.

The way in which transfers are provided is very important to ensure an efficient use of public money. This leads us to the question of which taxes can be assigned to local jurisdictions and which must remain the responsibility of the national government. By assigning specific tax bases to the local jurisdictions and by not making the grants received from the national government dependent on the taxes raised locally, the local jurisdictions would have, at the margin, the option of spending more if they could raise their own tax revenue. Their perception of the benefit cost of this action would presumably guide their decisions on spending and taxing.

The assignment of tax bases to local jurisdictions must take into account several considerations. The first is the importance of objectives (other than the basic one of raising revenue in the most neutral and efficient way) being pursued through taxation. The more important are these other objectives in connection with particular tax bases, the less advantageous it is to leave these tax bases to local jurisdictions. For example, the more weight the government assigns to the objective of income redistribution (through progressive taxation) or to stabilization (through the use of built-in stabilizers) the better it is to leave certain tax bases, such as the progressive income tax and the corporate income tax, to the national government. The reason is that progressive income taxes are the best tool to redistribute income through the tax system, and corporate income taxes (together with the personal income taxes) are the best tax tool to provide a built-in stabilizer to the economy.

Second is the mobility of the tax bases. If a tax base can escape taxation at the local level by moving to another jurisdiction, that base is not a good candidate for local taxation unless harmonization of tax

---

[1]Problems of this kind developed in Italy after 1978 when a reform centralized revenue collection but decentralized expenditure responsibility.

rates among local jurisdictions reduces or eliminates the mobility of tax bases. Thus, the more mobile is a tax base, the greater is the presumption to keep it at the national level. Incidentally, in an integrating world economy this problem reappears within an international context, especially for small countries.

Third, the more important are economies of scale in tax administration for a given tax, the stronger is the argument for leaving the tax base for that tax to the national government. Economies of scale may depend on informational requirements, for example, on a national taxpayer identification number, on technical requirements (such as the use of computers, and so forth), or on other factors. Fourth, the greater is the need to maintain a level field for the whole country (to avoid distortions created by different tax rates), the stronger is the presumption that the tax should be left to the national government.

Given the above premises we can quickly survey the assignment of tax bases starting with the simplest and moving to the more difficult ones. Obviously, this is a complex subject that requires much more space than is allocated here to provide complete treatment.

Import and Export Taxes

Economists generally consider import and export taxes inefficient and undesirable sources of revenue. Their importance in industrial countries is limited, but they still account for a large share of revenue in developing countries. However, to the extent that countries do decide to use them, perhaps because of strong revenue needs, they should always be imposed by the national government, so as to reduce the possibility that major distortions are introduced within the country by differential foreign trade taxes imposed by different jurisdictions.

Taxes on Land and on Real Property

Land and existing structures are among the most immobile of tax bases. Land in particular cannot move because of tax factors nor can existing buildings. Where they are used, taxes on real properties are often imposed by local jurisdictions. Apart from the fact that these tax bases are immobile, it has been argued that they are guided by a benefit-received principle, because spending by local jurisdictions benefits (and thus increases the value of) local properties. Of course, while land and existing structures cannot move, new structures will not be built if the jurisdiction taxes them considerably more than other institutions.[2] Also, the capitalization of property taxes in the price of the properties, that is, the reduction of the property values because of the imposition of taxes implies that, even though the base cannot move in a physical sense, it can move in a fiscal sense because property taxes that are not used to provide local services beneficial to the properties will often reduce the market value of the properties. In other words, given the revenue from this tax, the effective tax rate after the capitalization will be higher than the statutory rate before the capitalization.

Sales Taxes

Among the sales taxes, we must distinguish single-stage (excises and retail) from the multistage ones (turnover and value-added taxes). The issues that arise for excises and retail sales taxes are similar. These taxes can be given to local jurisdictions provided that jurisdictions do not levy these taxes with highly different rates. Thus, a jurisdiction that relies on general retail sales taxes or on excises on specific products will not encounter difficulty with these taxes if the rates at which it taxes the products are not so much higher than the rates imposed by neighboring jurisdictions. If the rates are higher, it may encourage its own citizens to shop in the lower-rate jurisdictions. Major factors in this case are the vicinity of the other jurisdictions, the cost of travel, and the value of the goods purchased. If jurisdictions with lower tax rates are near, if the cost of travel is low, and if the item purchased has a high value (e.g., consumer durables or jewelry), then the difference in tax rates cannot be too high or the tax base will migrate toward the low-rate jurisdictions. Generally, competition among jurisdictions limits the scope for rate differentials and thus limits the freedom of actions of local jurisdictions.

Retail sales taxes and excise taxes are generally simple taxes. However, in economies with many small sellers, retail sales taxes may be difficult to administer especially if the rates are high. High rates would promote high evasion, and evasion by retailers when a retail sales tax is in effect is more difficult to control and more costly in terms of revenue losses than, say, tax evasion by retailers under a value-added tax. The reason is that when retailers evade paying a retail tax, the whole tax is evaded while, for the value-added tax, only a share of the tax is lost.

---

[2]Some countries, for example, Italy, have at times given preferential property tax treatment to new construction. This policy not only reduces revenue but also creates serious equity issues because new buildings are often owned by wealthy people.

Value-Added Taxes

Value-added taxes imposed with a credit mechanism are generally rebated on exports and imposed on imports because they follow the destination principle. This principle stipulates that these taxes should be paid by the final consumers and should thus not distort trade relations. The application of the destination principle requires border checks by the jurisdiction that imposes the tax. It is neither feasible nor desirable, however, to impose border checks on trade within a country, because this would impose excessive costs and would impede trade flows within the country. For these reasons, value-added taxes are best left as a responsibility of national governments.

The European Community (now European Union) has been considering the use of value-added taxes based on the so-called origin principle, which dispenses with border tax adjustments by taxing production rather than consumption. But, as long as the tax rates in different jurisdictions diverge and as long as the balances of trade between jurisdictions are not in equilibrium, this alternative has many serious shortcomings.[3]

Personal Income Taxes

Personal income taxes can be *global* or *schedular*. In other words, they can be imposed on the total income received by a taxpayer—that is, by combining wages and salaries, interest and dividends received, and income from all other activities—or they can be imposed separately on each type of income.

Schedular Income Taxes

Schedular income taxes can be used by local jurisdictions with less difficulty especially if the taxes on some incomes, such as interest and dividend incomes and wages and salaries, are withheld at the source by those who pay these incomes and the taxes withheld are considered as final taxes. In this case, the taxpayer does not need to present a tax declaration and has no further tax liability. If these taxes are not considered final taxes but are related to the particular situation of the taxpayer, and especially if the incomes received come from jurisdictions other than the one where the taxpayer resides, then administrative problems arise because the tax authorities in the

---

[3]The possibility of sharing the base for sales taxes between the national government and the local governments is a realistic one, as long as, once again, it does not lead to widely divergent rates between, especially contiguous, jurisdictions.

jurisdiction where the taxpayer resides may not receive the necessary information to be able to tax the individual. At an early stage of development, most individuals derive only one source of income, and this income is generally earned in the same jurisdiction where the taxpayer resides. The more developed countries become, however, the greater is the proportion of individuals likely to earn different kinds of income (interest, dividends, and profits, in addition to wages and salaries). Furthermore, these incomes may be earned in different jurisdictions.

Global Income Taxes

For global income taxes to operate well in a modern economy, it is necessary that all the incomes that the taxpayer receives from different sources and different jurisdictions be combined before the tax is calculated. The tax administration of the jurisdiction where the taxpayer resides is unlikely to have information about income earned outside the jurisdiction. Therefore, tax evasion is likely to be significant. For this reason, it is better to leave this tax base to the national government, which is in a better condition to get the relevant information.

Should the local jurisdiction also wish to tax income, it would need to arrange with the national government the sharing of information. The easiest way of taxing global income locally is for the local jurisdictions to use the same statutory base for the national income tax and agree with the national government to share relevant information. This also reduces the compliance cost for the taxpayer because the same information can be used for both the payment to the national tax administration and the payment to the local jurisdiction. Tax competition among jurisdictions would ensure that no jurisdiction imposes tax rates that are much higher than those by other jurisdictions. If they did, some taxpayers, and consequently, some capital, would leave the high-taxed jurisdictions in order to establish residence in the lower-taxed ones.

Business activities may be associated with small establishments or with large enterprises. Small, family-type establishments often do not keep good records of their transactions and are thus taxed on the basis of presumptive principles. For example, they may pay a business tax that may be related to personal income often assessed on the basis of gross sales, or floor space in which the activity takes place, or on the basis of some other criteria. For this kind of activity, local jurisdictions often have as much as, or more information than, the national government. As a consequence, these taxes can be imposed as efficiently at the local level as at the national level. However, to reduce abusive or corruptive practices, careful monitoring of officials that determine the taxes is required.

For larger establishments, the situation is different. They often have branches in various parts of the country, may trade with other countries, and may buy inputs from businesses in other jurisdictions and sell their output in other jurisdictions. They are also more sensitive to tax factors. If these taxes were imposed locally, several difficulties would arise. The local jurisdiction would find it difficult to verify the information provided by the enterprises (related to the cost of the purchases from other areas and to the prices at which the produced output is sold). If the rates at which enterprises were taxed were highly different across jurisdictions, these rates would become an important factor in determining capital movements within the country and could generate serious distortions in the allocation of resources. For these and other reasons, it is good policy to leave the taxation of enterprises in the hands of the national government. Once again, the local jurisdictions can get a free ride by using the information from the national tax administration to tax also, at low rates, these enterprises using the same tax base. As long as the local rates are low, the local taxation of enterprises would not generate major difficulties.

Tax Assignments in Practice

There are many different patterns to be observed across countries in terms of tax assignments and own revenues accruing to various levels of government. To some extent these differences may be explained by varying constitutional and administrative arrangements. Some countries have unitary constitutions, whereas others are federal in nature; tax administration may be either centralized or decentralized. All these factors affect the patterns observed.

Nevertheless, some broad patterns do emerge. Property taxes are predominantly assigned to state or local governments (some Scandinavian countries, and others in the developing world, are exceptions). Income taxes are mainly, but not exclusively, assigned to the center, although there is some local "piggybacking." Some East European countries, such as Romania, are an exception.

Chinese Tax Reform Proposals

Much progress has been and is being made toward the solution of the fiscal problems in China. A major tax reform is being planned that will modernize the tax system making it more efficient, more productive, and more equitable. I heartily endorse the guiding thought for the tax system reform given in Chapter (9): a uniform tax code, equitable tax burdens, a simplified tax system, a rational division of powers, straightening out of the apportionment of tax monies between the national government and local governments, and building a taxation system that is consistent with the needs of a socialist market economy.

The unification of the enterprise income tax for all types of enterprises is an important step, although I would have had a slight preference for a single rate rather than two. Similarly, the standardization of the individual income tax should be supported, with the slight reservation that the monthly deduction of Y 800 for living expenses may be too high, given China's current personal income level, and may reduce excessively the revenue from this tax. However, if this deduction remains unchanged in nominal terms, the fast growth of nominal income in China will bring it to a more normal level. Limiting this tax "on people having fairly high incomes" may eliminate much of the potential tax base. Again, the standardization of proposed value-added tax (VAT) should be implemented as proposed. It will be important to limit the rates to two, and to keep the tax base as broad as possible. The proposed consumption tax is a useful complement to the VAT, although the number of taxed items should be kept low. I am unable to express a judgment with regard to the business taxes. I understand that these taxes are applied largely to activities that would not be covered by the VAT. Thus, in a way, business taxes would require or represent an erosion of the VAT base. Perhaps, at some future time, these activities could be added to the VAT base so that the business taxes could disappear.

As for the other taxes contemplated by the tax reform, in general, I would hope that (1) they be kept to a minimum, and (2) that the assignment of many of these taxes to local governments would not prevent the elimination of some in the future.

The most important feature of the tax reform will be the elimination of the contracting system, the shortcomings of which have been eloquently outlined in Chapter 2. This will, indeed, be an important change. The tax reform will be accompanied at the same time by the introduction of a tax-sharing system. Actually, the system will have several features of which proper tax sharing is just one. Some taxes, and especially the VAT, will be collected only by the central government. Others will be collected by and assigned to the local governments. Several questions will deserve close analysis before final decisions are made:

(1) Are the administrative mechanisms in place to allow each jurisdiction to administer the taxes for which it has the collection responsibility?

(2) Does the planned assignment of tax bases to different jurisdictions reflect the most rational criteria?

(3) Are the percentages agreed for the division of the revenues shared in common consistent (when added to their own taxes) with the expenditure responsibilities of the different jurisdictional levels?

(4) What formulas or criteria will be used to share the revenues subject to revenue sharing not just between the central and local governments but among the subcentral governments?

The determination of local governments' responsibilities will, of course, play a large role in this process. The above questions are clearly in the mind of the Chinese officials dealing with these issues. The answers will require a lot of hard analytical work and difficult political decisions. It will also require a lot of work in setting up the new institutions that will (1) collect revenue, (2) plan and manage public spending, and (3) monitor and allocate the collection and the disbursement of the shared taxes. Much progress will be required in tax administration, in budgeting, and in the setting up of an administrative structure to handle cash receipts and payments for the various institutions.

One point that I would like to make is that even when the current tax reform is carried out, the government should not tie its hands in reforming the tax system again at some future date, perhaps to reduce the still large number of taxes that would remain in the tax system. It is important to retain this flexibility. In other words, the tax-sharing and tax assignment system that is put into place should not become an obstacle to future tax reform. It, itself, should be reassessed periodically.

These are exciting times for China. Many of the changes proposed are fundamental and necessary. They are also difficult. The government should persist with these reforms to achieve the various objectives that it has set to achieve such as (1) better control over the country's fiscal policy to control inflation and other macroeconomic problems; (2) better allocation of scarce resources to better satisfy the needs of the people and to sustain a high rate of growth; and (3) to achieve a more equitable distribution of income so that all parts of China can share in the growth of the economy. The achievement of these objectives would make China a successful socialist market economy.

The experience of other countries that have carried out fundamental tax reforms or that have successfully dealt with problems created by different layers of governments within their frontiers can help by pointing to alternative options and by indicating the options with the greatest chance of success. Reform is always an endogenous product, however, and its characteristics can only be determined taking into account the special features of a country and its constraints as well as its strengths.

12

Local Taxation in an International Perspective

Giorgio Brosio*

Local taxes enhance the autonomy of local governments and their accountability. The joint effect is to enable citizens to influence the quantity and the mix of services provided by local governments and the mix of taxes needed to finance them. In particular, accountability requires that the cost of providing local public services should be passed on to citizens who utilize them through taxes and user charges. This process is facilitated when local governments have tax autonomy, that is, when they have their own taxes and are able to fix their tax rates with reference to their financing needs.

Pros and Cons of Local Taxation

All over the world, the funding of local governments has become increasingly difficult in the last decades. There are good reasons for this phenomenon. First of all, the revenue needs of local governments have increased faster than those of the central governments. One has to remember the spread of urbanization and the rapid increase of costs associated with the provision of urban services. Second, technical progress in transport and communications has constantly increased the mobility of both persons and goods.

This higher mobility produces in turn two main effects on local taxes. First, it allows "tax exporting," that is, it allows a local government to shift the tax burden from its citizens to those of other local jurisdictions. This takes place, for example, when a local government is

---

* University of Torino, Italy.

allowed to tax a natural resource that is sold outside its jurisdiction, or when a city government imposes a parking fee only on cars coming from other jurisdictions. Tax exporting is not only unfair but also inefficient. Local governments tend to increase excessively their tax revenues when the tax burden can be exported to other areas.

The second effect refers to "tax competition." Citizens can react to high local taxes by moving to another jurisdiction with lower taxes. In turn, local governments can use tax reductions to attract persons and firms from other jurisdictions. Tax competition is not necessarily evil. It is surely not evil from the point of view of the taxpayers, but it does constrain the choices of local governments regarding their tax instruments. The joint effect of tax exporting and tax competition has been to reduce the number of local taxes that can be administered by local governments without creating too many problems and conflicts.

The problem of funding local governments has been compounded by the growing spatial unevenness of economic growth that has exacerbated differences among local jurisdictions about their tax bases and thus their ability to finance expenditures. These differences have been used as an argument against a too large local tax autonomy; that is, local taxes may produce horizontal inequity. This happens because rich areas are able to finance a higher level of local services than poor areas, even by imposing a lower tax burden on their residents. Moreover, in some countries, the centralization of tax instruments has been considered beneficial from many points of view, like stabilization and economic growth policies.

Finally, some experts (see, for example, Groenewegen (1990)) argue that tax administration is both harder and costlier when performed by lower levels of governments. Empirical evidence does not completely support these claims. It is clear, however, that the broad-based taxes (on income or consumption expenditure, for example) that represent the pillars of modern tax systems can be better administered at the central level.

In most countries, some of these problems have been solved by reducing the role of local taxes and by increasing the share of grants from the central government in the revenues of local governments. Furthermore, local governments have increasingly relied, for their own financing, on nontax sources of revenue, primarily user charges and fees.

It is important to stress, however, that in recent years many countries have tried to reverse the trend toward tax centralization, partly as an attempt to trim their central budget deficit and partly to achieve a greater degree of efficiency in the operation of local governments. New taxes have been created, and the role of old ones has been expanded, as we shall see in the next sections.

The last remark is that practically all the problems mentioned here tend to decrease with the increase in the geographic size of local jurisdictions. For example, the problems tend to become less acute—if not disappear—when passing from local governments to regions or to states in federal countries. In fact, in Europe, some countries (e.g., the United Kingdom and Belgium) have proceeded in the last two decades to merge their small local governments, thus creating more viable units of government. Such changes were also important from the point of view of tax assignments and administration.

The Tax Assignment Problem

At the theoretical level the problems associated with the size and capacity of local governments have been taken into account in the literature on tax assignment. Musgrave (1983) has used equity and efficiency criteria to formulate the following broad principles:

- taxes suitable for economic stabilization should be the responsibility of the central government;
- taxes with a high redistributive potential should be also central;
- tax bases that are highly unequally distributed among jurisdictions should be left to the central government;
- taxes on mobile factors and goods are best administered by central governments;
- taxes on immobile (or scarcely mobile) factors and goods should be the responsibility of local governments; and
- taxes and user charges based on the benefit principle can be appropriately used at all levels of governments, but are especially suitable for assignment to the local level, inasmuch as they are able to capture the benefits of local expenditures.

These general principles can be translated into more detailed tax policy recommendations (see also Box 1 on local autonomy):

- the personal income tax and the corporation income tax should be assigned to the central government, the former for the redistribution and stabilization reasons already given, and both for discouraging the interjurisdictional mobility of factors of production;
- broad-based consumption taxes should be treated differently according to how they are levied: sales taxes levied at the manufacturing stage should be given to the upper tier of government and to subordinate levels of government only where geographical areas are large (as in the case of the states and provinces in the United

---

Box 1.
Local Taxes Ranked According to Degree of Autonomy They Provide to Local Governments

Own taxes   The base and the rates of tax are under local control. In other words, local governments can control the burden they impose on their citizens.

Overlapping taxes   The base is determined at the national level, but the rates are decided locally.

Shared taxes   The base and the rate are decided nationwide. No possibility of controlling locally the burden of the taxes. Local governments may, however, bargain with the central government the amount of the revenue they receive. Furthermore, as for the other taxes, they can stimulate with their policies the growth of the base of the taxes.

States and Canada); sales taxes levied at the retail stage can be given to local governments insofar as it is possible to restrict the tax to residents;

- selective excise taxes should be assigned to the central government if they fall on goods (to avoid tax exporting) or to local authorities if they fall on services (since much smaller tax exporting is assumed for them);
- land and property taxes are the most suitable for lower tiers of government, especially when they are imposed on residential property that is the least mobile; taxing commercial and industrial property, on the other hand, allows the possibility of exporting the burden and makes the property a less suitable tax base for local governments;
- benefit taxes, license fees, and user charges have an important role to play at the local level.

Structure of Local Taxation

Industrial Countries

As for the industrial countries, no common pattern exists in the structure of their local tax revenues (see also Owens (1992) and Brosio and Pola (1989)). In fact we can single out three modes, or groups of countries (see Table 1). The countries in the first group rely for more

Table 1. Tax Revenues from the Main State and Local Taxes as Percentage of Total Tax Revenues of State and Local Governments, Selected Countries

	Income and Profits			Property			General Consumption			Specific Goods & Services			Other		
	1955	1975	1990	1955	1975	1990	1955	1975	1990	1955	1975	1990	1955	1975	1990
Australia															
State				43.5	26.6	30.6				24.1	16.1	14.1	32.4	57.3	55.3
Local				98.3	100	99.8							1.7	0	0.2
Austria															
State	46.8	44.2	47.8	1.3	1.8	0.9	37.4	33.9	36.2	9.6	13.5	6.2	4.9	6.6	8.9
Local	47.7	38.9	40.4	16.2	11.2	8.9	13.0	19.7	21.6	9.0	14.1	10.4	14.1	16.1	18.7
Canada															
State	6.9	43.6	51.1	8.0	2.3	4.3	12.3	19.6	20.6	38.1	16.8	14.4	34.7	17.7	9.6
Local				88.2	88.5	84.5			0.2			0.1	11.8	11.5	15.2
Germany															
State	76.9	62.8	59.5	8.8	6.2	7.2		21.8	27.0	7.2	2.8	2.0	7.1	6.4	4.3
Local	50.3	69.4	80.3	26.8	20.3	18.6				5.1	0.4	0.4	17.8	9.9	0.7
Switzerland															
State	65.7	77.7	76.6	19.6	14.3	16.4				4.9	1.5	1.3	9.8	6.5	5.7
Local	80.9	86.5	86.4	17.7	13.2	13.2				1.2	0.2	0.3	0.2	0.1	0.1
United States															
State	15.5	31.6	39.2	6.2	9.2	10.6	22.3	30.8	33.1	37.4	23.6	15.9	18.6	4.8	1.2
Local	1.2	4.3	5.7	88.2	52.5	49.9	3.8	7.1	10.7	2.9	3.6	4.6	3.9	32.5	29.1
Belgium															
Local	82.7	72.9	90.4	25.1	13.2	7.3	17.3	0	0				10.0	27.1	9.6
Denmark															
Local	73.9	86.4	92.6				0	0	0	0	0.2	0.1	1.0	0.2	0.1
France															
Local	n.a.	23.0	13.2	n.a.	23.1	35.3	n.a.	0	0	n.a.	4.8	4.9	n.a.	49.1	46.6

Ireland Local				100	100	100	0	0	0	0	0	0	0	0	0
Japan Local	25.6	54.8	63.7	30.9	24.9	23.0	0	0	0	18.0	15.1	8.3	25.5	5.2	5.0
Italy Local	38.4	0	0	20.4	17.5	0	0	0	0	41.1	0	14.5	0.1	82.5	85.5
Netherlands Local	0	15.4	0	56.8	54.2	73.2	0	0	0	18.4	2.7	1.2	24.8	27.7	25.6
New Zealand Local	0	0	0	100	89.1	93.0	0	0	0	0	6.7	1.4	0	4.2	5.6
Norway Local	75.2	91.9	87.7	6.7	5.2	8.6	0	0	0	10.7	0	0	7.4	2.9	3.7
Spain Local	n.a.	57.3	17.5	n.a.	8.5	41.1	n.a.	31.0	12.0	n.a.	3.2	15.0	n.a.	0	14.4
Sweden Local	99.1	99.6	99.6	0	0	0	0	0	0	0	0	0.4	0.9	0.4	0
United Kingdom Local	0	0	0	100.0	100.0	26.6	0	0	0	0	0	0	0	0	73.4
Unweighted Average	35.8	40.0	39.7	39.2	32.6	31.4	4.8	6.8	6.7	10.4	5.2	4.8	10.3	15.4	17.4

Source: International Monetary Fund.

Table 2. Two Cases of Tax-Sharing Systems: A "Classical" One, Germany, and a New One, Belgium

	Shares of Revenue Attributed to		
	Federal government	State governments	Local governments
	(In percent)		
Germany			
Personal income tax	42.5	42.15	15
Capital income tax	50.0	50.0	0
Corporate income tax	50.0	50.0	0
VAT	65.0	35.0	0
Belgium			
Personal income tax	67.2	32.8	0
VAT	30.6	69.4	0
Tax on property sales	58.6	41.4	0

than two thirds of their local tax revenue on income taxes, on both individuals and companies. This is the case in the Scandinavian countries, Switzerland, Belgium, and Germany. (Belgium and Germany are examined further in Table 2.) Japan is also close to this pattern, as the share of income taxes is approaching the percentage mentioned above. The prevalence in subnational revenue of taxes on property characterizes the second group, that is, formed by the United Kingdom and its former colonies. Countries in the third group show no predominance of a single tax, but rather a large variety of solutions to the problem of raising local tax revenues. Consumption taxes are not the single revenue source in any country of the subnational level, but in most federal countries general consumption taxes (namely, value-added tax and sales taxes) are important sources of revenue for state governments.

The present structure seems to reflect only partially the criteria suggested by the theory. This is because of the importance of the income and profit taxes. At a closer look, however, the gap between practice and theory becomes much narrower. First, many countries, like Germany, Denmark, Austria, and Spain, adopt a tax-sharing arrangement for their income taxes. Under such arrangement, state and local governments are automatically attributed a fixed percentage of the overall income tax receipts within the country. The division of these receipts between individual units is usually made on the basis of the division of the tax base between these units. This implies that state and local governments have no autonomy in the administration of the tax; that becomes close to a general (block) grant. Second, in the other countries (the only exception is Switzerland), lower levels of government use a single, proportional, rate. The rate usually varies throughout the country but within limits. This allows local authorities to reduce the potential for competition between themselves, and the disparities in revenue capacity of the various units. In addition, the taxable income is determined with uniform rules all over the country (again the exception is Switzerland). The main advantages of income taxes from the point of view of their use by local government stem from the fact that their tax base is both wide and buoyant.

Taxes on immovable property are the second most important source of tax revenues for local governments (see also Box 2). Many reasons explain the use of these taxes by local governments. Although property taxes are predominantly local, subnational governments do not have complete discretion about them. Central governments tend to intervene in the specification of the assessment procedures and in setting limits on the tax rates that can be levied. For example, only in Sweden and the United Kingdom (although not in the last period in the 1980s in which the tax was in existence) were there no limitations on the rates, as in most parts of the United States (where the tax is governed by the individual states). The central government is usually also involved in the administration of taxes, because of the strict connection between these taxes and other important taxes, such as death, income, and capital transfer taxes.

The share of property taxation in total revenues has slightly decreased over the period considered in Table 1. The role of property taxes in financing local government has been subjected to conflicting trends. Some countries have decided that property taxes should be eliminated or substantially reduced. The United Kingdom replaced the local property tax ("the rates") with a poll tax, in order to increase the accountability of local governments (see Box 3). The experiment showed big flaws (see Smith (1991)), and the government was induced to revert to a new form of property taxation. Ireland abandoned its property tax in 1978, but for different reasons that were connected with the deemed insufficient equity of the tax. The tax was abandoned for only five years, however; Ireland reverted thereafter to the same kind of taxation, by introducing a tax on imputed income from residential property. In Switzerland some cantons, which are responsible for local taxes, as in every federal system, abolished the property tax during the early 1980s because of its high costs, especially when compared with its yield.

Mediterranean countries, on the contrary, have shown a growing interest toward property taxes as a source of revenue. Spain has given more autonomy over the tax rate to its local authorities. Portugal decided to introduce a new property tax that is destined to become

---

Box 2.
Four Main Types of Property Taxation

- *Annual or rental value of property.* In this system, the base is defined as the expected or notional value of the property. (Examples are the former British tax and the taxes still used in the former British colonies.) There are usually wide divergences between assessed values and the net market rent because of (1) legal deductions in annual value, (2) rent controls, and (3) assessment difficulties. The rates applied are in some cases flat, in others, progressive with respect to property value (especially in developing countries).
- *Capital values of land and improvements.* The tax base is defined as the assessed value of land and improvements. In theory, this value should be equal to the full market price. In practice, however, it is generally lower than that because of infrequent assessment and poor assessment practices. The rates applied are generally flat. This version of the tax is more difficult to administer than the former one. In fact, in the capital value type, higher levels of government are frequently involved in the assessment process both in developed and developing countries, whereas the annual type is usually administered by local governments only.
- *Site value of the land.* This is a special version of the former type: only the value of the land is taxed. The main attraction of this tax is its potential for improving the efficiency of land use. More precisely, since only the land is taxed the owner has no disincentive to developing the land to its most efficient use. This tax has been used in a number of developing countries (like Jamaica and Kenya) and in some parts of Australia, New Zealand, and South Africa. The tax has two main disadvantages. The first is the usual assessment problem, due in this case to the paucity of sales of vacant land, which imposes a need to evaluate the total property value and then deduct from it the value of improvements. The second is the restriction of the tax base when only the site value is considered.
- *Capital gains on property.* Increased value may be taxed on an accrual or realization basis. This second choice is better suited to individuals. The base of this tax is lower than that of the other types.

---

the pillar of its local taxation. Greece is also in the process of decentralizing and raising existing taxes on property. Italy introduced in 1991 a property tax (ISI, *imposta straordinaria sugli immobili*) as a national source of revenue. From 1994 it became a true local tax, as its revenue and the power to fix rates were completely devolved to local authorities, whereas the administration continued with the central government.

Box 3.
The "Failed Revolution" of the British Poll Tax

- The *main goals* of the tax were to increase the accountability of local governments by (1) ensuring that all citizens who vote for local government services contribute to their costs; and (2) establishing a clear link between changes in local expenditure and changes in local tax bills.
- *Structure of the tax.* Every adult (aged 18 or over) was subject to the tax. The average liability in 1990 was £252 (approximately $400). Persons with very low incomes received a subsidy of up to 80 percent of the poll tax.
- *Implementation problems.* There were high administration costs due to the registration of residents, who exhibited a high mobility, and the huge expenses for recovering unpaid debts.
- *Political difficulties.* Strong resistance to the tax from citizens, especially low-income persons, who perceived the tax as inequitable.

Of the remaining taxes administered by local governments, one has to mention local business taxes (see Bennett (1987) and Pola (1991)). Under this heading is included a wide range of taxes that allow local governments to generate revenues from economic activities located within their jurisdiction. Business taxes are widely used in socialist countries. In Western Europe, there are three main versions of these taxes:; (1) special taxes on inputs to a firm, like the French *Taxe professionnelle*, or on a combination of inputs, profits, and income, like the German *Gewerbe Steuer*, (2) taxes on profits, or income of professionals, like those administered in Switzerland, and (3) taxes on property used by business as a factor of production. In addition, businesses contribute to local revenues by paying fees and user charges that play a very important role in some cases.

Special taxes on inputs to a firm are an instrument for taxing business activities, and are being increasingly used in a number of countries. Germany and France are the most important cases, but similar taxes are now levied in Italy and Spain. These taxes have various bases. In the French version, the base is composed of two elements: (1) the rental value of fixed business assets and (2) one eighth of salaries and wages. According to French experts (see Gilbert and Guengant (1991)), the burden of this tax varies considerably among various activities and among jurisdictions. As for the former, capital-intensive firms are generally more burdened than labor intensive ones. The tax provides, however, a substantial share of local tax revenues, due to its wide coverage.

The base of the German tax is also very complex, even if it has been simplified recently by excluding, among other things, the payroll component. It is levied on business profits, plus 50 percent of interest paid on long-term debt and capital stock, plus 50 percent of long-term debt. The tax plays a very important role in the financing of German local governments, contributing more than 40 percent of their total tax revenue. Moreover, it gives flexibility to local governments' fiscal policies, since rates are fixed locally.[1] Negative features of the tax include its sensitivity to the general economic cycle and the extraordinarily large disparities in tax potential between various areas, which are corrected by means of equalization grants.

The Spanish tax that was reformed in 1992 (IAE, *Impuesto sobre Actividades Económicas*) is a kind of license tax, that is, a flat tax on businesses that varies according to different activities and sectors. The tax also takes into account the surface area of business premises. Its most attractive features are its simplicity of administration and its wide coverage, which ensure a potentially substantial revenue. It is clearly a kind of tax that is well suited to developing countries. Italy has had a local business tax since 1988; like the Spanish tax, the tax base also takes account of the surface area of business premises and is weighted according to the taxpayer's income.

Business taxes offer local authorities the possibility of weighing the burden imposed on their residents against that imposed on economic activities, that is, balancing the revenue potential of cities with a high concentration of business activities and that take benefit from this tax with that of cities that are predominantly residential and that benefit mostly from using local taxes on income or sales. Moreover, these taxes are perceived by local governments as an instrument for fostering local economic growth through tax incentives. Central governments are obviously more cautious in this respect, fearing the effects of fierce competition among local jurisdictions. In fact, in unitary states, the tax base, the main criterion for the administration, and ceilings on tax rates are specified at the central level.

Recent developments in local taxation include various new kinds of taxes. Of special interest is the reliance on utility charges to tax publicly provided goods. Italy, for example, introduced in the mid-1980s a local tax on electricity consumption. Electricity is sold by a national public monopoly. The local tax is in addition to the nationwide fixed price. The tax has three distinct advantages (the same arguments may apply to telephone bills and even water bills): first, electricity con-

---

[1] Most of the other sources of revenue for subnational governments in Germany are shared taxes.

sumption is a proxy indicator of income; second, the costs of administering such a tax are low; and third, the tax can be tailored to local jurisdictions of every size (even to the sub-units of a city).

A second important example of new forms of taxation, or of revitalization of old ones, is the special charge levied on the financing of urban infrastructure. In some cases (e.g., the Canadian "development charges" or the American "impact or development fees"), they are imposed on developers and are based on the costs of the project. In other cases, a tax is imposed on the increased value of property attributable to public investment projects. This kind of taxation is discussed more broadly in the next section, in reference to the valorization tax.

A final point is the increased reliance on charges and fees. A number of services that are provided at the local level (among the most costly are public transportation and kindergartens) can be charged individually, which helps increase the efficiency of their provision. It does so by stimulating consumers to express their dissatisfaction with what they receive. In addition, charges and fees are potentially a substantial source of revenue.

Developing Countries

A few remarks are in order with respect to developing countries. The first concerns the scope of responsibilities left to local governments. For both political and economic reasons, fiscal decentralization is generally less significant in developing countries than in the developed ones. Of course, cities (especially the big ones) in the developing world present even greater expenditure and revenue needs than those of the industrial countries, but, in general, subnational governments account for a lower share of all government expenditures, and local taxes play a lesser role—always with respect to developed countries—in financing local expenditures. In fact, in recent decades some government functions have shifted to higher levels of government. Quite often this shift has taken place through the creation of special national agencies charged with the provision of urban services.

On the revenue side, central governments have pre-empted the use of most, if not all, of the more productive taxes, such as broadly based income and sales taxes. Local governments have thus been forced to accept what was left, which, in most cases, is inappropriate for their rapidly rising financing needs. The structure of local taxation in developing countries presents a very wide variety of situations (see Bahl and Linn (1990) and Shah (1991)). Some examples of the existing problems include the following. The property tax in some countries (Brazil, India, Indonesia) is administered, exclusively by the central government, or jointly with local governments. Some countries still rely on excises—clearly not the best choice from the efficiency point of view—for the funding of their local governments (e.g., Argentina and Bangladesh). There are even a few cases (e.g., in some Indian states) where taxes on intermunicipal trade are administered by the local authorities.[2] Also the business tax continues to be used in some countries, such as Colombia, where administration poses difficulties.

In general, developing countries encounter bigger difficulties in the administration of local taxes than the developed ones. Second, mobility is a source of lesser concern in such countries. Both these factors help us to understand why developing countries still rely on traditional taxes.

Experts have suggested various ways of widening the range of tax instruments suited to cope with the financing of local expenditure in developing countries, especially in urban areas where problems and financial needs are concentrated. The suggestions include property taxation, which is already levied in a number of countries, as well as, valorization and automotive taxes (discussed below).

The valorization tax, which has been tried in Colombia (see Bird (1992)), consists of utilizing the rapid rise in property values produced by public investment projects to finance their costs by taxing the increase in value. It is not only a benefit tax but a truly earmarked tax in the sense that (1) its product is reserved for financing a specific expenditure, and (2) its tax base is derived from the realization of this expenditure. It presents some advantages with respect to the other types of property taxation mentioned above, namely, the tax on capital values of land and improvements, and with respect to the capital gains tax on increments in site values. As we saw, the assessment of the tax on capital values is difficult and the revenue it produces lags behind in respect to the public infrastructure expenditures. The same problem applies to the capital gains tax; that is, the payment is usually made only when the increment in value is realized by sale. This contrasts with the valorization tax where the payment is secured during, or even before, the investment is made, and the tax recovers only those benefits from public investment that enhance the value of the land.

The administration of the tax, however, presents some difficulties, which can be solved by appropriate skills and procedures. The Colombian experiment suggests that the tax requires the following: (1) careful study of the projects to determine those that will create an increase

---

[2]This is the case of the octroi, a tax levied on goods entering a city for the purpose of local processing or final consumption. It may curtail domestic trade and surely increase the price of "locally imported" goods.

in site value at least equal to the cost of the projects; (2) careful costing of projects; (3) freedom to establish formulas for apportioning the tax among property owners; (4) prompt construction of projects; and (5) prompt collection of all taxes assessed on the property owners during the execution of the project.

Taxes related to motor vehicle ownership and use, such as automotive taxes, constitute another potentially important source of revenue for local governments that is often neglected in developing countries. There are three main arguments in favor of this kind of taxation (see Bahl and Linn (1992) and also Box 4).

- it is a rapidly growing tax base;
- it allows local governments to match the costs on local governments due to automobile use; and
- it helps to control automobile use and the social costs produced.

Automotive taxes are also appealing from the equity point of view. In fact, they may improve the distribution of income.

Conclusions

Local taxes are a powerful instrument for accountability of local governments. Their use is subjected to increasing constraints, however, owing to the high mobility of persons and goods and to the unevenness of spatial growth, which enhances differences among local governments in their taxing power. Great care has thus to be exerted, when thinking about possible reforms of local tax systems, in the choice of proper taxes. Analysis of the existing tax systems shows that most industrial countries rely alternatively for the financing of their local governments on two kinds of taxes, namely, the personal income tax and the property business tax. The personal income tax is very attractive from the local government's point of view. Its potential revenue is large and buoyant. Some provisions have to be made, however, in order to face some of the problems created by their use at the local level, like the disparities in their potential and their procyclical character.

Some countries that have used the property tax for a long period, like the United Kingdom and Ireland, tried to replace the tax with other instruments but have reverted to it subsequently. Many Mediterranean countries have recently decided to increase their reliance on this kind of tax for financing their local governments.

Some attention has been devoted to business taxes, which are still (or even increasingly) popular in continental Europe, as a way to bal-

192 REFORMING CHINA'S PUBLIC FINANCES

Box 4.
Four Main Forms of Automotive Taxation for
Local Governments

- *Fuel taxes.* Fuel taxes consist of levying an additional fuel tax over and above the national tax accruing to the central government. Local fuel taxes may be used for controlling congestion costs, that is, for restricting vehicle use on congested streets. Their main advantages, however, reside in their considerable revenue potential, even by applying moderate rates and the moderate cost of administering them, especially if the production and distribution of fuel is made by a government-owned company, as is the most frequent case in developing countries.
- *Taxes on sales and transfers of motor vehicles.* In many developed countries this kind of automotive taxation takes place through stamp and registration taxes that are administered mainly at the central level. One may conceive of local governments utilizing this tax base. The revenue potential is substantial but clearly lower than that of the third form of taxation.
- *Annual license taxes.* These are taxes levied annually on the ownership or on the use of motor vehicles. Even with moderate rates, these taxes may substantially contribute to the financing of local governments.[1] They require careful administration, however, in order to avoid evasion.
- *Congestion taxes.* This fourth category consists of a variety of instruments, like area- and time-specific taxes designed to address congestion problems. Parking fees and tolls form part of this category, but the revenue potential is clearly smaller than that of the preceding ones.

[1]For example, Bahl and Linn (1992), p. 202 show that in Jakarta the motor vehicle license tax accounted for approximately 33 percent of all local taxes for fiscal year 1986.

---

ance tax revenues coming from individuals with those levied on businesses. This balancing allows equalization of the tax potential of residential areas with that of industrial and tertiary areas. While implementation may pose difficulties in developing countries, such taxes may be thought of as a proxy for the use of local services by businesses.

Less uniformity in local taxation is shown by developing countries, which are usually; more centralized than the industrial ones. Revenue needs of local governments are extremely high, especially in the large cities. Their satisfaction requires, among other things, modernization, if not simply the creation, of a local tax system. This paper has stressed the potential of property taxes and automotive taxes for local revenues.

For both industrial and developing countries—and for countries that are presently engaged in the transition from socialist to market economies—user charges and fees are an extremely productive source of revenue and an efficient one. One can observe an increased reliance on them in a number of countries.

References

Bahl, Roy, and Johannes Linn, Fiscal Decentralization and Intergovernmental Transfers in Less Developed Countries, paper presented to the 46th Congress of the International Institute of Public Finance (Brussels, 1990).

——, *Urban Public Finance in Developing Countries* (New York: Oxford University Press for the World Bank, 1992).

Bennett, Robert, "Local Business Taxes: Theory and Practice," *Oxford Review of Economic Policy*, Vol. 3 (Summer 1987), pp. 60–80.

Bird, Richard, *Tax Policy and Economic Development* (Baltimore: The John Hopkins University Press, 1992).

Brosio, Giorgio, and Giancarlo Pola, A Survey of Various Attempts to Explain the Distribution of Tax Revenues Among Levels of Government, in *Changes in Revenue Structure*, ed. by A. Chiancone and Ken Messere, proceedings of the 42nd Congress of the International Institute of Public Finance (Detroit: Wayne State University Press, 1989).

Gilbert, Guy, and Alain Guengant, *La fiscalité locale en question* (Paris: Monchrestien, 1991).

Groenewegen, Peter, "Taxation and Decentralization. A Reconsideration of the Costs and Benefits of a Decentralized Tax System," *Decentralization, Local Governments, and Markets: Towards a Post-Welfare Agenda,* ed. by Robert L. Bennett (Oxford: Clarendon Press, 1990).

Musgrave, Richard, A., "Who Should Tax, Where and What?" in *Tax Assignment in Federal Countries*, ed. by Charles McLure, Jr. (Canberra: The Australian National University, 1983).

Owens, Jeffrey, "Financing Local Government: An International Perspective with Particulate Reference to Local Taxation," in *Local Government Economics in Theory and Practice*, ed. by David King (London; New York: Routledge, 1992).

Pola, Giancarlo, ed., *Local Business Taxation: An International Overview* (Milano: Vita e Pensiero, 1991).

Shah, Anwar, *Perspectives on the Design of Intergovernmental Fiscal Relations* (Washington: The World Bank, 1991).

Smith, Peter, "Lessons from the British Poll Tax Disaster," *National Tax Journal*, Vol. 44 (December 1991), pp. 421–36.

13

Issues in Natural Resource Taxation

Tamar Manuelyan Atinc and Bert Hofman*

Resource taxation plays a small role in China compared with other forms of taxation. In 1991, it constituted 0.6 percent of total tax revenues. Introduced at the time of enterprise income taxation reforms in 1984, the resource tax differs from the tax in many other countries in that it is paid by the users of natural resources rather than the producers; it could thus be classified as a product tax rather than a natural resource tax. This is not to say that resource taxation has been absent: the pricing mechanism, which has maintained relatively low prices for raw materials, has acted as an implicit taxation on natural resource exploitation, combined with a subsidy for the user of these resources (Table 1). In fact, the implicit marginal tax rate on production of coal mining and oil drilling has contributed to the Y 12 billion in losses in that sector, or about one third of all losses by state-owned enterprises in 1991. In 1991, about 50 percent of total coal production was traded at planned prices, amounting to an implicit subsidy (or forgone tax revenue) of about Y 16 billion, or 1 percent of GNP.[1]

Planned prices are rapidly adjusted to market levels,[2] and during ongoing price reforms, a further alignment of resource prices with world market prices can be expected; rents from resource exploitation will accrue to the exploiting firms, if no further measures are taken; and

---

*World Bank. The views expressed in this paper are preliminary, and should not be considered as those of the World Bank.

[1]The calculation is based on a scarcity price of about 80 percent of long-run marginal costs (this takes into account potential efficiency gains in extractions), which would lead to a price of about Y 85 a ton at the mine. Table 1 quotes Beijing prices, which are higher than the mine price, due to transport costs.

[2]In fact, often underpriced transport services now have become the major obstacle to resource availability.

Table 1. Chinese and International Prices, 1991

	Beijing Retail[1]		International	Border Price[2]
	Price (Y/ton)			
	Plan	Non-Plan	(U.S. dollar/ton)	(Y/ton)
Steam coal	75–80	120–125	35	186
Gasoline	750–900	1100–1700	254	1346
Diesel oil	500–700	900–1300	182	965
Fuel oil	350–400	700	80–94	424–498

Source: World Bank, (1992).
[1]Prices quoted by fuel supply bureau, November 1991.
[2]Converted with official exchange rate of Y 5.3/US$1.

natural resource taxation will play an increasingly important role in guaranteeing to the government, as the owner of the resource, an appropriate reward for the depletion of the resource.

China's government recently announced that a resource tax would be levied on the recovery of petroleum and metallic and nonmetallic mineral resources,[3] a decision that should contribute to the optimal management of China's resource base. Changing from implicit to explicit taxation of natural resources raises a number of policy issues, to be discussed in this paper:[4] (1) the valuation of natural resource rents that should accrue to the government as owner; (2) the determination of the optimal depletion rate and the impact of tax policy on depletion; (3) the treatment of externalities of resource exploitation; and (4) the appropriate distribution of natural resource revenues among the different levels of government.[5]

In view of the pervasiveness of state ownership of natural resources in both developed and developing countries, the government has a dual role to play. As resource owner, it has to ensure that it receives a competitive return on its natural resource endowment. As tax authority, it has to be concerned with the overall allocative effects of tax policy and has to ensure that different sectors of economic activity receive

---

[3]"Tax Reform Will Affect Every Area of Economy," *China Daily*, March 12, 1993, p. 2.

[4]The paper is limited to a discussion of nonrenewable resources in view of China's endowment profile. While the economic issues raised here are valid for all natural resources, sustainability of asset use becomes a paramount consideration in the management of renewable resources, with consequent implications for government policy.

[5]The discussion reflects the treatment of the topic in the literature on natural resource economics and is also guided by current practice in the mineral sector. For extensive treatment of the topic, see Dasgupta and Heal (1979), Conrad and Shalizi (1988), Tietenberg (1992), Heaps and Helliwell (1993), and Nellor and Sunley (1993).

uniform treatment under the tax code.[6] For China, a third role can be distinguished: the role of owner of the resource-exploiting enterprise. There are many reasons to separate the role as enterprise owner from that of resource owner, and China is currently developing mechanisms by which state-owned enterprises work at arm's length from government.[7] Moreover, in the future, use of foreign or Chinese nonstate enterprises may be used for natural resource exploration. Therefore, we assume that the exploiting agent behaves as if it were a private sector agent, with profit maximization as its only goal.

Government as Owner of Resources

Economic Rents and Resource Rents

If resources are extracted, the government as owner of the resource needs compensation for the loss of resource reserves. Whether resources should be extracted depends on the value of the resource in the ground compared with the value of the resource exploited. The value of the resource exploited is the market value minus all costs necessary for exploitation, which is defined as the economic rent.

The value of resources in the ground equals the shadow price (or user costs) of the resource, which is determined by the theoretical price that should be charged to induce a program of exploitation that maximizes social benefits from exploitation. In an optimal program, the resource should in the end be completely exploited, and the returns made on exploiting the resource should equal those of leaving them in the ground. That revenues made with exploitation could be invested at the market interest rate implies that the shadow price of the resource should increase with the interest rate in an optimal extraction program.[8] If the rate of price increase is lower, the government would have an interest in increasing the extraction and investing the ensuing income flow in other assets with higher rates of return. If it is higher, the resources are better left in the ground and exploitation postponed until such time as the rate of return on the resource flow is higher than

---

[6]Corrective tax policy to adjust for externalities or noncompetitive market structures is appropriate and does not detract from the validity of the concept of uniform tax treatment across sectors.

[7]If the roles of enterprise and resource owner are not separate, the introduction of a resource tax makes no sense, as government as the owner of the exploiting firm will already capture all the rents.

[8]It is assumed here that marginal costs of extraction are constant. With increasing or decreasing costs, minor variations in the analysis would apply.

the (social) discount rate. Note that alternative uses of the land, such as agriculture, may yield higher returns than resource exploitation. In this case, the shadow price is too high to validate exploitation.

The shadow price of the resource is often labeled "resource rent," or "royalty." It is the minimum payment the government needs to be compensated for the loss of its natural resource and is similar to any factor payment. Resource rent and economic rent may differ, just like the market wage rate may be higher than the minimum wage an individual worker would accept for his labor. Resource rents and economic rents will also differ from project to project, since the costs of extraction, the quality of the resource, and the location of the mine or well differ, which makes economic rents per mine differ. The marginal mine yields just enough revenues to compensate for exploitation costs and resource rents.

In the absence of an asset market for trading mineral rights, how can the government determine the royalty price of natural resources? The royalty price, or the resource rent, is the opportunity cost of the resource in the ground, or the amount by which the present value of the stock declines when the unit is removed. Under competitive conditions, this would be given either by present value of the net benefit stream associated with exploitation, adjusted for risk, or by the alternative uses of the land, whichever is higher. The unit value of the resource at the minegate can be determined with reference to the world market price. If the opportunity cost of exploitation is higher than the valuation of the resource at the mine, the resource is better left unexploited, until such time that world market prices are sufficiently high to cover the opportunity costs.

Extracting Rents

The government needs to ensure that it will at least receive the opportunity costs of the resource. The way this is done, however, could influence the behavior of the exploiting enterprise, and with that the total amount of economic benefits generated. The government thus needs to take account of the incentives it offers for the exploiting enterprise. Before undertaking an investment, the exploiting enterprise has to determine whether the income generated by the project yields a competitive rate of return on physical capital employed, adjusted for risk, after payment to third parties, including remuneration of other factors (labor, resources) and taxes. Its evaluation will be based on the objective that maximizes the net present value of the project, which will involve judgment about the optimal extraction rate given the expected evolution of prices, costs, and government tax policy. Each tax diminishes returns to the enterprise and increases it for the government, but if the enterprise is taxed too high, the project will no longer be financially viable to the firm. The government and the exploiting enterprise engage in an explicit or implicit contract that includes tax payments, regulatory policies, and possible government equity participation; each party to the arrangement needs to be interested in the arrangement over the duration of the project. The ideal arrangement would induce the enterprise to exploit the resource such that it maximizes social benefits from exploitation.

What Tax?

Ideally, the government should tax the resource rents with a tax that takes economic rents as a base. A pure rent tax does not distort investment and production decisions: thus it carries no excess burden. Unfortunately, it is virtually impossible to calculate economic rents, because this requires information on accrued costs, including imputed capital costs to the firm that are not directly observable, such as real depreciation of assets, depletion of resources, real financing costs, and risk.[9] Moreover, these costs may differ substantially among firms and among resource bases. *Cash flow taxes* are an attractive alternative, both economically and administratively. They are simple to calculate because they do not involve imputation of capital costs; capital costs are taken into account as they occur and deductions are taken in full up front for depreciable assets. Economically, cash flow taxes are equivalent in present value to rent taxes calculated on accrued net income.[10]

In practice, cash flow and rent taxes are rarely used to capture resource rents. Cash flow taxes reduce tax liabilities up front, which might be problematic for some governments. Moreover, both types of tax are susceptible to manipulation by international, vertically integrated companies through transfer pricing practices or debt-equity choice, and both taxes imply a high degree of risk for the government. The cash flow tax can be modified, however, and the development costs may be capitalized and depreciated once the cash flow from the natural resource exploitation becomes positive. This smooths out the tax obligation of the resource-exploiting enterprise. If interest over the full book value of the capitalized development costs can be deduced, the system approaches an ideal cash flow tax. The *modified cash flow*

---

[9]See Boadway and Flatters (1993).

[10]This equivalence holds only when negative cash flows either are fully refundable or can be carried forward at market interest rates.

taxation differs from a profit taxation in that income taxation usually does not allow capitalization of all costs.

Royalties (severance taxes, production taxes, stumpage fees) that are levied on each unit extracted can theoretically be constructed such that they capture only rents of exploitation. The ideal (maximum) royalty would then be the difference between the mine gate price and the costs of extraction.[11] Actual *royalties* or *severance taxes* hardly meet the requirements that would make them a rent tax. They can be levied either as ad valorem or per unit taxes on production. Both types of tax reduce economically recoverable reserves and create incentives for "highgrading" of deposits, leaving economically profitable lower-grade deposits unexploited. *Unit taxes* do not take account of either the value of the resource or the extraction costs. They induce producers to change the quality selection or extraction profile in order to reduce the present value of taxes. Flat unit taxes postpone extraction, while the effect of progressive unit taxes depends on the rate of increase of the tax compared with the interest rate used by the producer to discount future income flows. *Ad valorem taxes* do take account of the value of the resource but they induce the producer to allocate extraction to periods with lower prices in present value terms, and thus future resource prices determine acceleration or deceleration of extraction. In addition, ad valorem taxes create risk sharing between government and producer as tax revenues are dependent on market prices. *Production sharing* is analogous to an ad valorem tax when the government simply appropriates a certain share of total output. As such, production-sharing arrangements have an element of risk sharing.

When the country is a price taker, *export taxes* have the same effects on the producer as do production taxes, discussed above. Export taxes, however, have the additional disadvantage of diverting resources for domestic use, representing an implicit subsidy from the government to processing industries (e.g., Cameroon for timber). In China, where the internal price differs from the world market price, the imposition of an export tax may be necessary in order not to distort against domestic supply. However, the first-best solution to stimulate domestic processing would be to liberalize prices and subsidize processing directly.

Modified Royalties

The output taxes discussed above result in suboptimal extraction profiles, because typically they ignore some extraction costs. Pure

---

[11]Nellor and Sunley (1993), p. 5.

rent taxes should be levied on net revenues after deduction of all operating and capital expenses. Some production taxes and production-sharing arrangements allow for the deduction of some costs (typically, operating costs) and thus approximate a rent tax. Notwithstanding the disadvantages of simple royalties or production taxes, they are often used by government to capture part of the rents. The main advantage is that they are easy to monitor, and no assessment needs to be made on the costs incurred by the exploiting enterprise. However, more complex royalties that take some cost factors into account could be based on relatively simple, transparent formulas that limit monitoring difficulties.

Income-based taxation is sometimes used for rent taxation. Resource properties are usually subject to general income taxation, but taxes specific to the resource industry are sometimes based on an income concept. If some allowance for the capitalization of the development costs is made, this approaches the cash flow taxation. Colombia uses an income-based tax for coal and Indonesia, for hard minerals, the United Kingdom for oil, and in Canada and the United States, the corporate income tax makes special allowances for resource-exploiting firms. In some of these countries, however, the rate of return on equity in resource exploitation firms has been very high, and the rents have apparently not been captured very effectively.[12]

Nontax Instruments

An *auction* or competitive bidding for the sale of exploitation rights offers a mechanism for the government to capture rents. If there are sufficient bidders to prevent collusion and information is uniformly available, the bids reflect the present value of the future net benefit stream, adjusted for risk. This is exactly how resource rents were defined earlier. Thus, a properly designed and implemented auction system can capture 100 percent of resource rents for the government and would solve the government's problem of assessing the rents of a certain resource project. *Leasing* is sometimes used by governments to allocate exploitation rights, for example, in the petroleum sector. Leasing has the same effects as an auction and therefore a rent tax if the leasing period is indefinite. Shorter periods will distort incentives for extraction rates, but may be chosen for political reasons, if non-state ownership of the resource is considered not acceptable. For an investor, however, leases and auctions may not be the ideal way to pay the rents that are due to the government. Because the auction or lease

---

[12]Boadway and Flatters (1993), p. 48.

price is paid up front, the exploiting firm becomes vulnerable to expropriation of the profits after the investment has been made. This would reduce the price the enterprise is willing to pay for the right of exploitation.

Direct *equity participation* in production is another way for the government to appropriate resource rents. The price at which the government purchases equity relative to its market price determines the level of rents captured by the government. The government's equity participation can be structured and priced such that it is equivalent in effect to a pure rent tax,[13] but direct participation exposes the government to the risks associated with the exploitation of natural resources. It is in this aspect the same as a cash flow or rent tax. The notable difference is that equity participation confers an active role on the government as shareholder, while taxation relegates government to a passive role typical for a tax authority in a mixed economy.

Externalities

Proper remuneration for the exploitation of resources may involve more than payment of the royalty price, reflecting the scarcity value of the resource. The opportunity cost of extraction may also involve externalities generated by the extraction process (e.g., land erosion, environmental degradation due to open pit mining) that reduce the value of other assets. These economic costs should be taken into account, and tax policy in the mineral sector should be modified to induce socially optimal adjustments to extraction profiles.

Dutch Disease

An economic cost reminiscent to externalities is the "Dutch disease," the negative impact of mineral production on the development prospects of the rest of the economy.[14] The problem arises when the increase in wealth experienced by the discovery of natural resources induces an appreciation of the real exchange rate. The change in the country's comparative advantage and the increase in the real ex-

---

[13]At one extreme, if the government obtained free equity with entitlement to an equivalent share in net current revenues, this arrangement would represent a tax both on resource rents and on private returns to capital. A pure rent tax would require that the government either purchase its equity at the proportional cost of capital investment (corresponding to its share in net revenues) or reimburse the private operator for an imputed return on capital investment.

[14]See Conrad and Shalizi (1988) for the development of the arguments related to Dutch disease.

change rate reduce the competitiveness of traditional exports, potentially leading to unemployment and idle capacity in this sector. If the traditional export sector shows increasing returns in production, a temporary reduction in production due to the resource boom may permanently affect competitiveness. The relative importance of Dutch disease depends on the extent of the economy's dependence on natural resources. A diversified economy with a relatively small share of its output and exports derived from natural resources is unlikely to experience serious problems, while for smaller resource-dependent economies, it may wreak havoc with their agriculture sector in particular.[15] While a country will be unable to avoid the problems generated by a sudden increase in wealth, the government can compensate for the associated costs in the traditional sectors and prepare the economy for the transition away from a resource-dependent production structure.

Production taxes will induce producers to take externalities into account. While these taxes increase costs and therefore influence investment and extraction decisions, the modification in behavior is desirable in the presence of externalities, and thus welfare improving. The cleanup costs of environmental damage require the accumulation of production taxes, or the posting of a bond by the exploiting enterprise; otherwise the enterprise will be tempted to walk away from those costs by going bankrupt.

Risk

The government as owner of the resource is exposed to risk arising from the uncertainty on, inter alia, the size and quality of the stock and the future evolution of natural resource prices and extraction costs. Various possibilities exist for risk-sharing arrangements between the owner and the exploiter of the resource. The government's willingness to share risks depends on the level of diversification of the economy and on access to international capital markets.[16] More diversified economies will experience smaller income fluctuations because of resource price fluctuation. Economies with greater access to capital markets are better able to sustain greater exposure to the natural resource sector than less creditworthy economies, because income fluctuations

---

[15]Examples of countries that have suffered from Dutch disease abound. In addition to the classical example of the Netherlands (natural gas) for which the phrase was coined, Bolivia (tin), Zaïre (copper), and Indonesia (petroleum) have all been affected to varying degrees.

[16]See Conrad and Shalizi (1988).

can be smoothed out. The risk attitude of the government will have an impact on the design of the contractual relationship with the producer, as well as on the acceptable rate of return on resources. With uncertainty, the government maximizes the *expected* rate of return on its assets. The government equity participation is one way of risk assumption, while ex post rent taxes and ad valorem and ad rem output taxes have different implications for the extent of risk sharing.

In conclusion, government as owner of the resource has to be concerned with putting in place a policy framework that will provide adequate renumeration for the loss of an asset and compensate for any economic costs associated with mineral development. The rate of return that the government is willing to accept on its natural resource endowment will be related to the rate of return on other assets, adjusted for risk. Proper evaluation of natural resource rents and economic costs will lead to the optimal rate and timing of extraction to maximize economic welfare.

Government as Tax Authority

In its role as tax authority, the government has to be concerned with the overall allocative effects of tax policy. As discussed above in the section on externalities, tax policy can have an efficiency-enhancing impact when used to correct for market imperfections. This important governmental role notwithstanding, tax policy is typically concerned with devising a system for generating sufficient revenues to finance public expenditures in a manner that minimizes distortions in decisions of economic agents regarding investment, output, and production techniques (relative use of inputs). The previous section discussed the problems caused by certain taxes levied for capturing resource rents on incentives within the resource industry. In this section, the treatment of the resource sector in the economy-wide tax system is discussed, underlining the importance of uniform treatment across sectors.

A typical feature of the system of direct taxes in most economies is taxing capital income in addition to personal income. As part of the net of economy-wide taxes, natural resource industries are subject to the corporate income tax, which represents a tax on capital income earned in corporations. To preserve the neutrality of economic incentives for the allocation of investment capital among the different sectors, industries should be taxed in a homogeneous fashion. In practice, however, resource industries face a reduced rate of effective taxation, as they benefit from special privileges including rapid expensing of exploration and development expenses when the rest of the economy is operating on the accrual method of determining taxable income. Additional provisions including depletion allowances and interest deductibility reduce further the rate at which equity income is taxed relative to other industries. This has implications for investments across sectors.

Other Goals

Governments often seek to achieve other goals than rent appropriation with natural resource taxes. The taxes on resources are often set differently for different uses, most notably a lower tax for domestically processed resources. Local employment goals are often pursued, and resource-exploiting enterprises may be "taxed" by forcing more people than necessary onto their payroll. Also, taxes may be set lower than the opportunity costs of the resource, in order to develop resources that are not economically viable, but may secure supply of a crucial resource. In general, taxation is less suited to achieve such goals, as they only indirectly influence the behavior of the exploiting enterprise, and more direct measures, such as direct subsidization of the desired activity, are often the better policy.

Use of Revenues

The government should realize that, in using the natural resource in exploitation, it loses an asset, which cannot be used in the future, and in an economic sense this is equal to accumulating debt. If no alternative assets are bought for the revenues, which are instead used for government consumption, the net worth of government will fall, and future generations will have fewer assets than the present one. The distribution over time of the benefits to some extent is a moral issue, but a good rule of thumb is that the revenues from natural resources should be spent such that a constant stream of future income is generated. This would, for instance, imply that most of the revenues should be invested or international debt repaid with it. The decision on spending the revenues should not be restricted by earmarking them for a certain purpose, but should be decided upon within the overall budgetary process. Appropriate spending of the revenues would also reduce Dutch disease effects.

In conclusion, the government as tax authority should ensure that different industries in the economy receive uniform treatment under the corporate income tax. There is no economic justification for providing preferential treatment to resource industries. As discussed in the first section of the paper, however, there are good economic reasons why resource industries should be afforded special treatment in the tax system. This has to do with the fact that natural resources generate rents that should accrue to the government as owner, requiring fiscal instruments that tax resources over and above the levies implicit in general income taxes.[17] The important public policy issue is to devise a system for the extraction of resource rents that takes into account all economic costs as well as the relative risk profile of governments and private sector agents.

Distribution of Resource Taxes Among Levels of Government

Once it is decided how to tax natural resource rents, the question is what level of government should control natural resource taxation. The feasibility of optimal taxation of resource rents is not independent of this issue. The regional dimension of taxation is highly relevant to the Chinese context. The revenues from China's existing resource tax belong to the taxes that are shared according to the tax contracts. In the present tax experiments, the tax is shared, with 50 percent to local government, or 70 percent for local governments of minority areas, bringing in a redistributive element in the resource taxation.

China's fiscal system is de jure a unitary system, with both rates and base decided by central government. However, because of its decentralized control of tax collection, the system operates akin to a federal system. In addition, the recent tax experiments are moving away from the traditional tax contracting system and in the direction of a tax assignment system, with only limited sharing of taxes. Moreover, central government has recognized the need for increased local control over a number of taxes. New taxes, like the natural resource tax, are proposed, and this broadening of the tax base may break the present deadlock between central and local governments. In this context, it should be decided what level of government will obtain control over the tax, and aspects of efficiency, stabilization, and equity need to be considered.

Efficiency

The accrual of natural resource rents to a subnational government would induce movements of production factors and migration into

---

[17]Where resources are privately owned, taxing resources is still an economically desirable form of taxation, because, when properly designed, rent taxes generate no distortions.

that jurisdiction, in order to capture part of the rents. From a national perspective, the costs involved in such relocation, including the crowding of the locality with the resource rents, are wasteful, as the rents could be distributed by other means, among which are equalization schemes administered by the central government. Moreover, production efficiency would be violated, if local government could lower enterprise taxation, because of natural resource revenues. In China, migration is strongly discouraged by existing regulation, but this has not stopped many people from moving out of the inland rural areas to the coastal cities in order to benefit from the prevailing higher wages. A similar movement could be expected to localities that generate substantial resource rents. However, empirical evidence from the United States suggests that the efficiency losses due to rent-induced factor movements remain limited.[18]

Local governments may be less inclined to levy the optimal resource tax than the central government, as local governments have a stronger interest in such goals as reducing unemployment than in the optimal use of the natural resource.

Contrarily, natural resources would be the ideal local tax base from the perspective of excess burden: because the tax base cannot move, no excess burden from interjurisdictional movement of the tax base would arise. Moreover, the local government may be better able to determine the optimal tax, which, as shown above, depends on the productivity of the extracting firm, which in turn depends strongly on local conditions of extraction. Better information on local conditions is the standard argument for the devolution of government,[19] and in this context this could imply that at least part of the authority over the tax rate could be left to local governments.

The development of natural resources can raise considerable demand for local public goods. Negative externalities from natural resource development in the form of pollution are usually strongly spatially concentrated. The cleanup costs of at least part of this would fall on local budgets. Moreover, the rents attached to the natural resource may depend on local government input, such as roads and waterway maintenance; thus giving the local government a share in these rents may align its interest with those of the central government.[20] However, this compensation for the provision of local public goods to develop natural resource extraction need not take the form of taxes: the central

---

[18]Miezkowski and Toder (1983).
[19]Oates (1972).
[20]Scott (1978).

government as an owner could provide fees or grants for local governments to achieve this goal.

In China, the present tax administration would argue against central assignment of the natural resource taxation. The double subordination of the tax bureaus means that they operate to a large extent as a local government institution. Since the local government would have only little interest in the collection of a natural resource tax that accrues to the central government, the effective tax rate would differ from the optimal tax, which would induce too high a rate of depletion of the natural resources. If the exploiting firm is locally owned, the natural resource tax would even be strictly against local interests, and exemption of the tax may occur. Thus, in present circumstances, a local share in the tax seems unavoidable from a collection point of view. If the central government succeeds in its efforts to establish an effective national tax administration,[21] centralizing the revenue of a natural resource tax may become more feasible.

Stabilization

Local assignment of natural resource taxation may complicate economic stabilization. World market prices for natural resources are highly volatile, and so are the rents that should accrue to the government under a rent taxation arrangement. Moreover, natural resource prices tend to be high in cyclical upturns and low in cyclical downturns. Since China is opening up more and more to the outside world, the economy will fluctuate more and more in step with the international business cycle.

Local government in China does not have legal access to capital markets, and is thus more likely to base expenditures on short-term revenue considerations. The procyclical pattern of natural resource revenues is therefore likely to lead to procyclical government expenditures. To avoid this, centralization of at least a substantial portion of the revenues seems advisable. However, some of the procyclical spending pattern could be avoided, if regulated access of local government to capital markets was developed. Apart from stabilization considerations, local governments' regulated access to borrowing would also enhance intertemporal efficiency. Besides, the local government has considerable unregulated access to borrowing in any case, owing to the intertwining of state-owned enterprises and the government. As an al-

---

[21]A state administration of taxation was created in 1994 to administer national and shared taxes. Full implementation of this measure is expected to take a number of years. *Ed.*

ternative to borrowing for mitigating stabilization problems, China's authorities could regulate the accumulation and decumulation of reserves for local governments, and in this way avoid procyclical spending of natural resource revenues. Finally, a national windfall profit taxation, like the one in the United States, could reduce the procyclical effect of locally accruing natural resource taxation. Of course, the auctioning of mineral rights may completely isolate local governments from price fluctuation.

Equity

The standard literature on the allocation of revenue sources maintains that tax bases that are highly unevenly distributed among regions should be taxed centrally,[22] because fiscal equalization would become impossible if fiscal capacities of subnational governments are highly unequally distributed.

The inequality of fiscal capacity, however, is not unique to natural resource taxation alone; thus, solely centralizing this tax for that reason may give rise to distortions. Moreover, in China, fiscal equalization is only weakly developed, and "quota grants" have been eroded by inflation over the last five years. This has substantially reduced the poor provinces' capacity to provide an efficient package of public goods. At the same time, the internal provinces that are the main suppliers of natural resources in China belong to the poorest states. Introduction of a local natural resource tax or giving local governments a substantial share in the revenues of a central resource tax would enhance the fiscal capacity of these provinces substantially.

To illustrate the size of possible changes in tax capacity, let us assume an efficiency price of coal of Y 85 at the mine, the coal-producing provinces that export half their production are giving the rest of the country a subsidy of about Y 8 billion (1988 data). The main losers of taxing coal up to its efficiency price are Beijing, Liaoning, Jilin, and Tianjin, who together received an implicit subsidy of Y 3 billion, or about 1.5 percent of provincial GNP in 1988. The main benefactors of a tax, if revenues were tobe assigned at the provincial level, would be Shanxi, with Y 4.3 billion (14.5 percent of provincial GNP); Ninxia, with Y 0.2 billion (4 percent); and Henan, with Y 0.6 billion (0.8 percent).

The first-best solution for the equalization problem is to establish an equalization scheme that takes into account total fiscal capacity and then redivides this among provinces according to objective criteria. The natural resource tax could then be one of the taxes taken into ac-

---

[22]Musgrave (1983).

count in local fiscal capacity. Alternatively, with a central natural resource tax, the receipts could be used to replenish an equalization fund, which is disbursed according to needs criteria. The development of natural resources could then be seen as a needs factor.

International Practice

International practice on the assignment of natural resource taxation shows a variety of approaches, but in many at least part of the revenues, and sometimes the control of natural resource taxes, is assigned to subnational governments.

The United States allows states to tax natural resources, with severance taxes (production taxes, license taxes, conservation taxes), which amounted to 4.3 percent of total state revenues in 1981. The average rate for oil severance tax is 5 percent, with a range of zero to 12.5 percent. The states also benefit from natural resource exploitation through mineral rights leasing. For instance, in Alaska, the collection of mineral lease revenues amounted to $1,119 million, almost as high as the severance tax collection of $1,170 million. Further resource-related revenues for states are the corporate income tax as part of the general enterprise taxation; finally, the local government collects property taxes on the assets of natural resource enterprises.

Canada has constitutionally assigned the ownership of subsurface mineral rights to the provinces and collects royalties from them. The federal government as regulator of interprovincial trade can also tax natural resources, but traditionally, the corporate income tax is the main means by which the federal government benefits from natural resource exploitation. Alberta is the main benefactor of natural resource revenues.

Australia assigns to the states all rights not explicitly mentioned in the constitution ("residual rights"), and the ownership of natural resources is understood to be among these rights. The federal government has the rights to offshore drilling, on which it collects a royalty of 10 percent, 60 percent of which is passed to the states. In 1979, 20 percent of total revenues of the states came from natural resource taxation, as compared with 9 percent of federal revenues. The strong regional differences due to resource taxation are redressed by strong equalization components in federal grant schemes.

In 1992, Russia established a severance tax of 8–20 percent of the production value based on the domestic price, which is about one sixth of the world market price. In addition, petroleum is subject to an export tax ($50 a ton) and a "fee for the reproduction of resources" of 10 percent of production value, which is earmarked for petroleum sector investment. The export tax is a federal tax, the royalty is shared between the federation (20–40 percent), oblast (20–30 percent), and city (30 percent). The fee for reproduction of resources is assigned to cities. The substantial accrual of resource tax revenues to the local level has been primarily motivated to counter the centripetal forces in the Russian Federation.

Options for China's Natural Resource Tax

As China's government moves toward market-based pricing of natural resources, and resource-exploiting enterprises become more independent from government, the natural resource tax will become an important instrument for the government to appropriate resource rents.

Resource rents should ideally be taxed by pure rent taxes, but China's low tax buoyancy may make the necessary up-front payments infeasible. Simple royalties and severance taxes would distort the production incentives for the exploiting firm, adding to an environment that is already prone to distortions due to the incomplete nature of China's reform. The alternative of auctioning exploitation rights may not be efficient, given the limited number of Chinese bidders, the political reluctance to allow foreign firms, and the hesitation foreign firms may have in owing natural resource rights to China, due to the risk of (explicit or implicit) expropriation of the benefits.

China may want to consider a modified cash flow tax as a means to appropriate rents for the state. The concepts needed to effectuate such a tax have been developed in the context of new income tax laws, and thus natural resource tax legislation can lean heavily on the income tax law. Administration of the tax could be done fairly easily by those branches of the tax administration specializing in income taxation, and thus no separate collection units for natural resource tax need be developed. Explicit, transparent definitions of rents should be formulated and codified, which may seek a compromise between the goal of fully capturing accrued rents and limiting administrative difficulties. Although practice has shown that the adjusted cash flow tax is often unable to capture all rents, government ownership of the exploiting firm makes this less of a problem. The adjusted cash flow tax would require explicit, transparent laws and regulations.

China's current plans seem to lean toward the introduction of royalties or severance taxes to appropriate rents. Suitable allowances for costs, both current and capital, should be made, in order to closely mimic the pure rent tax. Production taxes could be used, however, to address the negative externalities of exploitation, in which case the adjustment in exploitation profile is desired. For such taxes, no deduction of costs should be allowed.

Although the assignment of tax revenues is in the end a political decision on how much autonomy localities are allowed to have, a number of arguments favor giving the local government at least a share of the resource tax revenues. Local governments need compensation for the negative externalities natural resource exploitation brings with it and need incentives to develop local infrastructure needed for development. The negative externalities from production could best be addressed with a local production tax. However, as long as the local branches of the State Tax Bureau act, de facto, as local tax bureaus, a substantial stake for local government seems desirable for tax effort reasons. The local government's share can be established in two ways: (1) through a share in a nationally determined tax or (2) by a locally determined rate or surcharge on a nationally determined tax base. Which should be chosen depends on the overall direction China's tax system takes.

For rent taxation, the tax rates and bases should be determined by national tax laws, in order to avoid suboptimal rate setting by localities. However, for product taxes used to internalize externalities, local rate setting would be an option, in the context of national guidelines.

Local assignment of resource tax revenues in any form makes a sound system of fiscal equalization among localities all the more urgent. Different assignment of shares in natural resource taxation among provinces for equalization purposes seems undesirable. Rather, China should in the reform of the intergovernmental fiscal relations provide for a broad-based equalization scheme, with objective criteria for eligibility and contributions. If this policy is established, differential rates per locality as they exist now should be abandoned. To counter possible procyclical effects of local resource revenues, China's government should consider regulated local access to the capital market.

Independent of the tax chosen to appropriate rents for government, and independent of the assignment of the tax over levels of government, resource exploitation enterprises should be subject to the other taxes levied in the Chinese tax system, in order not to distort the allocation of investment among sectors. Furthermore, the arrangements made for resource taxation should be stable, transparent, and consistently applied over all projects, although actual rates may differ due to the characteristics of individual projects. The room for costly negotiations and rent seeking should, however, be minimized. Stability and predictability are essential for investments in long-gestation projects, such as natural resource exploitation. These arguments argue for a strong legal basis for resource taxation.

References

Boadway, Robin, and Frank Flatters, "The Taxation of Natural Resources: Principles and Policy Issues," Policy Research Working Paper, WPS 1210 (Washington: World Bank, 1993).

Conrad, Robert F., and Zmarak Shalizi, "A Framework for the Ananlysis of Mineral Tax Policy in Sub-Sharan Africa," Policy, Planning, and Research Working Papers, WPS 90 (Washington: World Bank, 1988).

Dasgupta, Partha, and G.M. Heal, *Economic Theory and Exhaustible Resources* (Welwyn, England: J. Nisbet, 1979).

Heaps, Terry, and John F. Helliwell, "The Taxation of Natural Resources," Chapter 8 in *Handbook of Public Economics*, by Alan J. Auerbach and Martin S. Feldstein (Amsterdam; New York: North-Holland, 1993).

Miezowski, Peter M., and Eric Toder, "Taxation of Energy Resources, in *Fiscal Federalism and the Taxation of Natural Resources*, ed. by Charles E. McLure and Peter M. Miezkowski (Lexington, Massachusetts: Lexington Books, 1983).

Musgrave, Richard A., "Who Should Tax, Where, and What?" in *Tax Assignment in Federal Countries*, ed. by Charles E. McLure, Jr. (Canberra: Centre for Federal Financial Relations, The Australian National University, 1983).

Nellor, David C.L., and Emil M. Sunley, "Taxation of Mineral and Petroleum Resources" (mimeograph, Washington: International Monetary Fund, 1993).

Oates, Wallace E., *Fiscal Federalism* (London: Harcourt Brace Jovanovich, 1972).

Scott, Anthony, *Central Government Claims to Natural Resources,* Occasional Paper, No. 8 (Canberra: Centre for Research on Federal Financial Relations, The Australian National University, 1978).

Tietenberg, Thomas H., *Environmental and Natural Resource Economics* (New York: Harper Collins, 3rd ed. 1992).

World Bank, *Price Reform in China*, Report No. 1041–CHA (Washington: World Bank, May 1992).

Grants and Transfers

14

Theory and Practice of Intergovernmental Transfers

Anwar Shah*

The design of intergovernmental transfers in developing countries is often a contributing factor to fiscal imbalances at subnational levels and an impediment to efficient and equitable provision of public services. The structure of these transfers in developing countries usually emerges from ad hoc decisions without adequate consideration of economic criteria and political and social objectives of member units. Thus, basic principles of equity, benefit-cost spillovers, allocative efficiency within government, autonomy, certainty in planning, ease of administration, transparency, neutrality toward grantsmanship, consistency with federal and state objectives, equalization, and so on, often do not receive adequate attention in grant design. Reform of fiscal arrangements at the federal-state and state-local level could be an important step in fiscal adjustment and finding a long-term solution to the twin problems of subnational deficit and debt reduction. Intergovernmental fiscal transfers are also often the single most important source of revenue for state and local governments in most developing countries, and, as a result, they play an important role in shaping expenditure priorities and have implications for the fiscal health, autonomy, and tax effort of recipient governments and for the efficiency and equity of public services provision.

This paper provides a selective survey of the theory and practice of intergovernmental transfers with a view to developing a broad agenda for reform. It discusses the economic rationale for intergovernmental transfers and its implications for the design of transfers. Issues and options in the design of equalization programs to reduce regional fiscal

---

*The World Bank.

disparities are also presented. Existing mechanisms for fiscal transfers in selected developing countries are also reviewed.

Economic Rationale for Intergovernmental Transfers

Five main economic reasons are suggested as economic rationale for grants (see Boadway, Roberts, and Shah (1993)).

(1) *Fiscal imbalance.* Unmatched revenue means and expenditure needs at various levels—a fiscal gap—create structural imbalances resulting in revenue shortfall usually for lower-level government. Reasons for this imbalance are:

- Inappropriate expenditure and tax assignment.
- Limited or unproductive tax bases available to lower levels of government, making tax rates inefficiently high.
- Regional tax competition among state and local governments fearful of losing capital, labor, and business to other jurisdictions.
- Level of federal government taxation limiting state and local revenue-raising potential.

To correct problems associated with the first two kinds of imbalance, joint occupancy of some tax fields or decentralization of some taxes are advocated. Unconditional grants or revenue sharing based on the principle of origin are also appropriate solutions. To deal with tax competition, a higher revenue effort by the federal government and unconditional grants are required. Finally, to deal with the last type of imbalance some form of tax abatement by the federal government is necessary to provide more tax room in fields jointly occupied with the lower levels of government.

(2) *Minimum standards of services.* For certain services, expenditure assignment to state and local governments may be based on efficiency of public service provision and responsiveness to local needs and concerns, even though it may conflict with national equity and efficiency objectives. Musgrave (1976) argues that the redistributive role of the public sector is best performed by the federal government. In a federation, mobility of factors severely limits the redistributive role of local governments; New York City is a prime example. Redistributive policies adopted by the city in the 1970s created a major fiscal crisis, and the federal government had to reverse these policies to restore the financial health of the city.

Some public services typically assigned to state and local governments for efficient accountability are strongly redistributive. Social insurance, health care, education, and welfare are examples of such services. Health and educational services are quasi-private goods and in terms of technological efficiency are best provided by the private sector. In the United States, health care is by and large treated as a private good. Some economists have advocated private provision of health and education services in developing countries based on this view of economic efficiency. Such a viewpoint completely ignores information asymmetries such as moral hazard and adverse selection. Fiscal federalism literature argues that informational inefficiencies alone do not provide a convincing case for the public provision of health care and education.

Most governments treat health care as a fundamental public responsibility and strive to provide these services on a uniform basis because they are considered redistributions in kind. The case for public provision of these services primarily rests on equity objectives. For example, the incidence of disease is directly correlated with the incidence of poverty and inversely with economic well-being. Thus, public finance and provision of health care enhances the redistributive role of the public sector. Similarly, public education, by improving access for the poor, serves to further equality of opportunity. The relative importance of expenditures on health, education, and social services further suggests that redistribution by the tax system or direct cash transfers pale in comparison with the in-kind redistribution made possible by public services.

In a federal system, lower-level provision of such services—while desirable for efficiency, preference matching, and accountability—create difficulties in fulfilling federal equity objectives. Factor mobility and tax competition create strong incentives for lower-level governments to underprovide such services and to restrict access to those most in need, such as the poor or the old. This is justified by their greater susceptibility to disease and potentially greater risks for cost curtailment. Such perverse incentives can be alleviated by conditional selective nonmatching grants from the federal government. Such grants do not affect local government incentives for cost efficiency but ensure compliance with federally specified standards for access and level of services.

A second justification for common minimum standards for public services in a federation is based on economic efficiency. Common minimum standards help reduce interregional barriers to factor and goods mobility and thereby contribute to efficiency gains. Establishing minimum standards for social services encourages labor mobility and for infrastructure capital, factors and goods mobility. Boadway (1992) has emphasized that harmonization of expenditures improves gains from interregional trade and helps foster a common internal market.

Common minimum standards for public services across different states can be encouraged through conditional nonmatching or conditional closed ended matching programs. Conditional nonmatching programs are preferred because they are nonobtrusive, allowing state governments to spend grant monies as they choose so long as they meet certain minimum standards of service and access. The higher-level government simply monitors compliance with these standards.

(3) *Interjurisdictional spillovers.* Intergovernmental transfers can be used to increase the efficiency of providing public goods and services. Their major contribution is to correct inefficiencies arising from interjurisdictional spillovers. Spillovers usually occur because the benefits of a locally provided good or service itself spill beyond the local jurisdiction to benefit those not contributing to the costs (air and water pollution control, locally educated students who relocate) and because nonresidents enjoy the services provided (parks; cultural, recreational, and transportation facilities; state universities; state welfare and health care systems). In planning and administering such benefits, state and local governments consider their own benefits and therefore under-provide public services. To compensate, governments may redraw jurisdictional boundaries or create separate jurisdictions for each service (McMillan (1975)), but intergovernmental transfers are often the most practical means of alleviating the inefficiencies of spillovers. Open-ended conditional matching grants that modify relative prices are the most appropriate kind of transfers for implementing these corrections. The extent of cost sharing by the higher level of government should be consistent with the degree of spillover.

(4) *Differential net fiscal benefits across states.* Net fiscal benefits vary from state to state for a number of reasons:

- Some states have more valuable natural resources and therefore better access to an enlarged revenue base.
- Some states or localities have relatively higher incomes and therefore greater ability to raise revenues from existing bases.
- Some states or localities have inherited higher-cost disability factors (low thresholds for economies of scale, difficult terrain) or higher-need factors (greater proportion of young, old, or poor).

The presence of differential net fiscal benefits encourages fiscally induced migration. Labor and capital may move to areas with positive net fiscal benefits for fiscal considerations alone. In the process, negative externalities, such as unemployment, imposed on the jurisdictions they leave and enter may be ignored. The result of fiscally induced migration is that too many of the factors will move, creating social and economic problems in resource-rich areas. Factor movement in response to fiscal considerations alone creates inefficiency. Treating identical persons differently by the public sector in various states creates inequity. National welfare is reduced by the externalities imposed by fiscally induced migration.

Fiscal equalization grants to eliminate or reduce differential net fiscal benefits across states can enhance the efficiency and equity of a federal system. An ideal form of such transfer is an interstate revenue pool providing negative and positive equalization grants to member states such that net transfers equal zero. Thus, the program by design becomes self-financing. Such a grant system must be unconditional and must not reward strategic behavior to enhance positive grant entitlement or minimize negative transfer by member states. Thus, grant design must incorporate factors over which states have little control. The German system is a fraternal one of equalization among the German states; the federal government simply acts as an observer and occasionally as a mediator. The Canadian and Australian systems are federal programs that are not self-financing. The Canadian system attempts to augment the fiscal capacity of member provinces up to a five-province standard. The system measures the fiscal capacity of a state by the revenue that could be raised in that state if it employed all of the standard revenue sources at the average intensity of use nationwide. The Australian system analyzes expenditure needs as well.

Another infrequently mentioned objective of these transfers is to advance stabilization policies of the federal government.

(5) *Stabilization objectives.* Intergovernmental transfers can also be used to help achieve economic stabilization objectives. Grants could increase during periods of slack economic activity to encourage local expenditure and diminish during the upswing of the economic cycle. Capital grants would be a suitable instrument for this purpose. Care must be exercised in ensuring that funds are available for operating expenditures associated with such initiatives.

Criteria for Design of Intergovernmental Fiscal Arrangements

Autonomy. Subnational governments should have complete independence and flexibility in setting priorities and should not be constrained by the categorical structure of programs and uncertainty associated with decision making at the center. Tax-base sharing, that is, allowing subnational governments to introduce their own tax rates on central bases, formula-based revenue sharing, and block grants, is consistent with this objective.

Revenue adequacy. Subnational governments should have adequate revenues to discharge designated responsibilities.

Equity. Allocated funds should vary directly with fiscal need factors and inversely with the taxable capacity of each province.

Predictability. The grant mechanism should ensure predictability of subnational government shares by publishing five-year projections of funding availability.

Efficiency. The grant design should be neutral on subnational government choices of resource allocation to different sectors or different types of activity. The current system of transfers in countries such as Indonesia and Sri Lanka to finance lower-level public sector wages contravenes this criterion (Shah (1990)).

Simplicity. The subnational government's allocation should be based on objective factors for which individual units would have little control, and the formula should be easy to comprehend so that "bargaining" for grants is not rewarded, as appears to occur with plan assistance in Pakistan and India.

Incentive. The proposed design should provide incentives for sound fiscal management and discourage inefficient practices. There should be no specific transfers to finance the deficits of subnational governments. The current system of central transfers to finance subnational government deficits in India, South Africa, and Sri Lanka, and state transfers for the same purpose in Malaysia, clearly violate this criterion.

Safeguard of grantor's objectives. The grant design should ensure that certain well-defined objectives of the grantor are properly adhered to by the grant recipients. This is accomplished by proper monitoring, joint progress reviews, and providing technical assistance, or by designing a selective matching transfer program.

It is quite obvious that various criteria specified above could be in conflict with each other and, therefore, a grantor would have to assign priorities to various factors in comparing various policy alternatives.

Intergovernmental Transfers in Practice

In general, the existing design of grants in developing countries is not consistent with economic principles enumerated earlier.

General nonmatching transfers, tax base sharing, and revenue-sharing mechanisms to deal with fiscal gaps. Revenue-sharing mechanisms are used in a number of countries but tax base sharing has generally not been tried. Revenue-sharing mechanisms vary considerably. In Brazil,

India, and Nigeria, for example, complex grant allocation formulas are employed using factors such as population, per capita income, school enrollments, backwardness (India), and "minimum responsibilities" (Nigeria) indices. In other countries the criteria are quite simple; for example, Mexico and Pakistan use population and derivation (point of collection), while Malaysia and China use derivation as the primary basis for revenue allocation. General unconditional transfers are not popular, but deficit grants have been tried in a number of countries, including India, Pakistan, South Africa, Malaysia, and the former Soviet Union.

Conditional nonmatching or equal per capita transfers to ensure minimum standards of service across the country. Few such transfers are used in developing countries. Central government transfers to provincial and local governments in Indonesia and the capitation grant to Malaysian states come close to the concept of such a transfer.

Benefit spillover compensation using selective open-ended matching transfers. Although benefit-cost spillover is a serious factor in a number of countries, such transfers have not yet been implemented in any developing country.

Equalization transfers to reduce or eliminate differential net fiscal benefits among subnational governments. Despite serious horizontal fiscal imbalances in a number of countries, explicit equalization programs are untried, although equalization objectives are implicitly attempted in the general revenue-sharing mechanisms used in India, Pakistan, Brazil, Mexico, and Nigeria. These mechanisms typically combine diverse and conflicting objectives into the same formula and fall significantly short on individual objectives. Because these formulas lack explicit equalization standards, they fail to address regional equity objectives satisfactorily.

Conditional open-ended matching transfers to encourage certain expenditures. Generally, open-ended matching transfers are not in use in developing countries although India, Pakistan, and Malaysia use conditional closed-end matching transfers.

Revenue-Sharing Mechanisms

In Brazil, one of the main instruments for federal-state revenue sharing is the State Participation Fund. The federal government transfers a specified share of certain federal taxes to a pool, and the Council of States determines state shares using a formula that incorporates population and per capita income as its main components. A proposal currently under discussion extends the components to include such factors as land area, interstate trade, and fiscal effort. In recent years, shares determined by this formula have been unacceptable to the Council, which has resorted to a compromise allocation based on an arbitrary adjustment to formula shares.

The principal merits of this program are the consistency of its design with objectives of transparency, predictability, and local autonomy. The program addresses some fiscal equalization objectives but has design flaws that inhibit achievement of its objectives. For example, one measure of fiscal capacity is state per capita income; this is an imperfect guide to the ability of a state government to raise taxes, because a significant proportion of income can accrue to nonresident owners of factors of production. Furthermore, only a small portion of total state revenues is raised from income taxes. Estimates of state per capita income are subject to significant errors and are available with a long lag. For example, estimates are available only through 1980. These difficulties diminish the usefulness of per capita income as a determinator in a program of fundamental importance to federal-state fiscal relations.

The State Participation Fund further combines diverse and sometimes conflicting objectives, such as revenue sharing and fiscal equalization at the state level, into a single formula in a multiplicative manner and therefore falls significantly short on individual objectives. The program is redistributive in its overall impact but does not assure consistency of individual state shares with the formula objectives, so states with similar fiscal capacity receive widely different entitlements. Since the formula lacks an explicit equalization standard, it also fails to address regional equity objectives satisfactorily. These failings explain why the Council of States finds it easier to strike political compromises rather than accept results of the formula.

The program to channel federal revenue-sharing monies to municipalities is the Municipal Participation Fund (FPM). This program considers municipal population and state per capita income to determine the shares for individual municipalities. The program has two major drawbacks: first, the formula for the program fails to incorporate differential fiscal capacity of the municipalities in a meaningful way, and therefore does not result in a fair and equitable distribution of funds. Because there is no local income tax in Brazil (and none is called for because of capital and labor mobility), per capita income is a poor indicator of a local government's ability to raise revenues. Furthermore, in each state, rich and poor municipalities exist side by side: state per capita income, by definition, cannot distinguish between the two classes. Second, this program discourages local fiscal efforts by meeting nearly two thirds of municipal revenue requirements from federal reve-

nue sources. Such overwhelming dependence by municipal governments on outside revenues creates a dichotomy between spending and
revenue raising decisions, and contributes to reduced financial accountability at the local level.

In 1990, Mexico restructured its assistance to states and municipalities, allocating 18.1 percent of sharable federal revenues to a general
fund, 6.5 percent of sharable federal revenues, until 1997, to a contingency fund, and 2 percent of sharable federal revenues to a municipal
fund. The allocation criteria for the general fund give equal weight to
population and previous state shares adjusted by annual increases in
federally administered excises on petroleum, motor vehicles, alcohol
and tobacco, and locally administered water charges and property
charges. The contingency fund is designed to compensate states that
lose allocated funding through this restructuring. The municipal fund
uses an inverse of the allocation for the general fund to provide states
with pass-through funds intended for final distribution to their municipalities. Using population as a criterion for determining general fund
revenues is a welcome change, because it enhances autonomy and equity objectives. Reliance on adjusted historical shares to allocate remaining funds perpetuates anomalies created by high petroleum
revenues accruing to certain states in the early 1980s, and will clearly
favor oil-rich states. The municipal fund makes only a minor contribution toward rectifying this problem.

Nigeria shares 45 percent of federal revenues with states and municipalities. Ninety-five percent of revenue shared with states uses minimum responsibilities—population, primary school enrollment, and
internal revenue effort—as formula factors; the remaining 5 percent is
distributed to mineral-producing states on the basis of origin. Transfers
to municipalities are based on equal shares (25 percent to recognize
minimum needs) and population (75 percent). Several aspects, equalization to a standard and instability associated with resource revenues,
require further attention in fine-tuning existing revenue-sharing arrangements. The former can be addressed by adopting some form of
the representative tax system and the latter by establishing an oil fund
managed jointly by the federal and state governments.

In India, a significant proportion of revenues is returned using population and some measure of income relative to the average; therefore,
some degree of implicit equalization is attempted by the formulas. Because the formulas embody factors to get a handle on multiple objectives, the extent to which each of the objectives is accomplished
requires further analysis. The formulas do not pay any special attention to fiscal capacity (revenue means) of individual states in grant
determination.

In Pakistan, revenue sharing is based on population and revenue collection by origin. Equalization to a standard by considering the revenue means of the provinces has not yet been tried.

In Papua New Guinea, minimum unconditional grants are based on expenditures in the base year, fiscal year 1976. Some revenues are shared using the derivation principle. It is not clear why base-year expenditures should be consistent with the priorities and economic-demographic dynamics two decades later.

In the Philippines, population, land area, equal shares, and derivation are factors used to determine revenue-sharing allocations. While the factors are objective and reasonable, they do not correct for horizontal imbalances. Revenue-raising potential of subnational governments should be incorporated into the formulas.

Federal Transfers

In a federation, specific-purpose transfers support important policy objectives; benefit spillover compensation; bridge fiscal gaps; ensure minimum standards of public services across the nation; fulfill the redistributive function of the federal government; create a common internal market; reduce net fiscal benefits across jurisdictions; and achieve economic stabilization objectives. In most cases, grant objectives determine grant design.

In developing countries, funds for specific-purpose transfers are usually distributed in an ad hoc manner, at the discretion of the central government. The practice of intergovernmental transfers is, therefore, at variance with the economic principles enunciated above and significant opportunities exist for the reform of these arrangements in developing as well as in transitional economies.

In Brazil, the federal and state governments engage in many specific-purpose programs or "convenios." For many of these programs, program objectives are typically not specified or are specified vaguely, and in some instances, grant objectives are determined after funds are released. In recent years, specific-purpose transfers have increasingly served not to safeguard federal objectives but as vehicles for pork-barrel politics, and only a handful of programs have desirable features. One such program is for unified, decentralized health care, in which federal financing is provided to achieve certain minimum standards of health care across the nation. The intent of this program is for the federal government to specify policies and for state and local governments to implement federally mandated programs. In practice, however, the federal government is heavily involved in program administration, and decentralization has not been fully achieved. The existing program also gives preferential treatment to private contractors over state and local government agencies. New fiscal arrangements are likely to constrain federal funding for this program.

Bangladesh offers a number of closed end matching and nonmatching grants for upgrading infrastructure, with allocation based upon verifiable indicators of general assistance. These grants provide general budgetary support to lower-level governments rather than special incentives for higher spending on infrastructure, as matching rates are small and nonbinding. Bangladesh also provides budget deficit grants that create incentives for running higher deficits.

India offers specific-purpose grants that provide assistance to relatively less prosperous states and encourage tax efforts at subnational levels. The complex review and approval processes work against some of these goals. India also provides budget deficit grants.

In Indonesia, central grants currently finance about 64.9 percent of expenditure at the provincial level and 71.4 percent of expenditure at the district level. There are two kinds of transfers: block grants, for general purpose local spending subject to some broad central guidelines; and specific grants, for expenditure on uses specified by the center and subject to relatively detailed central controls. The former include sectoral block transfers to each of the three main levels of local government: provinces, districts, and villages. The latter include a transfer that covers virtually all local government personnel expenses, and sectoral transfers for specific development expenditures on roads, primary schools, public health centers, and reforestation. As part of its policy of gradual decentralization, the Government has incrementally raised the share of block grants in total transfers (it increased from 15.9 percent in 1986/87 to 20.3 percent in 1993/94) and has also allowed local governments somewhat greater flexibility in the use of some specific grants.

There are several positive features in the design of the Indonesian intergovernmental grant system: the distribution of grants is transparent, determined by formulas utilizing objective criteria; the structure of grants is simple, as both the grants and the criteria used for distribution are few in number; and the grants achieve an overall equalizing effect on regional revenue availabilities. In its transparency and simplicity, the Indonesian grant system compares favorably with the grants systems typically found in other developing countries.

Nonetheless, there are several improvements to consider in the design of the Indonesian grant system that would allow it to achieve its efficiency and equity objectives more effectively. First, the recent trend toward increasing the share of block grants in total grants should continue. Second, regional disparities in overall fiscal capacities (revenue-raising potential) could be better reflected in the distribution formulas for block grants, by including a fiscal capacity equalization factor. The criteria currently used for distribution, area, population, or equal shares, all focus primarily on capturing the differential needs of local administrations. Better capturing of differential fiscal capacities to meet those needs would contribute to making the distribution of grants more equitable.

Third, an element of incentive to local governments to improve their own revenue effort could be included in the grant allocation formulas (the present set of criteria do not include such an incentive element). This could be achieved by supplementing the fiscal capacity indicator by one and capturing the extent to which that capacity is actually being utilized. Appropriately designed matching grants could also stimulate the local revenue effort (the Indonesian grant system includes only a very limited matching element). Fourth, the SDO grant could be consolidated with the general purpose block grants to the respective levels of government. As presently designed, this grant creates strong incentives for a higher government employment/wage bill at the local level. The center tries to circumvent this perverse incentive by retaining major control over government employment at all levels, but this undermines local autonomy and flexibility in allocating budgetary resources between personnel and other expenditures.

Fifth, the main improvement that can be made in the specific sectoral grants is to continue the shift toward using broad guidelines rather than detailed controls and physical targets in influencing the use of these grants. The allocation criteria for these grants are broadly appropriate, as they adequately serve their main objective (ensuring minimum standards of the targeted basic services across regions); one improvement would be to change the allocation of the reforestation grant from a project to a formula basis, as is done for the other specific sectoral grants. Sixth, consideration could be given to assigning provinces a role in the allocation of central grants to the lower levels, by making some of the grants pass through them. The rationale for doing so is that provinces are better placed than the center, especially in a large and diverse country, to assess the needs and fiscal capacities of individual lower-level jurisdictions.

In Malaysia, most transfers are based upon objective criteria except for deficit grants through the state reserve fund, which are only granted in exceptional circumstances.

In Mexico, criteria specific-purpose transfers lack transparent criteria and have often been mired in political controversy and debate.

Nigeria has a mixed record on the design of transfers. Some specific-purpose grants to states follow objective criteria, and the federal government sets standards of service to be achieved. Other programs lack any transparency in the allocation of funds. In China, Colombia, the Philippines, and Thailand, specific-purpose grants lack transparent criteria for allocation.

In Pakistan, federal transfers have worked as vehicles for federal bureaucratic control over provincial spending priorities. Most central transfers do not consider objectives, fiscal needs, or relative fiscal capacities at the provincial level. Examples include deficit grants (discontinued in 1992), which encouraged provinces to run higher deficits in order to have a greater claim on central resources, or education grants, to finance provincial expenditures above their 1983 level, that encourage excessive spending. Most are capital grants with no provision for financing maintenance expenditures. As a consequence, the grant structure encourages capital-intensive technology, which deteriorates because of inadequate funds for upkeep. Central grants are unpredictable and discourage long-term planning at lower levels. Economic criteria, efficiency, equity, spillover compensation, and autonomy are not usually recognized in current grant programs, but additional provincial spending and bargaining for grants is rewarded.

State-Municipal Transfers

The same economic principles govern state-municipal fiscal relations as those for center-state fiscal relations. In many countries, local governments are simply extensions of state governments and are subject to a high degree of interference and control. In turn, the dependence of local governments on state transfers is usually greater than the dependence of states on central transfers. In industrial nations, local governments typically account for more than 20 percent of general government spending and finance, with less than 30 percent of their expenditures coming from higher-level transfers. Property taxes are the mainstay of local governments, which also rely heavily on local income taxes.

In developing countries, local governments typically account for less than 10 percent of consolidated general government spending but derive more than two thirds of their revenues from higher-level transfers. In some instances, increased revenue-sharing transfers contribute to reduced local tax effort. For example, in the early 1980s, Mexico more than doubled its transfers to municipal governments and gave them exclusive access to property tax revenues. Nearly half of these transfers were directed to increased local expenditures; the rest were used as tax relief to municipal residents. As a result, municipal reliance on self-generated revenue declined from 75 percent of total spending in 1980 to 40 percent in 1984. In Brazil, high federal transfers to municipal governments in 1989 and 1990 also led to a lower tax effort (Shah (1991)). In many countries, the property tax is a state responsibility with proceeds shared with local governments and sometimes with the central government. The property tax is generally not a productive revenue source because its base can be eroded by exemptions and dated assessments. In principle, it should be easy for state governments to structure their transfers to local governments objectively, in view of easy access to their economic data. In practice, state transfers to local governments are arbitrary and discretionary. Only a few countries—Brazil, India, and Nigeria—have made serious attempts to structure at least part of their assistance in a nondiscretionary fashion.

Borrowing by local governments remains a major issue in most developing countries, where local governments are not permitted to borrow in credit markets and must rely on transfers for undertaking capital investments. This is an area where possibilities exist for autonomous bodies to supervise and assist local borrowing for capital projects. State governments can establish municipal finance corporations or a municipal loan council to provide technical assistance in project selection and appraisal and to assist in securing loans on preferred terms with state guarantees.

Except for Brazil and Mexico, information on state-local transfers is scant and not suited to detailed analysis. In Brazil, state-municipal transfers have two important components. One is the constitutionally mandated state-municipal, revenue-sharing arrangements, or state-municipal tax transfers. For the most part, distribution of such transfers follows the origin principle: 75 percent of municipal share of state value-added tax revenues are distributed in proportion to the value added in each municipality. For the remaining 25 percent, states have discretion to incorporate other fiscal need factors; population and area are the most common. Some states have also used fiscal effort as a special factor. A major criticism of the existing arrangement is that current formulas do not address fiscal equalization by varying a proportion of funds inversely with fiscal capacity (municipal tax bases). In fact, municipal tax bases hardly enter into consideration. The fiscal effort component is usually poorly designed, benefiting larger municipalities without regard for their fiscal effort.

A second component of state transfers to municipalities is specific-purpose or negotiated transfers. Most states have a large number of "convenios"—usually thousands—to provide project assistance. The sheer number of these transfers defies analysis, but anecdotal evidence suggests that political considerations dominate in the distribution of grant funds.

In Mexico, several states use the derivation principle, while others follow the former revenue-sharing formula of the United States, which varies grant funds directly with population and tax effort and inversely with per capita income. Municipal fiscal capacity is not considered in these formulas, and in some states, grant allocation is arbitrary. In many states, criteria for allocating grants are approved by state legislatures annually, making it difficult for municipalities to carry out a long-term projection of revenues and expenditures.

Concluding Remarks

Industrial countries offer examples of grant programs that recognize some of the economic principles discussed above. German experience suggests that a well-thought-out revenue-sharing system can obviate the need for many specific-purpose transfers. Canadian federal transfers for health and postsecondary education recognize the redistributive, in-kind nature of these public services and provide per capita transfers to provinces conditional on universal access to these services. Canadian experience with federal equalization transfers based on the representative tax system approach suggests that an objective equalization program that helps members establish minimum standards of basic services can endure and strengthen the federation. Australian experience with equalization is also instructive but much more difficult to replicate elsewhere.

The U.S. experience with road transportation assistance holds important lessons in structuring specific-purpose transfers. The program used objective indicators of need in allocating funds among states and established matching provisions to induce local participation.

Switzerland provides spillover compensation and equalization transfers to its cantons (Dafflon (1990)). The Canadian provinces and Australia (the U.K. and Victoria Grants Commission) use objective criteria in their transfers to local governments (Shah (1988)). Many of these models can be readily implemented in developing countries, and ample conceptual and practical guidance is available on the design of these transfers. Specific circumstances in each developing country require tailoring and adapting this guidance. Few developing countries have devoted serious attention to the design of these transfers, and therefore monumental and important work lies ahead.

Blueprint for Restructure and Reform

In this section, the major results of the previous sections are brought together to provide an overview. An analyses of fiscal systems in developing or transitional economies reveals certain common themes.

Fiscal federalism literature states that every objective specified by a granting authority requires a different form of grant. For example,

- To deal with fiscal deficiencies arising from expenditure needs being greater than revenue means that nonmatching transfers, changes in taxing responsibilities, or revenue-sharing mechanisms are needed.
- To address differential net fiscal benefits across jurisdictions or horizontal fiscal imbalances, general equalization transfers are needed.
- To compensate for benefit spillover, open-ended matching transfers are needed with the matching rate determined by the benefit-spillout ratio.
- To ensure minimum standards of services across the nation, conditional nonmatching transfers are needed.
- To stimulate public expenditures in areas with high national but low local priority, conditional open-ended matching transfers are needed.

A review of grant objectives and design in developing or transitional economies suggests that for the most part such conceptual guidance continues to be ignored.

Tax-base and revenue-sharing mechanisms are customarily used to address fiscal imbalances or disparities arising from constitutional assignment of taxes and expenditures to different levels of government. Tax-base sharing means that two or more levels of government levy rates on a common base. Tax-base determination usually rests with the higher-level government levying supplementary rates on the same base. Tax is collected by one level of government, generally the federal or central government in market economies and the local government in centrally planned economies, with proceeds shared upward or downward depending on agreements on revenue yields. Tax-base sharing is quite common in industrial countries and almost nonexistent in developing countries.

A second method of addressing vertical fiscal imbalances is revenue sharing, whereby one level of government has unconditional access to a specified share of revenues collected by another level of government. Revenue-sharing agreements typically specify how revenues are to be shared among federal and lower-level governments, with complex criteria for allocation and for eligibility and use of funds. Such limitations run counter to the underlying rationale of unconditionality. Yet revenue-sharing mechanisms are quite common in developing countries. They often address multiple objectives, such as equalization or regional development. If properly structured, specific-purpose transfers can support important policy objectives in a federation. Such objectives include:

- benefit spillover compensation, where the benefit area for public service is larger than the political jurisdiction;
- bridging fiscal gaps;
- ensuring minimum standards of public services across the nation;
- fulfilling the redistributive function of the federal government;
- creating common internal markets; and
- reducing net fiscal benefits across jurisdictions and achieving stabilization objectives.

Grant objectives should determine grant design. Almost without exception, a typical developing country has many specific-purpose programs for which objectives are either not specified or specified vaguely. In some instances, grant objectives are reviewed only after the release of funds.

There are some obvious reasons for this state of affairs. Central governments can exercise complete discretion over these funds without any accountability. Enhanced flexibility is achieved at the cost of transparency, objectivity, and accountability, and specific-purpose grant programs are used for local political expediency rather than in the pursuit of key national objectives. Some specific-purpose grant programs are structured to provide perverse economic incentives. For example, several developing countries provide transfers to cover deficits or public sector wages at subnational levels. Such grants—contrary to the intentions of the grantor—encourage lowering taxation efforts, thereby raising deficits and spending on public sector wages in order to qualify for higher grants. A review of these grant programs should be high on any agenda for public sector reform.

The most striking observation to come from this review is that despite simplicity and practicability of design and a high priority in most countries for limiting interregional fiscal disparities, not a single developing or transitional economy has adopted a program of equalization transfers to disadvantaged subnational governments that takes into consideration their fiscal capacities in determination of their entitlements. More sophisticated attempts at equalization have been adopted in Brazil, India, and Nigeria, but design flaws have made them less successful. Although the formulas adopted by these countries lack explicit equalization standards and fail to address regional equity objectives satisfactorily, most countries do not even attempt to go as far.

Federal-local and state-local transfers in most developing countries need major restructuring. In none of the countries reviewed here do these transfers consider the fiscal capacity or revenue potential of local governments. Allocation of funds is usually on an ad hoc discretionary basis—negating transparency, predictability, and autonomy objectives. Major increases in revenue-sharing funds from national governments to municipalities in Brazil and Mexico have reduced local tax efforts. The cause may be failure to recognize fiscal capacity (tax bases for municipal sources) and inappropriate design of fiscal components in the allocation formulas. Furthermore, the government of a large country usually does not have the administrative capacity to monitor finances of individual municipalities closely, making a weak case for direct federal transfers to local governments. Such transfers should naturally be the responsibility of state governments. State governments can likewise restructure their transfers to local governments objectively, since they have easy access to local economic and fiscal data. Recognizing municipal taxable capacity would also help the state level monitor utilization of local revenue bases, thereby offering corrective action on a timely basis. Much useful guidance on restructuring these transfers is available from the experience of industrial countries.

Reform of intergovernmental fiscal relations requires complementary adaptations in the institutional arrangements for intergovernmental coordination, planning, budgeting, and implementation. Intergovernmental coordination and consultation are critical to improved public sector management. This could be accomplished through regular meetings of officials. The structure of transfers should be periodically reviewed either by intergovernmental committees or by autonomous grant commissions. For decentralized institutions to succeed, it is important to loosen the grip of central planning over subnational governments. Such planning imposes a central view of public investment requirements at local levels and often works as an impediment to innovative responses to local issues by local governments. In general, it is best to avoid detailed central control over local government use of funds and financial management. Instead, there is need to strengthen higher-level monitoring and audit of lower-level government performance. These functions are often conducted by several agencies in an uncoordinated fashion. Consolidation of these tasks in a single agency would improve effectiveness of these audits and inspections.

Decentralization of responsibilities and rationalization of intergovernmental transfers must be further supported by the strengthening of institutional capacities at the local level. Higher-level governments can play a crucial role in this capacity-building effort by identifying training needs, offering training programs, facilitating staff transfers, providing guidance on organizational structure and management issues, and providing technical assistance and operational tools for use of personnel management and service planning, monitoring, and delivery.

In conclusion, there is now universal recognition that the way taxing, spending, and regulatory authorities are determined and the manner in which intergovernmental transfers are structured have an important bearing on the efficiency and equity of the provision of public services. Fortunately, much useful guidance in the design of intergovernmental fiscal relations in developing and transitional economies is available from the theoretical and practical literature on fiscal federalism. It is also apparent from a review of the developing country literature that very few developing countries have paid serious attention to this guidance in the design of their transfers. Making this guidance accessible to policymakers in developing countries and adapting it to suit individual developing country circumstances are essential. This paper takes a small step in this direction. Significant work lies ahead.

References

Boadway, Robin, *The Constitutional Division of Powers: An Economic Perspective* (Ottawa, Canada: Economic Council of Canada, 1992).

————, Sandra Roberts, and Anwar Shah, "The Reform of Fiscal Systems in Developing Countries: A Federalism Perspective," paper presented at the Conference on Fiscal Reform and Structural Change sponsored by the International Development Research Center and the Indian Statistical Institute at New Delhi, August 25–27, 1993.

Dafflon, Bernard, "Intergovernmental Equalization in Switzerland" (mimeograph, 1990).

McMillan, Melville, "Towards the More Optimal Provision of Local Public Goods: Internalization of Benefits and Grants." *Public Finance Quarterly* 3 (July, 1995), pp. 229–261.

Shah, Anwar, "Capitalization and the Theory of Local Public Finance: An Interpretive Essay," *Journal of Economic Surveys*, Vol. 2, No. 3 (1988), pp. 209–243.

————, "A Linear Expenditure System Estimation of Local Fiscal Response to Provincial Transportation Grants," *Journal of Economics and Business* (1989), pp. 150–168.

————, "Intergovernmental Fiscal Relations in Sri Lanka," paper presented at the 46th Congress of the International Institute of Public Finance, Brussels, August 27–30, 1990.

————, "The New Fiscal Federalism in Brazil," World Bank Discussion Paper Series, No. 124 (Washington: World Bank, 1991).

Musgrave, Richard, *Public Finance: in Theory and Practice* (Toronto: McGraw-Hill, Ryerson, 1987).

————, *Essays in Fiscal Federalism* (Washington: Brookings Institution, 1965).

15

Implementing and Managing Grants—
Institutional and Data Requirements

Ehtisham Ahmad, Jon Craig, and Dubravko Mihaljek*

The previous chapters have described the principles for the establishment of grants, along with illustrations from a number of diverse
countries. In this paper, we seek to describe the alternate administrative and institutional mechanisms that would be needed to determine
grants on an analytical basis and to list the main information flows
and data requirements that would be needed for effective management
of a grants mechanism.

Reformed Revenue-Sharing Arrangements

It is the intention of the Chinese government, as described in the
papers by Gao Qiang and Xu Shanda, to generate levers of macroeconomic control. Thus the new revenue-sharing system, to be implemented over time, requires that the share of the central government in
the total revenue collection increase from 40 percent to 60 percent. To
enhance the feasibility of the above measures, reforms would also have
to be introduced in the system of grants and transfers from the central
to local governments.[1]

While the revenue shares accruing to central and local governments
are likely to change over a relatively short period of time, changing
expenditure assignments and responsibilities may take somewhat
longer to implement. This is because clarity in expenditure assign-

---

*International Monetary Fund.

[1]Local governments in China are taken to refer to all subcentral levels of administration.

ments requires the completion of price reforms as well as the delineation of property rights—defining the role of the state—that would enable a more meaningful discussion of expenditure responsibilities at each level of government than at present. A flexible role for grants can be seen that would facilitate the required changes in revenue shares with the existing expenditure assignments, thus avoiding a major dislocation in investment and activity levels. The grants mechanism introduced should be capable of adapting to changing expenditure assignments over the medium term.

Options for Grants and Revenue Sharing

This subsection summarizes some key features of a grants and revenue-sharing system (see also Chapter 14), and the associated policy instruments available to a central government.

Some General Principles

The revenue and expenditure assignments adopted in a country may lead to deficits at various levels of government, which stem from inadequacy of *own* revenue sources assigned to a particular level of government. Such deficits are termed *vertical imbalances* (see Chapter 16, for an algebraic formulation). The estimation of vertical balances should be done against an established benchmark level of revenues and expenditures that smooths out short-term or cyclical fluctuations in revenues or expenditures. Grants (including tax-sharing arrangements) are needed to resolve differences in fiscal capacities between different levels of government.[2] Thus, deficits at some levels are compensated by surpluses at others, in a manner that meets the government's distributional and macroeconomic objectives.

In formulating grants and revenue-sharing arrangements, the central government's objectives may include efficiency in resource allocation,[3]

---

[2] Usually, it is the central government that has a *structural* surplus, with structural deficits at lower levels of government. However, some countries, such as Germany, display little or no vertical imbalances.

[3]In many countries, particular attention is given to regional spillovers of expenditure programs. The spillovers occur because the benefits of a locally provided good or service "spill" beyond the local jurisdiction, to benefit those not contributing to the costs (e.g., beneficiaries from control of air or water pollution and locally educated students who relocate) and because of migration from other regions to the locality (due to benefits of parks, cultural, recreational and transport facilities, regional universities, and, most important, regional health and welfare services). Regional governments usually consider only their own benefits and, because of such spillovers, underprovide public services, hence, yielding a case for supplementary central government grants.

support for backward regions, and assuring the equity of access of various regions to public services. In the short term, the central government may also seek to pursue stabilization goals, such as by making payments designed to offset regional differences in unemployment during a general downturn in activity.

The main transfer mechanisms used to tackle these various goals can be grouped into the following transfer categories (see also Chapter 14):

Conditional
- Matching grants
  open-ended or subject to limits
- Specific purpose grants
  open-ended or block grants

Unconditional
- Specific purpose grants
  open-ended or block grants
- General purpose equalization
  grants
- Revenue-sharing arrangements

The choice of transfer mechanism involves three choices. The first choice is whether the central government wishes to impose conditions on the use of funds, or the performance achieved in the programs, or both. Clearly, imposing conditions detracts from the autonomy of regional or local governments. It may be seen, however, as an essential means of imposing central government influence over spending for items of vital national concern (e.g., air or water pollution control) in areas that are primarily the responsibility of regional or local governments. Similarly, the central government may seek to attain national minimum standards in some areas of public concern (e.g., access to types of health or education programs). One of the major risks with conditionality is that it can distort decision making by lower-level governments, requiring them to allocate funds and administer programs in ways they would otherwise not do. In turn, this can lead to an absence of accountability for funds spent, resulting in waste and inefficiency. Conditionality thus places a heavy onus on the central government to specify its objectives clearly and ensure that it has the capacity to enforce and audit performance criteria.

Second, within the category of conditional transfers, the central government might require some matching of program funding by lower-level governments. While some cost sharing by lower-level governments may induce a greater effort in areas considered to be of particular importance by the central government, there is a risk that cost sharing will simply lead to lower expenditure elsewhere. If the objective is to boost net spending through incremental effort on particular programs, then it may be necessary to impose additional provisions to ensure that other spending is sustained. Such provisions are often difficult to enforce. A further disadvantage of matching arrangements is that they do not work well when there are large differences in the relative fiscal capacities of different regions. Matching may impose severe constraints on poorer regions, while richer regions can meet the requirements with little, if any, additional effort.

Third, within both conditional and unconditional transfer mechanisms, there is a choice of whether the grants should be open ended or subject to some limit. While open-ended grants may be favored by proponents of central government programs seeking to expand central government influence in areas of particular concern, budget control considerations often favor some limit on the size of grants.

An Equalization Framework?

A major question running through each of the choices outlined above is the degree of equalization of fiscal capacity that is to be attempted in a country. The objective is not to equalize regional incomes, but rather to equalize the *fiscal capacity* of each region to provide for a basic range of public services, taking into account its own revenue resources. Specifically, full equalization would require that each region should have the capacity to provide the same standard of public services as the other regions, provided it makes the same effort to raise revenue from its own sources and conducts its affairs with an average level of operational efficiency. This concept is known as *horizontal equity* across regions.

The absence of equalization grants in large and regionally diverse countries (particularly those with limited labor and capital mobility) may lead to a fracturing of a unified economic space, since local governments may be tempted to secure their own interests by erecting additional barriers to interregional trade. The United States is the only large industrial country that does not utilize explicit horizontal equalization; instead it relies on factor mobility (particularly for labor) to achieve the same objectives.

The relative importance attached to equalization can have a major bearing on the form of unconditional grants from the central government to lower-level governments. If a specific equalization goal is set, then two alternatives are available. First, an unconditional block "equalization" grant can be made from the center and distributed to regional governments on the basis of formulas that calculate regions' relative fiscal capacities. This is the approach used in Australia and Canada. Second, the equalization of fiscal capacities can be achieved through interregional grants from regions with above-average fiscal capacity to regions with below-average fiscal capacity. This approach is used in Germany.

Unconditional block grants from the center are generally to be favored when large vertical imbalances exist at lower levels of government. This is because efforts to resolve the vertical imbalance will inevitably have an impact on the horizontal fiscal capacities of different regional governments. In this context, it should be observed that revenue sharing on a derivation basis (i.e., according to amounts collected in each region) is equivalent to an unconditional transfer that does not equalize fiscal capacities across regions. Revenue-sharing arrangements on a derivation basis tend to favor relatively prosperous regions.

Interregional grants are favored where the vertical fiscal imbalances at different levels of government are small. Given the central government's limited ability to finance grants, horizontal balances are achieved by transfers from richer to poorer regions. Cooperative transfer arrangements, as in Germany, would be involved.

Regardless of the institutional approach used, a method of estimating equalization grants can be formulated (see Chapter 16 for an algebraic formulation).

International Perspectives

The extent of the transfer problem depends on the magnitude of the structural vertical fiscal imbalances at different levels of government. As Table 1 shows, there are substantial differences in these vertical balances in some major countries.

The industrial country experience covers a whole spectrum, from countries, such as Australia, with a large vertical imbalance favoring

Table 1. Vertical Imbalances in Some Countries, 1990

(Ratio of Own Source Revenues to Own Source Outlays)

	Level of Government		
	Central	State	Local
Australia	1.51	0.56	0.83
Brazil	0.84	0.77	0.27
Canada	1.11	0.88	0.53
Germany	1.09	0.98	0.74
India[1]	0.96	0.99	na
Switzerland	1.00	0.73	0.87
United States	0.92	1.26	0.66

Source: IMF, *Government Finance Statistics Yearbook* (Washington: IMF, 1993).
[1]Data relate to 1988.

the central government and requiring grants from the center to the regions, to those countries, such as Germany, which have small vertical imbalances with interregional (rather than central) transfer mechanisms to tackle horizontal equity and related issues.

In Australia, the major taxes accrue to the national government. As a result, about 75 percent of the national revenue is collected by the central government, and central expenditures account for only about half the national expenditures. Own account revenues of lower levels fall well short of the expenditures assigned to these levels of government in the Constitution. The vertical surplus at the center is then used to finance a wide array of function-specific and general revenue grants to the state and local governments. The grant structure is formulated within an equalization framework designed to enable state and local governments to achieve the fiscal capacity to provide a standard level of basic public service.

The Indian federal system has some similarities to the Australian system. Most of the major taxes are assigned to the central government, yet many of the expenditure responsibilities rest with the state and local governments. The central government collects two thirds of national revenues, yet undertakes less than half the national expenditures. The central government therefore makes both general revenue and specific purpose transfers to state and local governments. The general revenue transfers take the form of grants and tax shares, which are allocated on the basis of recommendations by two bodies—the Finance and the Planning Commissions. Neither body employs an explicit equalization formula, although both use criteria such as population, per capita income, and fiscal performance indicators to allocate grants to the states. As a result, the Finance Commission's allocations have been related more to filling actual fiscal gaps than to an assessment of relative fiscal capacities.

Canada has a small vertical imbalance at the center, because the central government shares its tax bases with the provincial governments through overlapping income and sales tax.[4] Nevertheless, the central government makes substantial transfers (in the form of both grants and tax shares) to the provinces for various purposes. For the provinces as a whole, transfers amount to close to 30 percent of resources. Included among the transfers made from the center are equalization grants, to ensure that each province can provide *reasonably comparable levels of public services at reasonably comparable levels of taxation.*

---

[4]The use of overlapping tax bases is currently being reviewed by the new Canadian administration. In general, an overlapping tax base, with the coexistence of central and state level VATs, as in Brazil, would pose considerable problems with administration and compliance.

In Brazil, the revenue assignments and tax-sharing arrangements are specified under the Constitution and have tended to provide an advantage to the regional and local governments relative to the center. The central government has a relatively unfavorable vertical balance and uncontrolled local expenditures have handicapped overall stabilization efforts. The central government does make special purpose grants to the regions. Some grants include provisions that may be construed as having an equalization element; however, there is no formal equalization process in Brazil.

The United States has a system of overlapping bases, whereby the central government shares income and sales tax bases with state and local governments. As a consequence, each level of government may be seen as virtually self-funding. Indeed, for a number of years in the 1980s, the state governments experienced a favorable vertical balance. Notwithstanding its large structural deficit, the central government has continued to make a number of specific purpose grants to state and local governments. While there is no formal horizontal equalization process in the United States, some of the provisions of the specific grants, for example, school grants, have embodied elements of equalization through assurance of minimum needs.

As noted earlier, the Federal Republic of Germany can be seen as lying at the opposite end of the spectrum of revenue sharing and grants arrangements to Australia. While the central government does make some grants to its regions (Länder) the need for such grants is minimized by three mechanisms. First, a careful attempt has been made to align revenue powers to expenditure needs. Second, the share of the centrally collected value-added tax going to the regions as a whole has been varied over time to minimize the vertical imbalances at the regional level. Third, the German equalization process primarily involves payments by the regions with "above-average" fiscal capacity to those with "below-average" fiscal capacity, with a minimal involvement by the central government.

China's Current Grants System

A combination of different types of grants have been used in China. The central government has typically made the following grants to the regions: quota grants, also known as general or system grants; special purpose grants; and final accounts or settlement grants.

Quota grants are unconditional transfers to local governments, used for financing of local governments' base-year budget deficits. The legal basis for quota grants is a 1980 regulation of the State Council that defines the (subordinate) financial relationship between the central and local governments and specifies the division of revenues and expenditures between them based on 1979 budgetary figures. The size of grant is determined by the difference between expenditures and revenues in the base year and is fixed in nominal terms for a period of five years. The local government does not have to return any fraction of the grant if its financial position improves within this period. Quota grants were provided to 18 provinces and autonomous regions in the total amount of Y 10.1 billion in 1992. Of this amount, about 80 percent went to five autonomous regions and three ethnic-minority provinces.

The financial system regulation of 1985 allocated quota grants to regions where own (fixed) and shared revenues were inadequate to meet expenditures. Until 1987, such grants were subject to a nominal annual increment of 10 percent to the eight regions and minority provinces mentioned above. In 1988, the State Council implemented six revenue-sharing arrangements in 37 regions—and the quota grants method applied in 16 regions.[5]

Special purpose grants are given to local governments in order to finance specific tasks that arise in the execution of local governments' budgets. The following are examples of such grants:

- Routine grants for financing various administrative expenses. These grants are given uniformly to all provinces (e.g., a fixed nominal amount per administrative worker or retired military officer);
- Grants to assist provinces in the construction of enterprises and regional infrastructure. These grants have a fixed and a variable component, which can be changed at the central government's discretion;
- Reimbursement of local expenditures on price subsidies for food, oil, cotton, and coal. The amount of these subsidies varies from year to year depending on the pricing policy. The Ministry of Finance reports that such subsidies will be eliminated in the near future;
- Grants for relief of serious natural disasters;
- Matching grants for specific welfare and social purposes;
- Interest subsidies on loans given by the People's Bank of China to poor provinces. Such subsidies operate as grants.

Special purpose grants are included in the budgets of recipient local governments as a revenue item and in the budget of the central government as an expenditure item. The legal basis on which they are given is the 1980 regulation of the State Council mentioned above. This regulation stipulates that (1) the central government shall not give random instructions to provincial governments in respect of ex-

---

[5]See also Chapter 2.

penditures on production, education, and culture, so that provincial governments are made more responsible for their spending policies; and (2) in executing the budgets of different departments, a special procedure has to be followed for transfers from central departments to the same department at the local level. Since 1980, the relative share of special purpose grants has increased: the amount of special purpose grants in 1992 was five times as great (in nominal terms) as in 1980. In general, the amount of special purpose grants varies considerably from year to year because of changes in the pricing policy. Special purpose grants have been incorporated in the budgets of central and provincial governments for 1994.

Account-settlement grants are transfers between different levels of government that are given for settling of final fiscal accounts. In 1992, a total of 40 such grants were made, of which 29 were from the central government to local governments and 11 from local governments to the central government. There are three types of final accounts grants. The first refers to the revenue sharing from certain taxes. This type of grant could disappear following the implementation of a new tax system. The second type refers to the settlement of accounts following the change in ownership of certain assets (from central ownership to provincial ownership, or vice versa). The third type refers to grants given in compensation for the impact of certain central government measures on local governments' financial positions relative to guaranteed base revenue shares. For example, the tax on cigarette production normally belongs to the provinces. If the central government wants to limit the output of cigarettes in any particular year, then this may result in a revenue loss for the provincial government, which is compensated through settlement grants. Final accounts grants are not included in the budget plans submitted for approval by the relevant authorities. They are normally calculated in February and March for the preceding fiscal year.

Under existing laws, local governments cannot have budgetary deficits. Local own revenue and grants received must equal local government expenditure. If a local government cannot get sufficient grants to cover the deficit, it must adopt legislation on extraordinary measures to increase own revenues or reduce expenditures. Implementation by local governments has tended to be at variance with the legal stipulations. The main avenue used to circumnavigate the formal laws appears to have been extrabudgetary financing, often in the form of direct or indirect services provided by local state enterprises, which falls outside direct budgetary controls.

The main problem with the existing system of grants is lack of transparency, both in regard to the objectives of the grants and the basis of their calculation. In turn, these weaknesses appear to translate into some lack of control over the growth of some grants.

Special grants appear to lack well-defined objectives and are largely formulated on an ad hoc, gap-filling basis. The open-ended nature of some special grants, especially the various food and related grants to cover subsidy payments by local government, also undermines efforts at budget control. Quota grants, as well as special purpose grants, are expected to be reviewed with the introduction of a new revenue-sharing system in 1994.

Vertical Imbalance

A vertical imbalance at the central level preceded the introduction of contracting arrangements in 1989, whereas local governments had a vertical surplus in 1985 and 1987 (see Table 2). With the onset of a period of austerity in 1988/89, the central government's vertical imbalance fell, whereas that of provincial and local governments increased markedly. Since 1990, the vertical imbalance of the local governments has declined as a proportion of GNP, whereas that of the central government has continued to increase as a proportion of GNP. Note that Table 2 uses the Chinese definition of revenues (including borrowing). Thus the table underestimates the true vertical imbalances, particularly at the central level, since only the central government has formal access to borrowing.[6]

Horizontal Imbalance

Regarding the horizontal fiscal imbalances, only limited indirect evidence is available. Data on per capita provincial revenue and expenditure indicate that the deterioration in the fiscal position of the deficit provinces outpaced the improvement in the fiscal position of the surplus provinces.[7] This result, along with indirect evidence from other studies, lends support to the hypothesis that the fiscal contracting system has contributed to the widening of regional disparities. Of course, some of these differences in fiscal performance may reflect policy differences rather than underlying variations in fiscal capacities.

It is evident that the amounts transferred to the central government since 1989 have been entirely redistributed to the provinces, with an

---

[6]Table 2 does not include provincial and local access to resources through extrabudgetary funds. The true situation is thus even more favorable to the provincial and local governments than appears in Table 2.

[7]See the World Bank study *China: Budgetary Policy and Intergovernmental Fiscal Relations*, Vol. II (Washington: World Bank, 1992), Tables A-4.2, p. 232, and A-6.2, p. 236.

Table 2. China: Revenue and Expenditure of the Central, Provincial, and Local Governments, 1985–93[1]

	1985	1986	1987	1988	1989	1990	1991	1992	1993 Budget
	(In billions of yuan)								
Own revenue (excluding transfers received)[2]	186.6	226.0	236.9	262.8	294.8	331.3	361.1	415.3	443.5
Central government (Chinese definition)	69.0	91.7	90.6	104.6	110.6	136.8	140.0	164.9	177.3
Provincial and local governments	117.6	134.3	146.3	158.2	184.2	194.5	221.1	250.4	266.2
Own expenditure (excluding transfers made)	184.5	233.0	244.9	270.7	304.0	345.2	381.4	438.9	472.7
Central government	79.9	96.2	103.2	106.0	110.5	137.3	151.8	181.7	200.4
Provincial and local governments	104.6	136.8	141.7	164.7	193.5	207.9	229.6	257.2	272.3
Transfers									
From the central government to provinces	...	...	...	...	56.2	58.5	55.4	59.7	58.3
From provinces to the central government	...	...	...	...	45.2	48.2	49.0	55.9	57.4
Net transfers made (−) or received (+)									
Central government	...	...	...	...	−110.0	−10.3	−6.4	−3.8	−0.9
Provincial governments	...	...	...	...	11.0	10.3	6.4	3.8	0.9
Total revenue (own revenue + transfers received)									
Central government	69.0	91.7	90.6	104.6	155.8	185.0	189.0	220.8	234.7
Provincial and local governments	117.6	134.3	146.3	158.2	240.4	253.0	276.5	310.1	324.5
Total expenditure (own expenditure + transfers made)									
Central government	79.9	96.2	103.2	106.0	166.7	195.8	207.2	241.4	258.7
Provincial and local governments	104.6	136.8	141.7	164.7	238.7	256.1	278.6	313.1	329.7
Pure vertical balance (Own revenue—own expenditure)	2.1	−7.0	−8.0	−8.0	−9.3	−13.9	−20.3	−23.6	−29.2
Central government	−10.9	−4.5	−12.6	−1.5	0.0	−0.5	−11.8	−16.8	−23.1
Provincial and local governments	13.0	−2.5	4.6	−6.5	−9.3	−13.4	−8.5	−6.8	−6.1
Overall balance (including transfers)									
Central government	−10.9	−4.5	−12.6	−1.5	−11.0	−10.8	−18.2	−20.6	−24.0
Provincial and local governments	13.0	−2.5	4.6	−6.5	1.7	−3.1	−2.1	−3.0	−5.2

Table 2 (concluded)

	1985	1986	1987	1988	1989	1990	1991	1992	1993 Budget
Memorandum items									
				(In percent of GNP)					
Total revenue (net of transfers)	21.8	23.3	21.0	18.7	18.4	18.7	17.9	17.3	16.2
Central Government	8.1	9.5	8.0	7.5	6.9	7.7	6.9	6.9	6.5
Provincial and local governments	13.7	13.9	12.9	11.3	11.5	11.0	10.9	10.4	9.7
Total expenditure (net of transfers)	21.6	24.0	21.7	19.3	19.0	19.5	18.9	18.3	17.2
Central government	9.3	9.9	9.1	7.6	6.9	7.8	7.5	7.6	7.3
Provincial and local governments	12.2	14.1	12.5	11.7	12.1	11.7	11.4	10.7	9.9
Pure vertical balance (Own revenue—own expenditure)	0.25	-0.72	-0.71	-0.57	-0.58	-0.78	-1.01	-0.98	-1.06
Central government	-1.27	-0.46	-1.12	-0.11	0.00	-0.03	-0.58	-0.70	-0.84
Provincial and local governments	1.52	-0.26	0.41	-0.46	-0.58	-0.76	-0.42	-0.28	-0.22
Overall balance (including transfers)									
Central government	-1.27	-0.46	-1.12	-0.11	-0.69	-0.61	-0.90	-0.86	-0.87
Provincial and local governments	1.52	-0.26	0.41	-0.46	0.11	-0.18	-0.10	-0.13	-0.19
Transfers received									
Central government	...	...	...	...	2.8	2.7	2.4	2.3	2.1
Provincial and local governments	...	...	...	...	3.5	3.3	2.7	2.5	2.1
Net transfers made by central government	...	...	...	...	-0.69	-0.58	-0.32	-0.16	-0.03

Sources: Ministry of Finance; and IMF staff estimates.
[1]Revenue and expenditure data compiled according to Chinese definitions.
[2]Own revenue collections by the central government and local governments, excluding transfers received from another level of government.

additional transfer from central government resources. Net transfers received by provincial governments, however, declined in both absolute and relative terms since 1989, given the increasing vertical imbalance of the central government, central government own revenues that have declined in relation to GNP, and a falling revenue share received from the provinces. In essence, fiscal contracting between the center and provinces worked as a clearing mechanism through which the central government redistributed a part of provincial fiscal surpluses to deficit provinces. Thus, the central government's role in horizontal redistribution has become increasingly difficult to sustain.

The proposed tax assignments and revenue-sharing arrangements (see Chapters 2 and 9) are designed to increase the proportion of revenues accruing to the central government to 60 percent. In the short run, the provinces are assured at least their 1993 levels of revenue.[8] Incremental central government revenues may not be adequate in achieving the 60 percent target, and further revisions to tax assignments and revenue sharing may be needed. The establishment of an effective grants mechanism would assure the provinces that their capacity to provide assigned expenditures will be protected. Thus, the speed at which an effective grants mechanism is established will govern the pace at which the objectives of the fiscal reforms are achieved.

Institutional Arrangements

In establishing the grants mechanism associated with the reformed tax system, it will be necessary to carefully consider the appropriate changes in institutional arrangements. Such arrangements will have a decisive impact on the credibility of the reformed fiscal system by ensuring that legitimate interests of local governments and the minimum needs of the population in general are consistent with macroeconomic constraints. It is important to avoid piecemeal change, so that confidence in the institutional framework is quickly established.

It should be kept in mind that grants are given for many purposes, of which equalization is just one. Special purpose grants may continue for a range of activities, including inter alia environmental purposes. The options below focus on the equalization aspects of a grants system.

---

[8]For 1994, all taxes are assigned either to the center or to local governments, except the VAT, which is shared with 75 percent of the increment going to the center.

Options for Equalization Grants

Three broad institutional options are generally available to support the new system of intragovernmental fiscal relations in China.

First, the work could be entrusted to a specially created section of the central Ministry of Finance, reporting directly to the Minister of Finance, and through him to the Executive. This option would be relatively easy to implement but may be seen as imposing a solution on the provinces—which may not be politically desirable.

Second, a special ministerial committee could be established, including representatives of the local governments, possibly with its own secretariat. This option would generally be preferable to the first. It is sometimes argued that this option has the best possibility of implementation, since officials from all levels of government are represented. However, provinces may still feel that the process is "manipulated" by the Ministry of Finance, and the objection to the first option may continue to apply.

Third, an independent grants commission could be established. This option has the advantage that the proceedings are generally seen to be "fair." It is important for the credibility of any future system of intergovernmental grants that the recommendations adopted be seen as having been calculated on an informed, objective, and transparent basis. While the other options may in fact adhere to these criteria, it will always be more difficult to convince outside observers, or aggrieved provinces, that this is the case. A grants commission would "insulate" the central government from "recriminations" from some provinces.

Under all the options, the central Ministry of Finance will play an important analytical and educative role. It will participate in a key manner even if a grants commission is established.

If an immediate decision is taken to establish a grants commission, it will take some time to become fully functional. An independent chairman and members will have to be appointed, offices established, and staff recruited. It will also take time to establish procedures and grants calculation mechanisms, especially if—as might be expected—the commission decides to conduct hearings in each region about relative budget needs. Thus, in the short run, it is likely that the decisions concerning the composition and structure of grants will have to be taken by the Ministry of Finance.

Interim Arrangements

In the initial phase of development, it will be important that the Ministry of Finance establish a workable system of grants that can be seen to embody the main principles of equalization likely to underpin the longer-term grants framework. It will take time, however, to develop fully the methodology and statistical bases likely to be incorporated in the longer-term framework. In the short term, the grants recommendations made by the Ministry of Finance could be seen as interim arrangements, with the understanding that the allocation (but not necessarily the overall level) of the grants may be subject to retrospective amendment once a grants commission is fully operational.

Steps for Establishing a Grants Commission

The establishment of an independent grants commission would require a number of institutional measures. The scope of the work to be undertaken should be clearly defined. International experience suggests that the role of the commission might best be focused on *horizontal equity* issues, leaving taxation and expenditure assignments and resultant vertical fiscal balance, revenue-sharing, and borrowing issues to be resolved by the Ministry of Finance.

The emphasis of the commission should be on technical issues, including the development of an objective methodology and supporting calculations, with tightly defined terms of reference established by political leaders and their official advisers.

The personnel appointed to the commission should have a technical and professional background and orientation. Former senior public servants, trained academics, and other professional persons may offer the best recruitment pool for the commission. Clearly, a broad-based regional and central government representation is an important consideration.

In many, but not all countries, the grants commission holds public hearings on the issues set down in its terms of reference. The commission often prepares a publicly available report for the consideration of the government, setting out its recommendations and the reasons for its judgments, including an explanation of any uncertainties in its deliberations. Where disagreements between members of the commission exist, both majority and minority views might be published. To facilitate this process, it is often useful for the terms of reference provided to the commission to request a technical analysis of various options.

The final decisions on whether or not to accept the commission's recommendations will be taken by the government. Thus, it should be made clear to all parties at the outset that the commission's role is solely to examine technical issues and make recommendations to the government.

Ultimately, the success of the grants commission will be judged by the quality and relevance of its work and the seriousness with which its recommendations are taken. While governments should not feel bound to accept the recommendations of such institutions, it is important that they be given serious consideration, and that explanations be provided where recommendations are not followed.

Information Requirements

The first task in developing any future program of grants to regional governments must be to develop a comprehensive data base on (1) vertical and horizontal budget balances under present arrangements; (2) transfers under the existing system of grants and tax sharing; and (3) the means used to finance capital spending within the state budget and state corporations. This data base can then be used to produce simulations of how the fiscal structure at different levels of government will look after the proposed reforms of the tax system, revenue sharing, and tax administration. Those simulations, in turn, will serve to provide the information within which a revised system of grants can be formulated.

Calculation of Vertical Imbalances

As explained earlier, the calculation of the vertical fiscal balance in China would initially involve a study of the proposed revenue and existing expenditure assignments, and the resultant own account structural budget balances. Once expenditure assignments are revised (this exercise may take a number of years), the vertical imbalances would need to be reassessed.

Own account revenues are defined as those revenue items that accrue to the level of government concerned. This "beneficiary based" definition seeks to allocate revenues, not according to the collecting agency, but according to the government benefiting from the revenue source concerned. As a general rule, it may be useful to attribute tax and other revenue to a noncollecting beneficiary government where (1) when such government has exercised some influence or discretion over the setting of the tax or distribution of its proceeds; (2) when the provisions of the tax laws provide that the government concerned should receive a given percentage of the tax collected or arising in its territory; or (3) when the government concerned receives tax revenue under a tax law leaving no discretion to the collecting government.

Own account revenues do not include revenues collected by another government that has some overriding claim over the determination or use of the revenue collected.

Own account expenditures are similarly defined as those spent on activities that benefit the level of government concerned, such as wages paid to its own employees, purchases of equipment or supplies used by the government concerned, or pensions and transfers to persons or enterprises that are beneficiaries of the government concerned. Grants paid to other levels of government, which then become the property of that government, should be classified accordingly.[9]

The purpose of this exercise is to identify the magnitude by which the central government's own account revenues are likely to exceed its own account expenditures on an ongoing structural basis (i.e., after abstracting from surpluses or deficits arising from the impact of cyclical swings in economic activity on the budget), and the likely structural deficit on regional and local government activities. The assessment of the two sets of fiscal imbalances will provide a framework for constructing a system of grants to be paid from the center.

To construct such a picture within China, it will be necessary to obtain the data covering the operations of central, regional, and local government budget and extrabudgetary operations for the most recent three-year period. These data can then be used as a base to project the likely outcomes of different fiscal arrangements over the next three to five years. Ideally, the information should be compiled within the consistent framework provided by the IMF's *Manual on Government Finance Statistics*. The main items may be characterized as follows:

Central Budget

Revenues (excluding Debt-Issue Receipts, which should be included below under Financing)
> Budget Sector
>> Central Fixed Revenues
>> Central Revenues from Shared Taxes
>> Transfers from Lower-Level Governments
>>> —Central Taxes Collected by Local Governments
>>> —Adjustment Grants Arising from Transfer of Ownership of Public Enterprises from/to Central Government to/from Regions

---

[9]For further discussion of these issues see Chapter 2 of the IMF's *A Manual on Government Finance Statistics* (Washington: IMF, 1986).

Grants and Contributions from Enterprises
Extrabudgetary Revenues

Expenditures
Budget Sector
Final Spending on Goods and Services
Capital Spending
Transfers or Grants
Recurrent Transfers
To Households
Subsidies to State Corporations
For Urban Transport
For Water and Sewerage
For Other Purposes
To Other Levels of Government
For Specific Projects
Matching Grants
For Price Subsidies
For Social Relief Operations
For Health, Education, and Other Purposes
Budget Deficit Grants
Equalization Grants to Regions
Adjustment Grants Arising from Transfer of Ownership
of Public Enterprises
Interest Payments to/from Central Government from/to
Regions
Capital Transfers
To Households (for housing, etc.)
To Enterprises (for capital spending, etc.)
To Other Levels of Government
Lending Minus Repayments = Lending from the Budget to State
Enterprises and Others Minus Repayments of Such Loans
Extrabudgetary Expenditure

Deficit = Revenues Less Expenditures
Financing of the Deficit
From Other Levels of Government
From Overseas Sources
From Domestic Sources
—Banking System
Central Bank
Other Banks
—State Enterprises
—Other Sources

Local Governments

(For each provincial government, and also on a consolidated basis for all provincial governments. If possible, this information should also ultimately be collected for all sub-provincial governments within a region, with a view to determining intraprovincial vertical balances.)

Revenues (excluding Debt-Issue Receipts, which should be included below under Financing)
    Budget Sector
        Local Fixed Revenues
        Local Shared Taxes
        Grants from Higher-Level Governments for Specific Projects
            Matching Grants
                Price Subsidies
                Social Relief Operations
                Health, Education, and Other Grants
            Budget Deficit Subsidies
                Equalization Grants to Regions
                Adjustment Grants Arising from Transfer of Ownership of Public Enterprises to/from Regions from/to the Center
        Grants and Contributions from Enterprises
        Extrabudgetary Revenues

Expenditures
    Budget Sector
        Final Spending on Goods and Services
            Capital Spending
        Transfers or Grants
            Recurrent Transfers
                To Households
                Subsidies to State Enterprises
                    For Urban Transport
                    For Water and Sewerage
                    For Other Purposes
                To Central Government
                    Central Taxes Collected by Regions on Behalf of the Center
                To Lower-Level Governments Adjustment Grants Arising from Transfer of Ownership of Public Enterprises to/from the Center to/from Regions
                Interest Payments
            Capital Transfers
                To Households (for housing, etc.)

To Enterprises (for capital expenditure, etc.)
To Lower-Level Governments
Other Transfers
Lending Minus Repayments = Lending from the Budget to State
  Enterprises and Others Minus Repayments of Such Loans
Extrabudgetary Expenditure

Deficit = Revenue Less Expenditures

Financing of the Deficit
  From Other Levels of Government
  From Overseas Sources
  From Domestic Sources
    Banking System
      Central Bank
      Other Banks
    State Enterprises
    Other Borrowers

Horizontal Imbalances

Much of the data used for an initial assessment of vertical balances in revenues and expenditures will be useful for calculating horizontal imbalances—including the breakdown of the main tax revenues collected at the local level (i.e., a breakdown of the local fixed revenue aggregate). Similarly, a functional breakdown of recurrent expenditures in the form of final spending on goods and services, capital spending, and capital transfers would be important in assessing differences between fiscal performance across regions. Interprovincial comparisons are facilitated if expressed on a per capita basis—thus local and regional data on population will also be required. Ideally, this information should be collected from population census data supplemented by frequent sample surveys. However, approximate estimates may be prepared using birth and death statistics to obtain net movements in regional populations provided that interregional migration is not large.

It would also be desirable to obtain information on the costs of those enterprise activities that result in uncompensated benefits. One example is urban public transport, which generates spillover benefits in the form of lower levels of traffic congestion and pollution. A case can be made for sustaining losses of public transportation companies to compensate them for providing such benefits that cannot be included in the price of tickets.

In order to translate the information collected above to a basis that will allow interprovincial comparisons, it will also be important for the Ministry of Finance to obtain data on population in each province.

Estimate of Fiscal Capacities

The analysis of the relative fiscal capacities of regional governments for an equalization exercise will require the compilation of a body of information as described above. A *needs-based* approach would require much more information than a purely *revenue-based* option. The former might become feasible in China over a period of years, while the latter could be made operational relatively quickly. However, the arrangements chosen should be flexible enough to accommodate adjustments to the changing role of the state in China, the clearer definition of expenditure responsibilities, and better availability of information flows in the future. The main information flows are briefly outlined below.

The information should be prepared in the context of a "standard budget," which will enable per capita comparisons covering all the regional revenues and expenditures deemed to be subject to the equalization exercise. This must include all transfers and grants from the center to the regions and those from the regions to the center. It should also cover all revenues shared between the regions and the center.

Usually the standard budget will cover something less than the full gambit of existing budgetary and extrabudgetary activity. There will be some expenditures that are judged not to be relevant to the equalization exercise. As noted earlier, in a market economy the definition would be restricted to "public goods," such as education, health services, and the like, and would often exclude measures such as subsidies to assist enterprises. It may also exclude capital spending, which may be seen as too bulky and one-off to be included in the equalization exercise.[10]

Once the coverage of the standard budget is defined, the analysts must (1) collect information on all budgetary and extrabudgetary regional revenues and expenditures, and ensure consistency of this data; (2) define methods to estimate "horizontal" equalization (alternative models are discussed in Chapter 16); (3) establish the "standards" against which regional fiscal capacities will be assessed; and (4) develop methods to assess relative revenue capacities and relative expenditure needs.

---

[10]If capital spending is to be included in the equalization exercise, the comparison base will usually be the *stock* of facilities available in each region rather than the *flow* of spending in any one year.

With regard to item (1), the revenue information to be included in the standard budget follows that outlined above for regional governments. However, the expenditure information must be collected within broad functional rather than economic groupings, such as education, health, culture, sports, law and order, judicial services, and economic services, which are to be included in the equalization study. It should be noted that the definitions adopted in the standard budget must be the same in all regions. For example, if the education function is defined to include the cost of supplementary items, such as bus transport to and from school, milk supplements for diets, research work by teachers, or curriculum development by regional headquarters, then information on expenditure needs must be assessed for these items (together with information on actual spending) for all regions under the common definition. In this context, it will be important to obtain information on quasi-fiscal activities performed by state enterprises or state financial institutions. For example, if state enterprises provide schools for students of their own workers and are allowed to deduct the cost of such schools for purposes of calculating taxation liabilities, then it would be important to include such information with the "standard budget" used in the equalization calculations. Similarly, if state financial institutions provide free or highly subsidized housing to certain groups of people within some regions, then it would be important to include such information within the standard budget calculations.

For item (3), two approaches are possible—a performance standard or a capacity standard. Performance standards involve the exogenous determination of a set of standards, typically minimum standards, which are seen as "warranted" for various revenues and expenditures.

On the revenue side, the standard, R_s, may involve judgments about the number of taxpayers in a region and the amount of tax that they should be able to pay. On the expenditure side, the standard, E_s, may depend on the *product* of the number of units (e.g., students) the region is required to serve, and the *standardized unit cost*. The standardized unit cost is equal to the *standard cost* determined for *all* regions as a whole, *plus* an adjustment for the *differential cost* to the particular region arising out of its own special circumstances.

The fiscal capacity approaches followed in Australia and Canada do not require a region to meet *specific* standards. Rather, the purpose is to ensure that each region receives an equalization payment that enables it to provide an endogenously determined "standard" of revenue raising and expenditure. Typically, the standard is some per capita "average" of the actual measured fiscal performance of the regions. The "average" may be a simple or some weighted average covering all or some selected regions. In Canada, for example, the "standard" used is a weighted average of the five eastern provinces. In Australia, the standard used is a simple average of all the states and territories subject to the equalization exercise.

One advantage of the capacity utilization approach is that it usually does not involve the conditionality normally associated with performance equalization models, which would be attractive to local governments. Regions would be given grants that allow them to achieve certain standards, but *they can choose to do more* (by taxing at above-standard rates and spending those funds on above-standard expenditures) *or less.* Moreover, capacity utilization models are not usually concerned with minimum expenditure standards. The aim is to obtain an average standard based on the actual revenue performance and expenditure patterns of the regional governments. This "endogenous" derivation of the standard should avoid concerns that the standards might be dictated by the central government.

An example of the operation of a capacity equalization model is set out in Chapter 16.

Once the standard is determined, assessments must be made of the relative *revenue-raising capacities* of a region (e.g., existence of relatively less industry, lower incomes, higher unemployment, etc.) as well as its *relative expenditure needs* (e.g., relatively greater proportion of dependent aged or young persons, relatively harsher weather, etc.). In the case of China, separate calculations of relative revenue-raising capacities and relative expenditure needs would be required for each own revenue source and each expenditure item selected for equalization, for each region. The effective weights would be determined by the "standard" budget that brings together the various revenues and expenditures judged to be relevant to the equalization exercise.

The analysis of relative revenue capacities and expenditure needs can proceed in two ways. One is to identify location-specific relative disabilities, for example, the higher cost in region A relative to the standard. Such disabilities might be derived by applying factors thought to be important in underlying the differences in costs relative to the standard (e.g., differences in scale, climate, etc., that are derived from indicative supporting statistics). The second method is to observe actual revenues or expenditures and attempt to identify policy differences between regions that could explain all or part of the actual differences, thus deriving a cross-sectional series reflecting underlying revenue or cost disabilities. In concept, both approaches should yield similar results. In practice, this is rarely so. Experience suggests that identification of location-specific disabilities is a more fruitful course. However, calculation from each approach provides a double check on what may sometimes have to be a broad judgment on the differences in regional fiscal capacities.

The measurement of relative revenue capacities will involve a definition of the regional tax bases, over the period for which the equalization exercise is to be determined. For example, the number of and value of cars underlying motor vehicle taxes the value of property underlying property taxes, the value of taxable profit underlying corporate income taxes, and the personal income underlying personal income tax will have to be calculated. In the case of new taxes introduced under the tax reform process, which did not exist in the equalization period, it may be necessary to estimate their current tax bases and then project backward the tax bases (i.e., estimate what the tax bases would have been in previous years had the new taxes applied then). The calculation of relative expenditure needs will also require estimation of a number of the underlying factors. In the education area, for example, one may include the number of children by age group, the number of teachers, the size of schools (a scale factor that may differ by regions), the ethnic background of the children (possibly involving added expenditures on language training and other factors), and climatic differences necessitating different heating or cooling needs of schools in different regions.

Sequencing and Initial Simulations

The work program involved in preparing a system of equalization grants can be thought of as involving three phases.

The first, *exploratory*, phase involves the construction of some simple simulations (described below), which attempt to gain initial impression of the magnitude of the vertical and horizontal fiscal imbalances within China, and some indication of the factors explaining those imbalances. It serves as a framework for determining areas where additional or improved statistical data are required, and where a better understanding of the factors driving revenue or expenditure need to be developed.

To summarize, this phase can be conceived as involving (1) some approximate calculations of the vertical fiscal balance between the central and regional governments, (2) some initial calculations of the actual horizontal balance between provinces, (3) a preliminary "standard or model budget" that brings together the public goods and services over which it is judged that some equalization of public provision is required, and (4) initial calculations to see if broad patterns can be discerned that "explain" observable differences in revenue capacities and expenditure needs between regions.

These initial calculations do not have to be very precise but should seek to link revenue performance to the underlying bases determining collections. Thus, wages and personal consumption in each region may drive sales taxes and VAT collections, and the gross value of industrial output may help to explain differences in the enterprise profits tax. Similarly, in this initial phase one might gather data on population characteristics, such as the age, sex, density, and ethnic breakdown of the population, in each region. All of these factors might serve to provide clues as to the differences in per capita expenditure needs between regions.

In the *second phase* of preparing a system of equalization grants, the detailed problems identified in the first phase would be tackled, with assistance from experts in the respective fields of revenue collection and expenditure determination.

The *final phase* would involve bringing the details of various analyses together into an overall assessment framework, which might be used as a basis for any grants scheme to be implemented. The focus at this stage will be on methodology and consistency of the overall assessments.

Of these steps, the exploratory phase will probably prove the most difficult. However, it will also be the most important one, since it will help ministers and officials to gain an impression of both the magnitude of fiscal imbalances in China (both now and in the future) and the gaps in the information base used to assess the imbalances. This will permit them to make informed decisions on subsequent policy actions, including, most importantly, whether equalization grants are needed, and the degree of sophistication and coverage.

Borrowing and Capital Spending

To the extent that there remains an overall deficit on public sector operations, reflecting a need to finance infrastructure and other capital projects through borrowing, attention will also have to be given to the appropriate mechanisms for controlling borrowing by lower levels of government. The main issue is whether regional and local governments should be given, under supervision, power to borrow on own account, for example, from higher levels of government, and the use of particular approved instruments. The alternative is that all borrowing authority should continue to be vested in the central government. Analysis of this issue will also require the compilation of a comprehensive picture of the existing and likely future capital expenditure profile and its financing.

In order to build a complete picture of all regional requirements, it would be useful to build a separate picture of the overall borrowing to finance capital investment in China by constructing an overall capital appropriation account. This would trace the amount and structure of capital investment and, to the extent possible, its financing. This task involves the collection of data on the following variables:

Total capital spending in China
  By State Enterprises
    Centrally Owned
    Locally Owned
  By Governments
    Central Governments
    Regional Governments
  By Other Entities
    Cooperatives
    Joint Ventures
    State Financial Institutions
    Foreign Companies and Banks
  Other Capital Spending

Financing of Capital Expenditure
  By State Enterprises
    Centrally Owned
      Internal Reserves (including amortization reserves)
      From Budget
      From Overseas Borrowing
      From Banking System
      From Other Sources
  By the Budget Sector
    Internal Reserves (including surpluses from recurrent operations)
      From State Enterprises
      From Overseas Borrowing
      From Banking System
      From Other Sources
  By Other Entities
    Internal Reserves (including amortization reserves)
      From State Enterprises
      From Budget
      From Overseas Borrowing
      From Banking System
      From Other Sources

The issue of control of borrowing by lower levels of government is crucial in maintaining macroeconomic stability. This issue is not addressed here,[11] but the information described above will be impor-

---

[11]See Chapters 4 and 5 for further discussion.

tant in establishing a framework for monitoring and control of borrowing.

Phasing-In Equalization Arrangements

A full equalization of regional fiscal capacities, given the apparently large regional differences that already exist in fiscal capacities in China, may be difficult to achieve in the near term. Moreover, it may be inappropriate to seek to move rapidly in the direction of a historically determined standard, given the large shifts now occurring in the structure of the economy. Thus, an agreed "indicative" standard, rather than a historically based standard, may need to be used during the period of rapid structural change.

Which Government Should Pay the Grant?

The question is left open as to who should pay the equalization grant. In Canada and Australia, the "equalizing grant" is paid by the central government from the shares of total taxes available to it, made possible by a vertical balance favoring the central government. But in Germany, where the vertical imbalances are smaller, Länder with above-average revenue capacity make equalization transfers to those with below-average revenue capacity.

Possible Sequencing for China

A process of establishing a system for horizontal grants in China may involve action on a number of fronts. First, the vertical balance against proposed revenue-sharing arrangements and tax assignments, on the one hand, and existing expenditure assignments, on the other would need to be quantified. This will require an expansion and modifications of the simplified models in Chapter 16.

Second, these quantifications could be used to clarify options for the reform of intragovernmental fiscal relations. Depending on the size of the calculated vertical imbalance and the desired degree of equalization, these options may range from a marginal reform of the existing system of grants, to arrangements for horizontal equalization based on both relative revenue capacities and relative expenditure needs. Consideration must also be given to whether regional and local governments should be given power to borrow directly from capital markets and, if so, what controls and supervision mechanisms will need to be established.

Third, the process of collection and, if necessary, creation of data required as input in the equalization exercise would need to be initiated.

16

Horizontal Equalization Grants

Jon Craig*

Chapter 16 provides a broadly based rationale for the creation of a system of grants. This chapter concentrates on just one aspect of such a grants system: the implementation of equalization grants designed to offset differences in the fiscal capacities of different regions.

Putting Horizontal Equity in Perspective

Within a country with multiple levels of government, it is usual to have both vertical and horizontal imbalances in fiscal arrangements. Vertical imbalances within a fiscal system derive from mismatches in the relative revenue and expenditure assignments or responsibilities established for the two levels of government. The conference sessions on expenditure and revenue assignments yielded insights into the forces molding the relative responsibilities of different levels of government in market economies. Each country must wrestle with conflicting pressures: the need to centralize, to improve macroeconomic stabilization policies and management of overall expenditure priorities, and the desire to decentralize, to improve the quality of service delivery and allow the population to enjoy the benefits flowing from diversity.

While the solutions found for each country will differ, a number of countries have found that there are advantages in centralizing policy control, administration, and collection of broad-based taxes, such as value-added taxes, excises duties, and personal and corporate taxes, at the national level. As a consequence, these countries will normally

---

*International Monetary Fund.

Table 1. Vertical Current Balances[1]

(Ratio of Own-Source Revenues to Own-Source Current Expenditures)

	Central		State/regional		Local	
	Overall	Current	Overall	Current	Overall	Current
"Federal" countries						
Australia	1.45	1.48	0.53	0.59	0.83	1.05
Brazil	0.78	1.15	0.82	1.03	0.28	0.37
Canada	1.05	1.08	0.88	0.93	0.53	0.60
Germany	1.03	1.08	0.96	1.09	0.75	0.94
India	0.76	1.20	0.59	0.82	na	na
Spain	1.05	1.18	0.28	0.40	0.74	0.97
United States	0.93	0.97	1.24	1.41	0.66	0.75
"Unitary" governments						
Austria	0.97	1.05	. . .	. . .	0.90	1.24
Denmark	1.54	1.61	. . .	. . .	0.57	0.59
France	1.02	1.07	. . .	. . .	0.64	0.91
Netherlands	1.26	1.32	. . .	. . .	0.26	0.27
Sweden	1.21	1.23	. . .	. . .	0.76	0.81
United Kingdom	1.23	1.26	. . .	. . .	0.45	0.46

Source: IMF, *Government Finance Statistics Yearbook* (Washington: IMF, 1993).
[1] The data show average ratios over selected periods for each country. The periods chosen are Australia, 1987–91; Austria, 1987–91; Brazil, 1982–91; Canada, 1985–89 (excludes 1987 for capital balance); Denmark, 1987–91; France, 1988–92; Germany, 1983–91; India, 1985–92; Netherlands, 1988–92; Spain, 1987–90; Sweden, 1988–92; United States, 1987–92; and United Kingdom, 1985–92.

have a vertical balance favoring the central government. Table 1 shows the vertical balances in a number of major industrial countries.

By contrast, the horizontal balance within a multilevel system of government relates to the inequality of fiscal capacities between regional subnational governments. Those inequalities stem from differences in relative expenditure needs in different regions due to population compositions, scale, distance, and other factors, as well as differences in the relative revenue-raising capacity of regions from the tax base available to regional governments. The end result of such differences is that some regions find themselves unable to provide comparable levels of service to their citizens without imposing substantially different levels of taxation.

In principle, these two imbalances within a fiscal system could be resolved by separate policy measures: (1) vertical imbalances could be resolved by a variety of tax-sharing and grant mechanisms with the regional governments, constructed in such a way so as to leave any "desired" or "accepted" horizontal balance unchanged; and (2) horizontal imbalances could be resolved by payments from "richer" regions with higher fiscal capacity to poorer regions (a feature of the German intergovernmental relations).

In practice, the two issues are often intertwined. Measures taken to resolve vertical imbalances inevitably have effects on the horizontal balance, and pressures to resolve horizontal imbalance often call forth actions by the central, as well as regional, government, which affect the vertical balance.

The aim of the policymaker concerned with these imbalances in finances must be to develop measures that address both objectives simultaneously within an overall budgetary setting that allows fiscal policy to make some ongoing contribution to the stabilization of the economy.

Why Is Horizontal Balance Important?

In order to understand the case for horizontal fiscal equalization, it is useful to think of why various independent regions might agree to sacrifice some or all of that independence and choose to join together into a "nation" or some other common economic space. While there may be a number of historical and cultural ties behind such actions, the most likely economic factor driving such unions is a desire to create a national marketplace that generates a "surplus" over and above the real income generated by the component parts.[1] If this were not so, there would be an economic incentive for regions to become independent with their own laws and policies. Such arrangements would preserve their regional diversity at the expense of unity. The residents of such separate and independent regions could have no expectation of equity with their neighbors.

Assuming that there are demonstrable benefits sufficient to underpin an economic union, three possible forms of intergovernment arrangements might be considered. The first would be to abolish all regional governments and form a unitary government to control the whole area. All citizens would then be subject to the same laws and policies, with common taxes and service provision of public services. The goals of unity and equity would be achieved, but the nation

---

[1]The "surplus" generated may flow from a number of factors. For example, the economies of scale from production and distribution within a national market place; common legal and other standards (working standards, education standards, product standards, and so on); common infrastructure (e.g., transport systems); and a predictable central fiscal structure and monetary system, including some harmonization of tax bases and rates for major taxes and common access to national public services (e.g., defense, foreign affairs).

formed would lack decentralization and diversity in service provision and taxation.

The second approach would be to maintain regional governments but not to make any effort to equalize for horizontal inequities. The nation then has unity and some diversity but, to the extent that different fiscal capacities exist in different regions, no equity.

The third approach would involve the preservation of regional governments *plus* a set of horizontal fiscal capacity equalization arrangements. The unity of the nation is preserved. Regions maintain a degree of diversity yet the goal of interregional equity is preserved.

The economic "case" for equalization therefore rests mainly on the desire to build a national structure that can simultaneously attain the key goals of unity, diversity, and equity. The issue of "interregional equity" is not simply a question of perceived social justice, however, important as that issue may be in its own right, it is also necessary to maximize the efficient use of mobile resources in an economy. Failure to introduce fiscal systems that broadly treat "equals as equals" across regions can induce flows of population that lower the overall national productivity of the workforce.

To grasp the essence of this point, consider the case of two identical individuals living in different regions, each of which provides identical public services. Region A has access to natural resources and can fund its budget expenditure from mining royalties, while region B has to rely on local income taxes. The individual in region A receives the full benefit of public expenditures in addition to the benefits derived from retaining all his personal income, whereas the person in region B must pay through personal income taxes for the benefits derived from public expenditures. Clearly, a net fiscal benefit is conferred on the resident of region A. A horizontal inequity has been created because individuals who were equal in the absence of a public sector are treated differently after the injection of fiscal measures. If residents of region B respond to this horizontal inequity by migrating to region A, they may be leaving more productive activities for less productive activities to capture the higher net fiscal benefits. Such fiscally induced migration may be undesirable on the grounds of economic efficiency.[2]

The political aspect of equalization has also been important. Fiscal inequity as between regions, resulting from the absence of equalization payments, is likely to cause political disharmony, economic dislocation, and fiscally induced population and capital movements. It was such political instability in Australia, associated with strong secession

---

[2]See Robin W. Boadway and P.A. Hobson, *Intergovernmental Fiscal Relations In Canada*, Canadian Tax Paper, No. 96 (Toronto: Canadian Tax Foundation, 1993).

movements in three of the six states that led to the development of a fiscal capacity equalization under the oversight of an independent Australian Grants Commission in 1933. The continuation of the German and Indian systems of intergovernmental arrangements may also owe something to the presence of arrangements containing some elements of fiscal equalization.

Capacity Equalization and Performance Equalization

In the discussion above, equalization is defined in terms of the relative fiscal capacities of the regions. Specifically, the aim of the equalization process is to provide each region with a share of a general purpose unconditional grant such as to enable it to have the capacity to provide a comparable level of services to other regions, provided it makes the same effort to raise revenue from its own tax bases and conducts its affairs with an average level of efficiency.

Capacity equalization must be clearly distinguished from fiscal performance equalization. This approach relies on providing each region with a specific-purpose (usually) conditional grant capable of providing a specified minimum standard of public service.

Capacity Equalization Model

The most generalized model of capacity equalization can be formulated as follows:

$$G_i = E_i^s - R_i^s, \tag{1}$$

where

G = the per capita equalization payment to a region by the granting government;

E = the per capita expenditure of the regional government concerned;

R = per capita revenue collections from *own sources* of the regional government concerned;

i = this subscript denotes the regional government involved; and

s = a national "standard" against which E and R have been compared in order to eliminate differences that arise purely from policy decisions as opposed to underling regional differences in revenue-raising capacity or the cost of providing services.

The means used to set the national standard vary considerably between countries. In Canada, for example, the standard for nationwide revenue equalization is based on revenue capacity in 5 eastern provinces (out of 12 provinces). A similar approach was used by Australia in the initial phase of its grants system, but now the grants are calculated against a standardderived as a weighted average standard of actual per capita revenues and expenditures for the six states and two territories.

This general model effectively tells us that the equalizing grant to a region will be equal to its *relative expenditure needs*, E_i^s, on the one hand, and its *relative revenue capacity*, R_i^s, on the other—each being measured against a national (average) standard. But there are many variants to this basic model. Some models only involve equalization of expenditures, usually by way of some conditional grant mechanism. Others involve partial equalization just in respect of revenues and ignore the needs created by differences in the cost of providing comparable services.

Revenue capacities are assessed by investigating the potential tax bases available to each region for a number of standard taxes and then comparing estimates of the revenue that could be raised by each region if the region imposed taxes at a national standard rate[3] to its own tax base.

Calculating relative *expenditure needs* involves examining the underlying demand and cost factors that determine the cost of providing a standard level of service in each functional area in each region. In the case of education, for example, it may examine regional differences in demand and cost arising out of such factors as

- differences in the ratio of school-aged children to total population or in the proportions of students in different age classes;
- economies or diseconomies of scale arising out of administration of different school sizes;
- population dispersion resulting in different costs of providing services for scattered populations or populations in remote areas;
- socioeconomic factors, such as differences in the ethnic or socially disadvantaged composition of students in some regions and climatic or physical environment differences in the cost of maintaining school buildings, transporting students, and so on.

Performance Equalization Model

Performance models provide equalization grants against a set of externally determined standards—typically minimum standards—that are seen as "warranted" for various expenditure areas. Although the

---

[3]Usually calculated as an average effective rate derived by comparing potential total tax collected with the total national tax base for the tax concerned.

models are typically restricted only to expenditure analysis, it is possible to incorporate allowances that further adjust the grants according to the relative revenue-raising performance of a region.

The expenditure performance model usually determines the grant payable to a region as being equal to the product of the number of units (e.g., students) the region is required to serve and the standardized unit cost per unit. The standardized unit cost is equal to the standard cost determined for all regions as a whole plus an adjustment for the differential cost to the particular region concerned arising out of its own special circumstances.

The following example provides a formula that might be used for an education grant.

$$G_i = N_i \cdot t_s \cdot w_s \cdot k_s, \tag{2}$$

where

N_i = number of students enrolled with designated enrollment criteria for school "i";

t_s = standard teacher-student ratio;

w_s = standard average salary cost per student; and

k_s = standard ratio of salary cost to total cost.

Appropriate disability cost loadings may then be applied to each of the factors influencing unit cost, as follows:

$$G_i = N_i \cdot t_s (1 + v_{it}) \cdot w_s (1 + v_{iw}) \cdot k_s (1 + v_{ik}), \tag{3}$$

where

v_{ij} = differential cost of element "j" per unit met by grant recipient "i" in providing standard service "s."

Comparing Performance and Capacity Equalization

The difference between the two approaches lies essentially in the method of establishing the standard against which regions are to be "equalized." The performance approach sets the standard by reference to criteria that are exogenous to the actual revenue and expenditure operations of the regions as a whole. Typically, the standard will be set arbitrarily by the central government on the basis of judgments as to the desired minimum set of expenditure conditions within particular functional areas. One important corollary of performance models is that they are often associated with some conditionality on the grants provided. That follows because the granting governments want to make sure that funds are used to achieve the minimum objectives established. In that sense, they may be seen to be inconsistent with the concept of decentralized multilevel finances discussed earlier. A country employing conditional grants to its regions is behaving similarly to a unitary government; as such it may attain some degree of equity in its fiscal system, but it will sacrifice decentralized responsibility and diversity.

By contrast, the capacity models determine the standard endogenously. That is, the standard is usually some average or weighted average of the actual fiscal behavior by the regional governments concerned. In Canada, for example, the standard for nationwide revenue equalization is based on revenue capacity in 5 "wealthier" provinces (out of 12 provinces). A similar approach was used by Australia in the initial phase of its grants system, but now grants are calculated against a weighted standard.

In contrast to performance models, capacity utilization grants usually do not involve conditionality. Regions are given grants that allow them to achieve certain standards, but they can choose to do more (by taxing at above standard rates and spending those funds on above standard expenditures) or less.

In practice, the two approaches may not yield widely dissimilar results. Broadly similar information and judgments may be required for either approach, although the degree of precision required for capacity equalization is normally greater because of the necessity of constructing accurate measures about relative capacities of regions. Of course, that concentration on precision is itself directed at reducing the degree of judgment used.

Constructing Intergovernmental Relationships

In constructing intergovernmental relationships to deal with vertical and horizontal imbalances, it is important to develop an overall framework for analysis of these twin balances and, within that framework, to establish some priorities between the conflicting objectives, as it may not be possible to resolve both the vertical and horizontal balance issues satisfactorily within a shorter-term planning horizon. Seven steps can be defined.

First, the vertical balance must be quantified against proposed revenue and expenditure assignments. That quantification must be adjusted for any cyclical impact on revenue and expenditures to ensure that the resulting fiscal balance is sustainable over time.

Second, measures must be set down to resolve the vertical imbalance. Which revenues will be shared? What system of grants can be used? If some revenues are to be shared, will the items be shared regionally according to the source of derivation (e.g., a percentage share of all enterprise profit taxes collected within a region)? Or will some regional reallocation mechanism be imposed (e.g., revenue share "caps" or other differential sharing or grants formula) be introduced that leads to differences between collections of revenue and amounts retained within each region? Or will a mechanism be adopted that allows regions to "piggyback" on the back of national tax (e.g., to introduce separate personal income tax levies set by regional governments)? Similarly, will grants be on a simple per capita proportional basis or involve some reallocation between regions?

In performing this task, the implications of the measures chosen to resolve the vertical balance for the horizontal balance must be considered. For example, if regions are allowed to keep a percentage share of all collections made within their borders for particular taxes (the so-called derivation approach to tax sharing) or to impose a piggyback levy on a national tax base, it may benefit richer regions with higher-tax capacities relative to other regions.

Third, an objective statistical framework must be devised to measure the existing horizontal balance between regions. It is necessary to establish a reliable comparison base—often referred to as a representative or standard budget that allows valid interregional comparisons of fiscal capacities. Decisions must be made as to whether the comparison base should cover all revenues and expenditure functions or be restricted to certain items. And within each of these revenue and expenditure categories, will the coverage be restricted still further to include only items (e.g., education, health) that are seen as "basic public sector responsibilities" as opposed to items such as cultural activities or state public enterprise activities that might be performed by the private sector? Finally, whatever functional expenditure coverage is chosen, there is the decision on whether the comparisons should be restricted to recurrent items (which can be more easily measured and compared) or extended to cover capital items also.

Fourth, with the coverage of the comparison base determined, it is then necessary to reduce the regional aggregates to a per capita basis by dividing by an accurate and up-to-date measure of regional population to allow standardized comparisons of regional fiscal capacities.

Fifth, once a sound per capita comparison base for actual regional revenues and expenditures has been established, attention must turn to investigating whether differences in these budget aggregates can be justified by underlying differences in relative revenue capacities and relative expenditure needs and costs.

In practice, the analysis of relative revenue capacities and expenditure needs can proceed in two ways. One approach is to identify the impact of location-specific disabilities on relative revenue and expenditure needs. On the taxation side, this may involve definition of a standard base for each revenue category and determination of a "standard national tax rate"—often calculated as an average by comparing actual revenue collected to a measure of the national tax base. On the expenditure side, it may involve identifying and collecting of statistical data of demand and cost factors affecting relative needs in each region. Examples of such factors include variations due to differences in demand arising out of the relative size, age, sex, or socioeconomic characteristics of relevant user population, cost differences arising out of the scale of delivery or administration in different regions, differences in degree of urbanization or industrial structure, and variations in the dispersion of the user populations.

Alternatively, an attempt can be made to identify policy differences between regions that could explain all or part of the differences in the actual budget figures. Once the impact of these policy factors is assessed, they can be deducted from the actual data to derive a cross sectional "needs" series that will reflect underlying revenue or cost disabilities. In concept, both approaches should yield similar results. Experience suggests that identification of location-specific disabilities may be a more fruitful course. Calculation from each approach, however, would provide a double check on what may sometimes have to be a broad judgment on the differences in regional fiscal capacities.

Of course, in some expenditure or revenue categories, it will be found that actual expenditures reflect actual need quite well—in which case, there may be no need to adjust the actual per capita regional budget figures in the needs calculation. In other budget categories, it may be found that needs are broadly similar on a per capita basis in each region—in which case, needs for each region can be assessed by including an equal per capita needs calculation for the items concerned in each region.

A sixth task involves decisions on the treatment to be accorded to any existing nonequalization grants to regions from the central government for specific purposes (e.g., education). Should these grants be continued once an equalization framework is established, and, if so, will they be taken into account in the overall calculations of revenue availability used in determining any equalization grant?

The last task relates to the choice of an "equalization model" to be used to formalize the measurement of horizontal balance. The formula for a general capacity equalization model is shown in the appendix, but a number of variations would be possible to take account of specific considerations. For example, it would be possible to take account of relative tax "efforts"—in addition to relative underlying revenue capacities—by each region and the specific allowance can be made for specific purpose nonequalizing grants. Both cases are discussed in the appendix.

Who Should Conduct the Equalization Studies?

No generalization is possible. In Australia, an independent Grants Commission has been appointed to advise on the distribution of grants. This system has worked successfully. The Commission has made its deliberation very open to scrutiny by the state and territory governments affected by its judgments, as well as the public generally. Public hearings are conducted and comprehensive reports published. The central government retains responsibility, however, for the final decisions on grant allocations. Normally, the Commission's recommendations are accepted, but the government retains the right to vary them or to make other compensating adjustments in the total payments structure to the states and territories.

By contrast, the Canadian Ministry of Finance conducts the equalization grant calculations; however, there is again considerable emphasis on consistent methodologies and public scrutiny of the results obtained.

Who Should Pay the Grant?

One question that may need to be addressed is who should pay the equalization grant. In Canada and Australia, the "equalizing grant" is paid by the central government from the shares of total taxes available to it. This approach reflects a vertical balance favoring the national government to pay grants to lower levels of government. But the grants could equally be made from regions with above-average fiscal capacities to those with below-average fiscal capacities. This practice is followed in Germany where the vertical balance is small, leaving the central government with a limited role in equalization grants.

Timeframe of Equalization

It is important that equalization grants be calculated on a three-to-five-year average basis so that the effects of particular random events (e.g., a natural disaster, such as fire, flood, drought) or disparate economic trends (e.g., energy price fluctuations) are evened out. Experience in Canada and Australia suggests that regular updating of studies of regional capacities is essential, and therefore a process of rolling averages may need to be used.

The inevitable delays in designing and collecting the vast amount of data required for objective measurement of horizontal imbalances in fiscal capacities, however, usually means that any system of equalization grants must be based on historical data—possibly up to five years old. In other words, the implementation of equalization is usually a retrospective rather than forward-looking exercise. This could be a problem in a country such as China, which is undergoing rapid structural change.

Phasing-In Equalization Arrangements

Given the large horizontal imbalances that already exist in fiscal capacities between regions in countries such as China, it may not be realistic to seek to obtain full equalization in the near term. Indeed, it seems probable that a goal of full equalization may make little sense given the distortions in public and resource allocation that are still being eliminated as China makes the transition to a market economy.

Over time, however, these concerns should diminish, and it may still be possible to set an intermediate goal such as assisting each region to achieve a fiscal capacity equal to, say, at least 70 percent of a visible national standard. That standard itself may not be a national average (which may be skewed by large rich provinces) but rather a subset of, say, larger eastern regions. Grants could be phased into achieve that goal, with poorer provinces achieving gradually greater shares of the total and richer provinces gradually reducing shares.

Appendix

A Generalized Capacity Equalization Model

A formal equalization model is:

$$G_i = \left[P_i \cdot \frac{R_s}{P_s} \cdot q_i \right] - \left[P_i \cdot \frac{E_s}{P_s} \cdot v_i \right], \tag{1}$$

where

G_i = equalization grant to region i;

P_i = population of region i;

R_s/P_s = a national per capita revenue collection standard;

q_i = the differential revenue-raising capacity of region i;

E_s/P_s = a national per capita expenditure standard; and

v_i = the differential cost of providing standard services in region i.

The per capita revenue term in equation (1) can be rewritten as

$$\frac{R_s}{P_s} \cdot q_i = \frac{R_s}{Y_s} \cdot \left[\frac{Y_s}{P_s} - \frac{Y_i}{P_i} \right],$$ (2)

where

R_s/Y_s = the national standard for regional government tax rates;
Y_s/P_s = a national standard tax base; and
Y_i/P_i = the tax base of the region.

This term tells us that the revenue-raising capacity of a region is derived by applying the national standard regional tax rate to the difference between the tax base of the region and that of the nation as a whole. The calculation is normally carried out in per capita terms and may be applied to each of a number of individual taxes raised at the local government level and then summed to derive a total for each region.

The expenditure per capita term on the right-hand side of equation (1) can also be rewritten to explain relative expenditure needs for each region as a function of a number of independent factors, such as

$$\frac{E_s}{P_s} \cdot v_i = \frac{E_s}{P_s} \cdot (u_i \cdot s_i \cdot d_i \cdot e_i - 1),$$ (3)

where

u_i = differential coverage of population eligible for services relative to the total population;
s_i = differential costs arising out of scale factors;
d_i = differential costs arising out of concentration or dispersion factors; and
e_i = differences in cost arising out of social, physical and economic factors.

Once a per capita measure is derived for each region, it is multiplied by the population of the region, P_i, to derive the contribution of relative revenue-raising capacity or expenditure need calculation to the total grant payable for each region.

Separate calculations would be required for each own revenue source and expenditure, the effective weighing being determined by a standard budget that brings together the various revenues and expenditures judged to be relevant to the equalization exercise.

Including a Fiscal Effort Adjustment

Although the fiscal capacity models set out above do not impose performance conditions on recipients, it is possible to insert a fiscal effort adjustment factor to the grant entitlement calculation if that were judged to be appropriate. There will be three components of the grant instead of two in equation (6).

$$G_i = P_i \cdot \frac{R_s}{Y_s} \left[\frac{Y_s}{P_s} - \frac{Y_i}{P_i} \right] + \left[\frac{Y_i}{Y_s} \cdot R_s \right] \cdot \left[\frac{R_i}{Y_i} \Big/ \frac{R_s}{Y_s} - 1 \right] + P_i \cdot \frac{E_s}{P_s} \cdot v_i. \tag{4}$$

A variant of this model, which would have the objective of imposing a penalty for below-standard, revenue-raising effort but not of rewarding above-standard effort, would restrict the fiscal effort adjustment to negative amounts so that the equation above would be subject to the constraint that

$$\left[\frac{Y_i}{Y_s} \cdot R_s \right] \cdot \left[\frac{R_i}{Y_i} \Big/ \frac{R_s}{Y_s} - 1 \right] \le 0. \tag{5}$$

Treatment of Nonequalization Grants and Tax-Sharing Arrangements

If the central government wishes to continue to make nonequalizing specific-purpose grants, the calculation of equalization grants would need to take account of the impact of these transfers on the initial pre-equalization position of each region. Equation (1) must be reformulated as follows:

$$G_i = \left[P_i \cdot \frac{E_s}{P_s} \cdot v_i \right] + \left[P_i \cdot \frac{R_i}{P_s} q_i \right] - \left[\frac{O_s}{P_s} \cdot \sigma_i \right], \tag{6}$$

where

$\dfrac{O_s}{P_s} \cdot \sigma_i =$ the differential specific-purpose grant.

This adjustment acts to nullify any relative advantage or disadvantages differential of existing nonequalizing specific purpose grants. Because the equalization calculations are undertaken with a lag, the adjustment is retrospective. Of course, if it were judged appropriate for regions to retain some or all of the advantages conferred by existing specific-purpose grants, it would also be possible to adjust the formula accordingly.